CH

MW01626833

GENDERQUEER

GENDERQUEER

AND OTHER GENDER IDENTITIES

This is a Genuine Barnacle Book

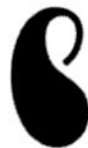

A Barnacle Book | Rare Bird Books
453 South Spring Street, Suite 531
Los Angeles, CA 90013
abarnaclebook.com
rarebirdbooks.com

FIRST HARDCOVER EDITION

Set in Lato
Printed in the United States
Distributed in the US by Publishers Group West
Art Direction by Alice Marsh-Elmer

10 9 8 7 6 5 4 3 2 1

Publisher's Cataloging-in-Publication data

Naz, Dave.
Genderqueer : and other gender identities / Dave Naz.
p. cm.
ISBN 978-1-940207-26-1
Contents: "Introduction: Identity" by Dave Naz, "Now Tell Me, What Kind of Man Are You?" by Morty Diamond, "Toying With Pleasure: Can Gender Be A Sex Toy?" by Jiz Lee, "Gender In Stereogram" by Ignacio Rivera, "A Nine Gender Valentine" by Jenny Factor, "Noah Enaction" for Sarah Burghauser

1. Transgender people—Pictorial works. 2. Transgenderism. 3. Gender identity. 4. Photography, artistic. I. Title.

HQ77.7 .N39 2014
306.76/8—dc23

Dedicated to Carlos Batts

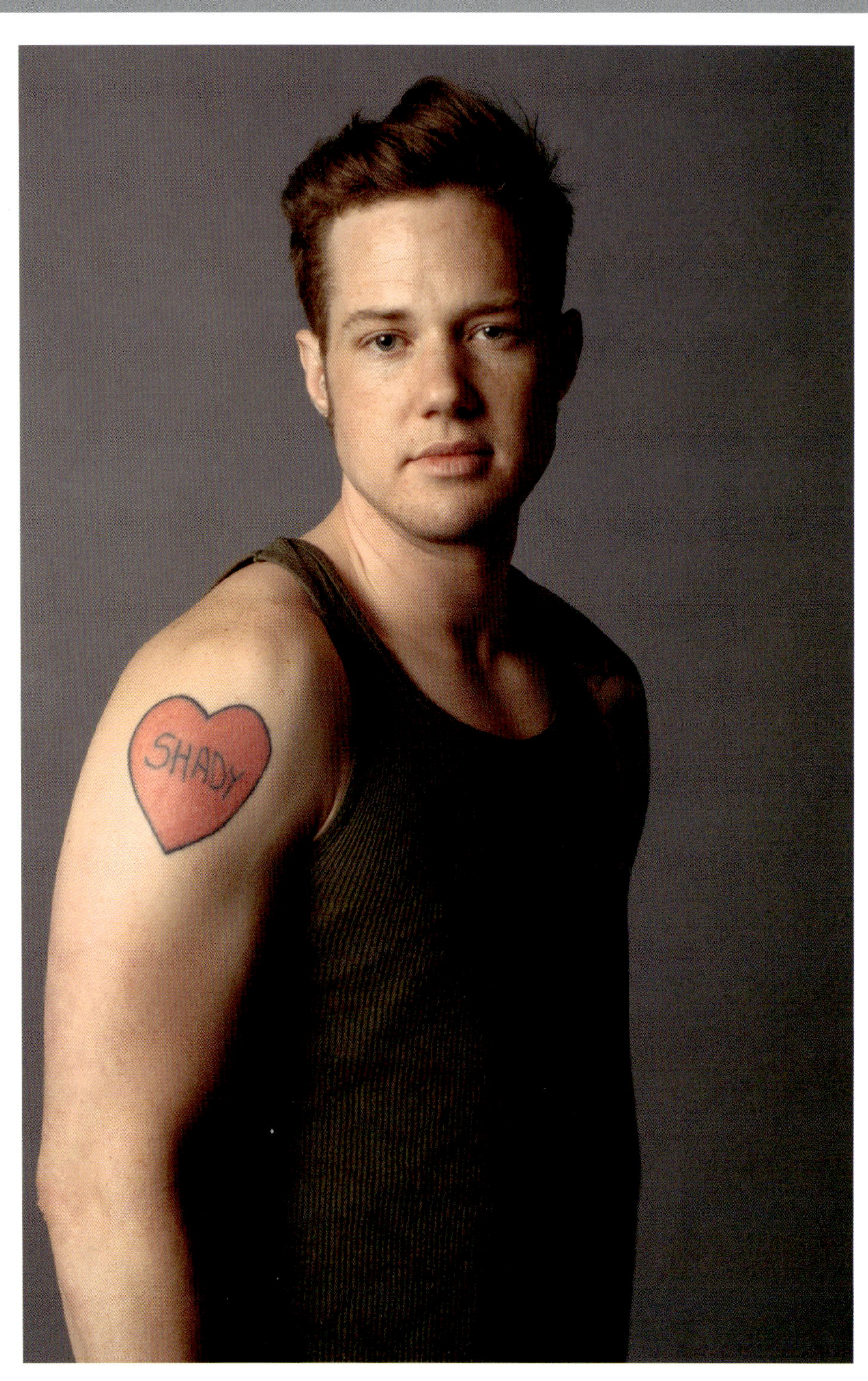
SHADY

INTRODUCTION: IDENTITY

I hear Poly Styrene shouting the lyrics. Everybody needs an identity. It helps define us. The subjects in this series helped me better understand this. I spoke to them as I took their portraits and in the emails we exchanged leading up to the shoots. Some were excited about being able to express themselves in this way and it made me more excited about the project.

I was inspired to start the series in 2009, after getting an email from Drew DeVeaux about modeling for me. I felt her look had a lot of depth; pale skin and a pretty face (without makeup) that defied gender. Shortly after that, I saw photos of Jiz Lee and Syd Blakovich and I wanted to take their photos, too. All three were breaking the usual gender boundaries, looked confident, and had a great sense of style.

I love that many people in this community have taken terms usually used derogatorily and claimed them. Terms like queer, sissy boy, and faggot. During the interviews for this series I heard some of the models proudly using these terms. It was powerful. Some of the models I shot came from supportive, artistic families and others were outcasts that moved to San Francisco to be around people who were tolerant and shared their interests. Some had never modeled before and others, like Pig Pen (possibly one of the most stylish people on the planet), had been in front of the camera many times.

Choosing the correct title for this series proved to be challenging. Genderqueer seemed like the right unifying term, since many people I photographed identified as genderqueer. However, some identified as trans, queer, or male rather than genderqueer, and this is why I was reactive in deciding a final name—with feedback from the models I added the subtitle: *And Other Gender Identities*. Mike Kelley approached some of his work this way and I always thought it was a good idea; put it out there, see how people respond, and fix it accordingly. After all, identities and terminology change. In ten years the term genderqueer could sound dated. But for now, it's what we've got.

Dave Naz
February 2014

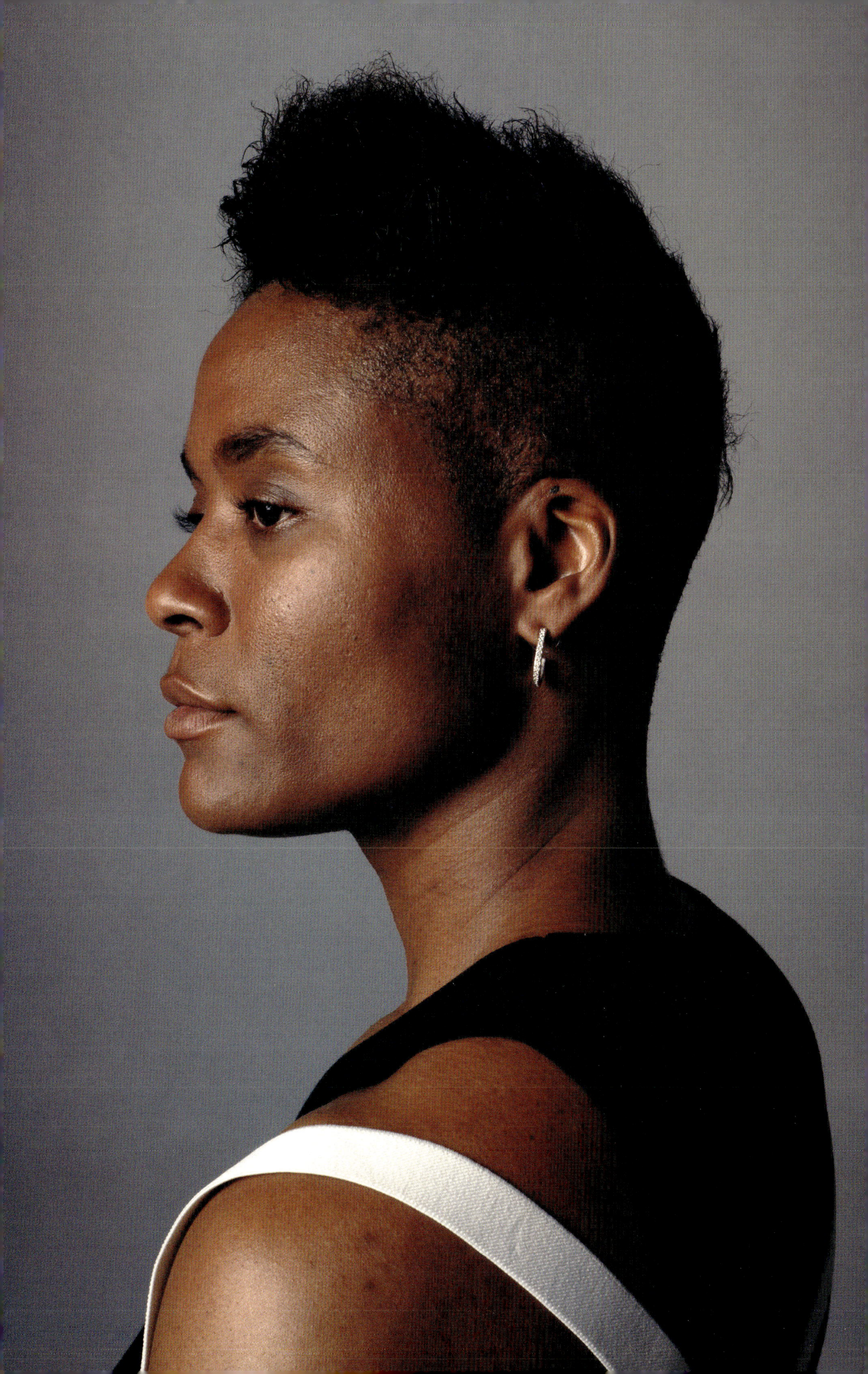

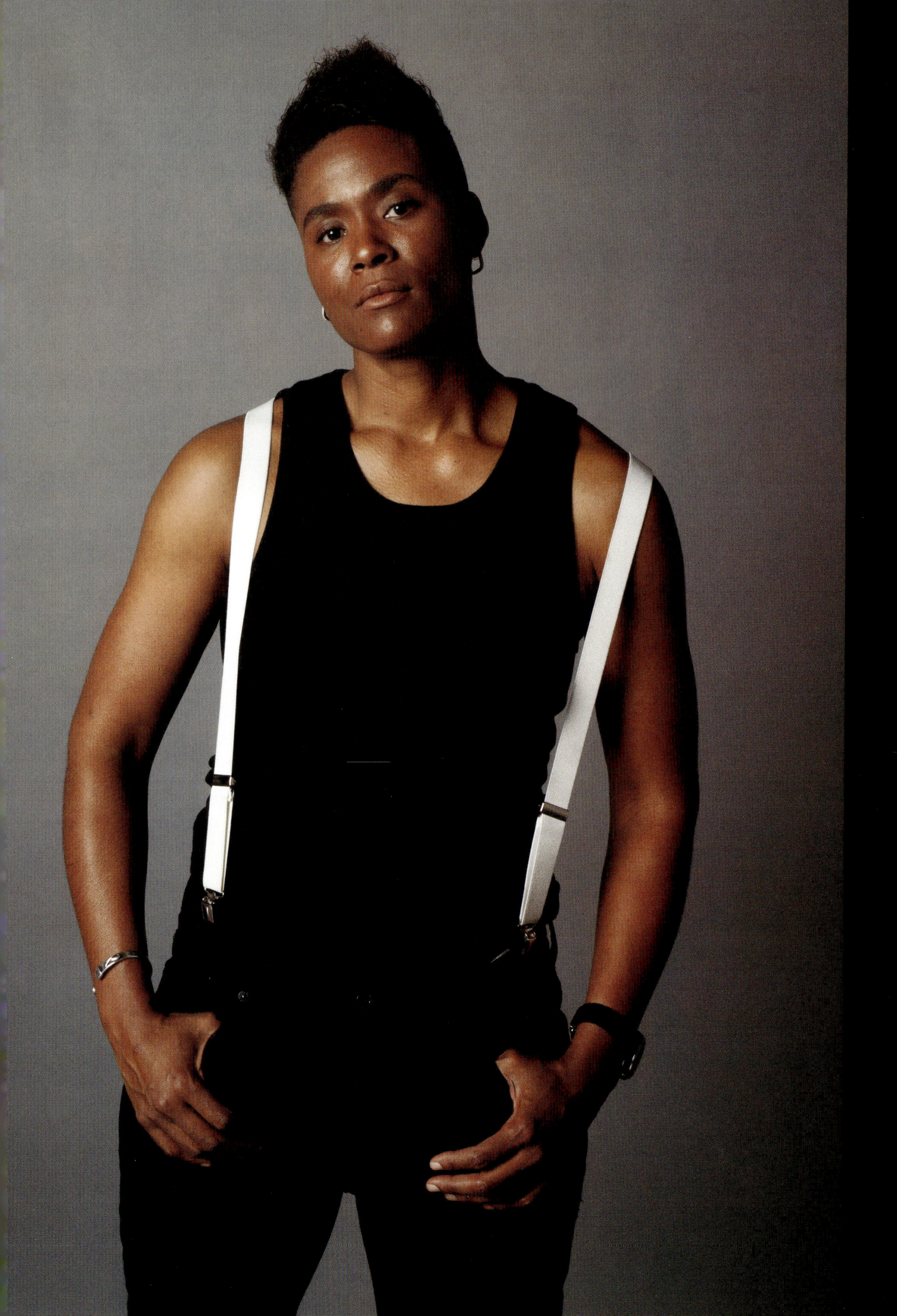

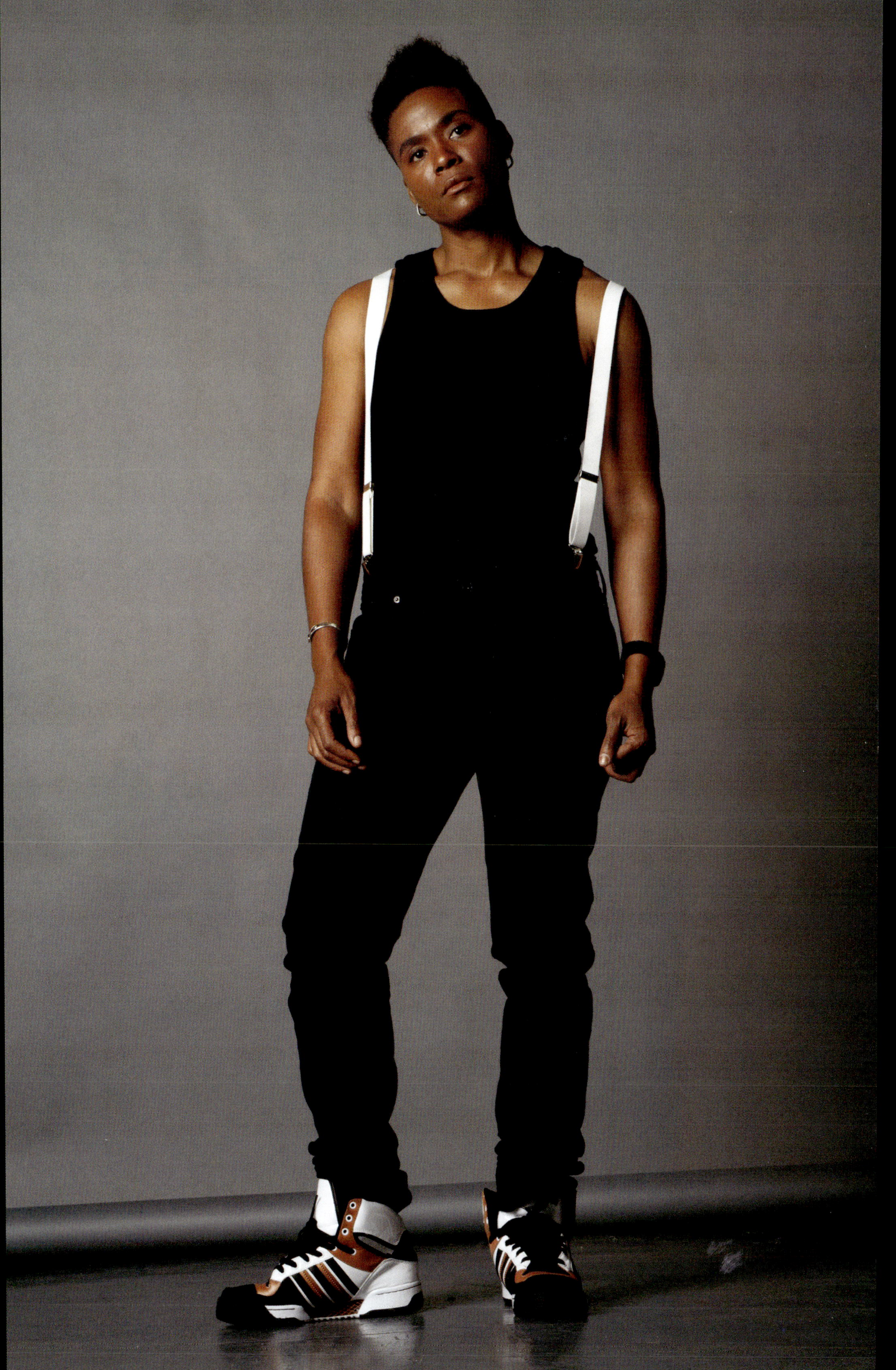

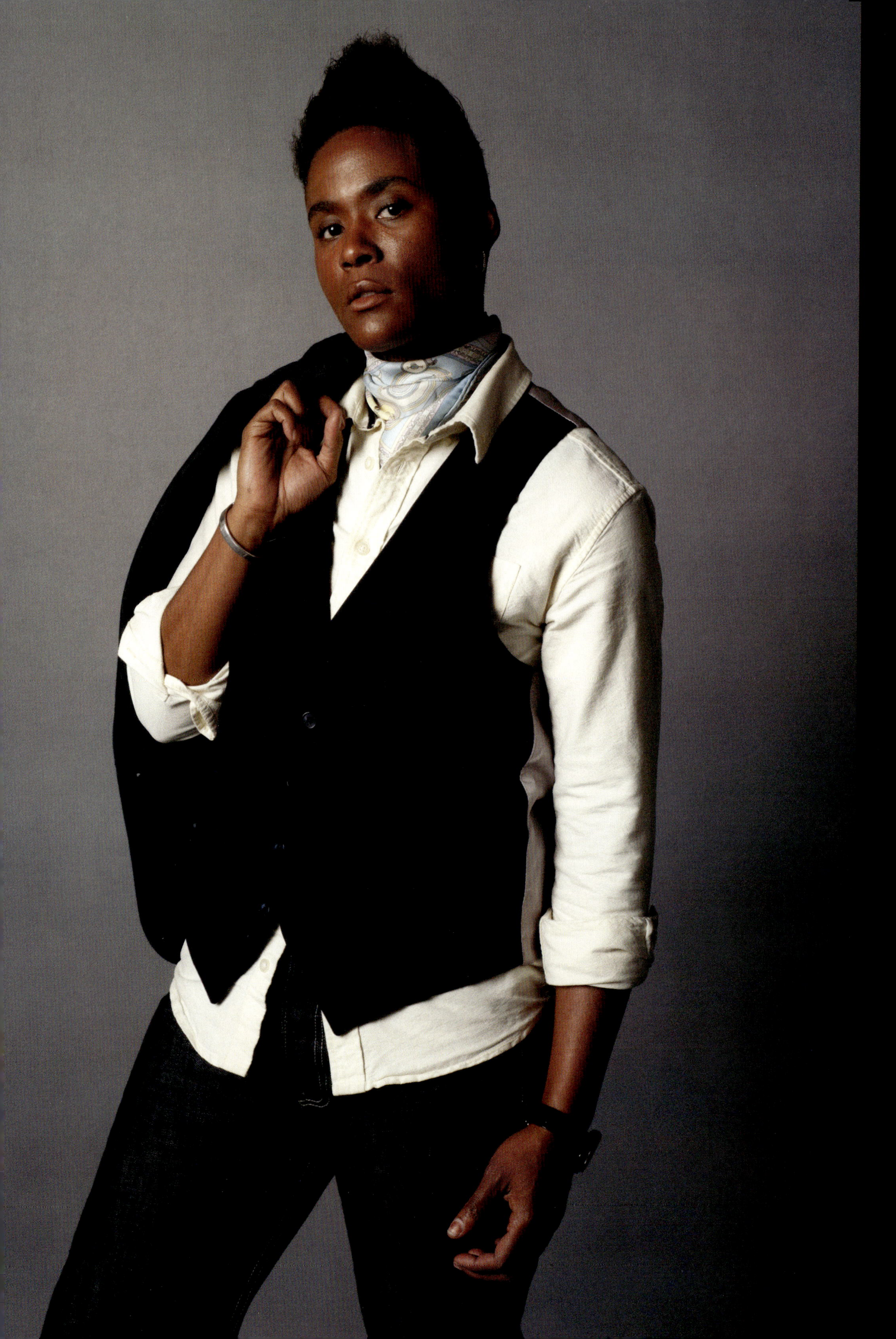

NOW TELL ME, WHAT KIND OF MAN ARE YOU?

Lately, it has been a complete wonderland to be in my skin. I caress the stubble on my face, run my hands over the soft black hairs on my belly, and revel in the fact I am only an inch from my original hairline. More so than the physical changes that have come with my transition and the twice-weekly testosterone injections I began fourteen years ago, my spirit and my soul are finally delighted with the man I've become. Not so long ago I was a miserable, self-flagellating, noncommunicative person with a slew of proverbial chips on my shoulder and an anxiety level so high it often kept me from going outside to get the mail. Of course, this is where you're supposed to inquire, "How did you make such an important and life-saving change?" Well, let me tell you, I feel not one singular ounce of shame in saying it all began (mostly) in meeting the woman who would become my wife. The story begins with the end of our first date, when I came to the conclusion I wouldn't want to be with a person like me for the long haul. Drastic changes needed to be made. And quickly.

But I'm sure you'd first like to know about our disastrous first date: Let me indulge you.

Rachel and I met on Craigslist. I put up the ad in haste, having moved back to Los Angeles weeks before, after having a pre-midlife meltdown in New York City, replete with abusive girlfriend and a brief psych ward hospital stay. Meeting anyone of substance on Craigslist was not high on the agenda. I just wanted some comfort in my new city in the arms of a woman who wouldn't ask a lot of me. I received an extremely small number of emails (what I get for posting as a transsexual man in the Women Seeking Women). I came upon one that punched me in the gut. Rachel's email was well written, witty, and sexy. We had some exciting email exchanges, and spoke on the phone a few times before deciding to meet at a coffee shop for a date. I came a bit early, grabbed an iced coffee, ambled towards a cushy chair, and sat, slouched and disaffected. I wasn't dressed particularly well and forgot to wear deodorant. I convinced myself that trying too hard was the wrong thing to do. I rationalized about my willful ignorance of the way I looked by telling myself I didn't really know her and if the date turned sour the fallout would be minimal. But, in the first moment I encountered Rachel's smile, her voice, and her energy, I realized I had made a mistake. I was this slobbish, slightly rank creature standing next to a stunning redhead in skintight jeans and a lacy top. I quickly brushed off my gaffe with the thought, *Well, this is me, she'll take it or leave it*. And this, quite clearly, was the man that I was. Too wounded to care, too sad to admit defeat, too interested in covering the pain I held inside with bravado, and too aloof to understand what was actually transpiring. The whole date was a study in what not to do. By the end, it was obvious she was not impressed. Towards the end of our encounter I told her, in so many words, that I was better than this. She believed me and we set a second date.

In the coming weeks we would get to know each other through dinner dates and thrift store shopping adventures. When our conversations led us to mutual romantic histories, I admitted to never having had a relationship I would deem healthy. I began discussing my issues with women and how messy and painful all of my relationships had been. As Rachel asked more questions, I squirmed in my seat. All of my sentences began with "She did..." or "She was...", and at one point I stopped myself and thought, *Wow, I'm kind of an asshole.*

Years of injections, surgeries, and gym visits had me looking like a younger (albeit shorter) version of my father. I thought that all I needed to be secure rested on my body aligning with my gender identity, that the rest would be figured out with ease. But, when I began to pass as male and live my life as a man, it became clear that I had to admit to having an ill-conceived understanding of what it meant to be a man. There was no template I followed to become a man, but there was also no plan on what kind of man I wanted to become. My transition occurred with little parental support and the friends I leaned on were a small group of misfits, many of whom used drugs, alcohol, and trusty but brutal denial to maintain themselves.

Many of the women I dated were equally tied to these ways of dealing with life. Years after my transition, I was still a man who lacked coping skills while taking the privileges that came my way. Fast forward to the meeting with Rachel and all at once I knew there was nothing more I wanted to do with the disheveled mess that was my masculinity. So, how does one become a man? An exceptional man, a man worthy of a woman determined to give me unconditional love? The answer for me: therapy. Lots and lots of therapy. I found myself discussing a childhood with a distant father I saw for four days each month, and an alcoholic mother who couldn't guide me through the difficulties of being a young queer. With my therapist, I reconciled the lack of deep bond with my given family. I also found ways to broaden my understanding of the man residing inside my five-foot-two-inch frame. And, even as I write this, I am still foraging for what the man inside me looks like. Searching for what he wants to say and how exactly he wants to say it. I know this much: I am a feminist man who isn't interested in flailing my masculine energy around just to feel important and worthy. I've embraced a masculinity that's more "Let's cuddle after sex and here are flowers for no particular reason" than "Baby, go get me a sandwich." I'm interested in evolving as a man. And that requires an open heart, and a willingness to hold the door open for other folks entering the restaurant. That's the man I want to be.

MORTY DIAMOND

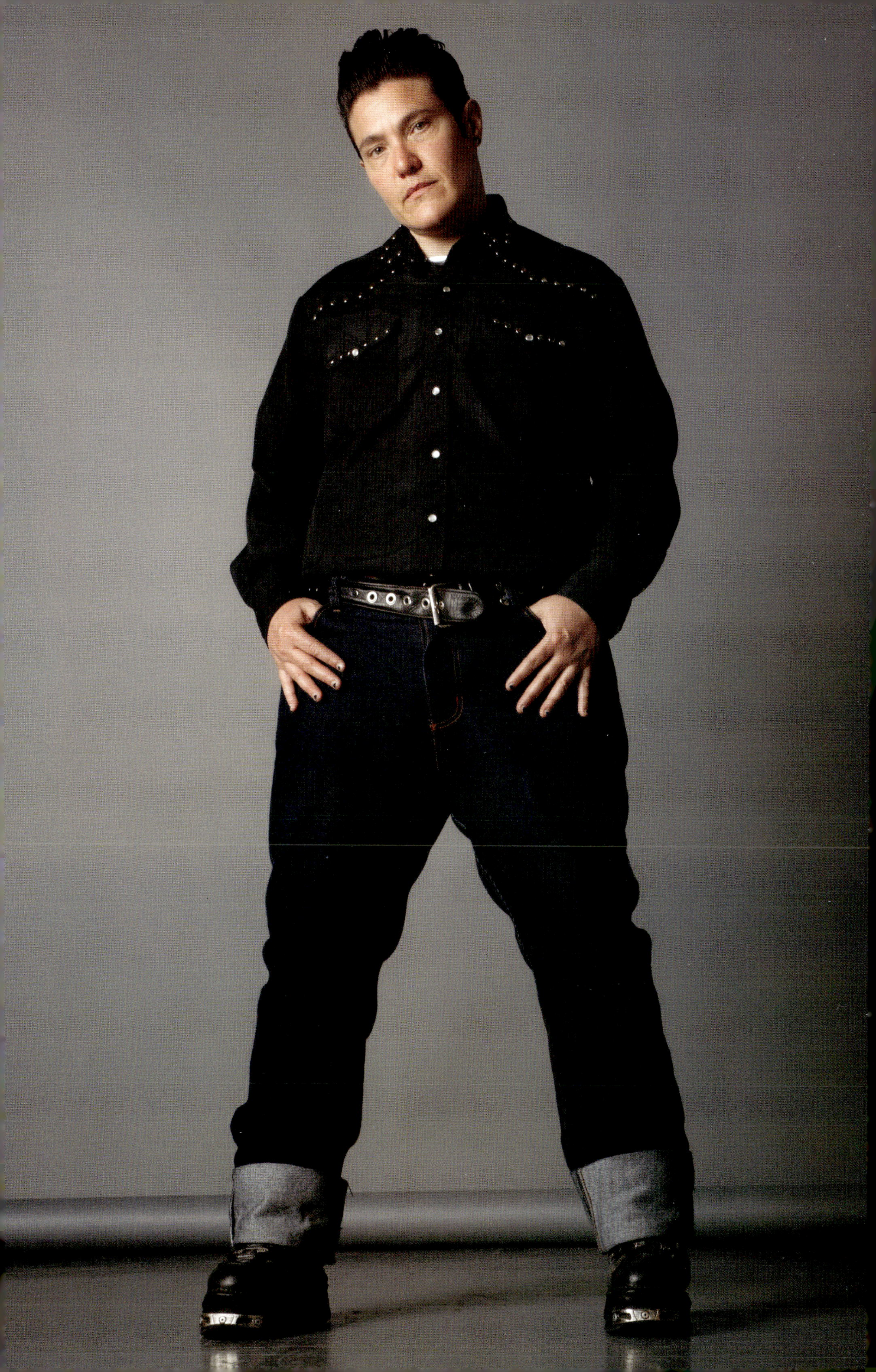

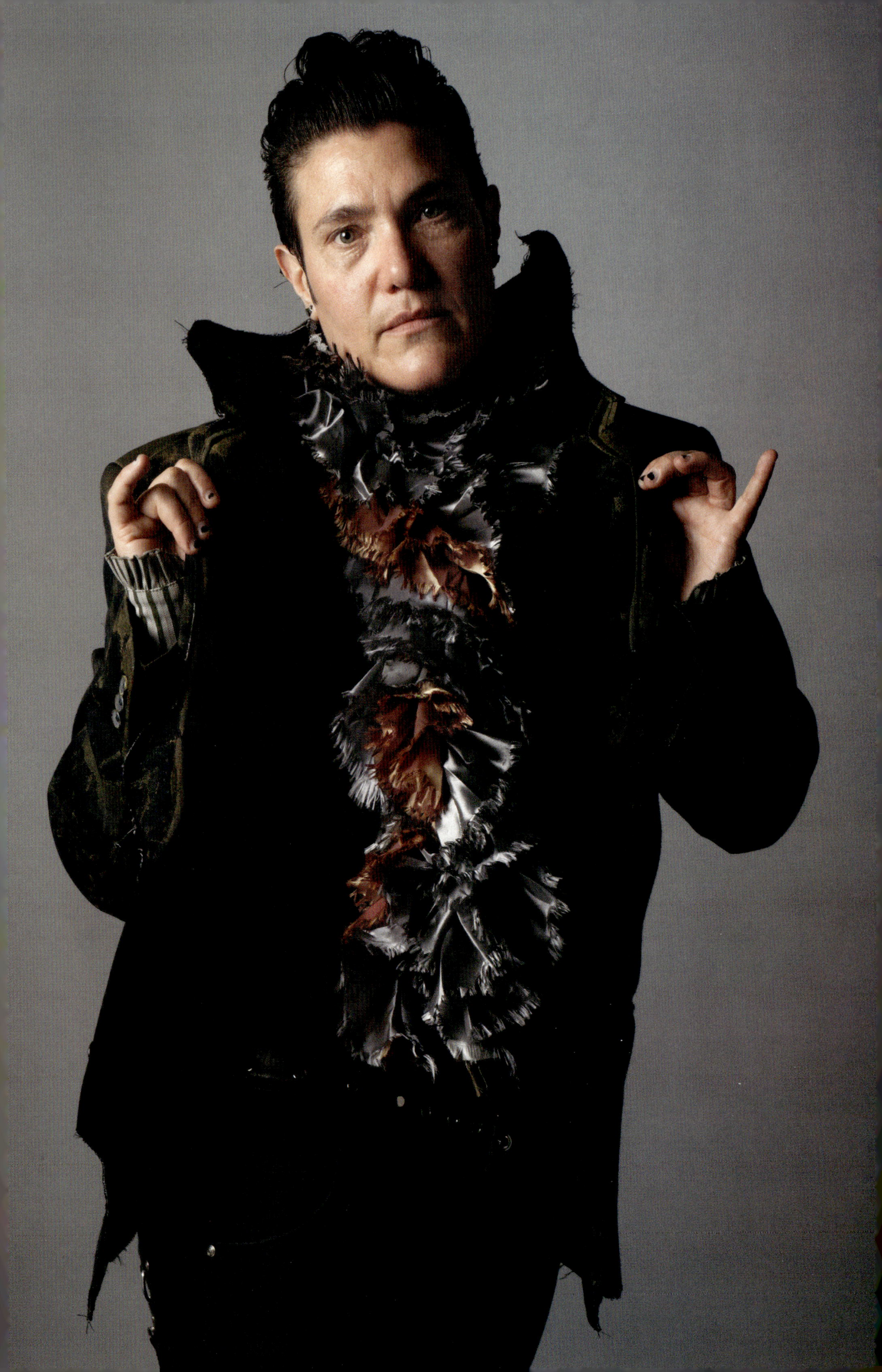

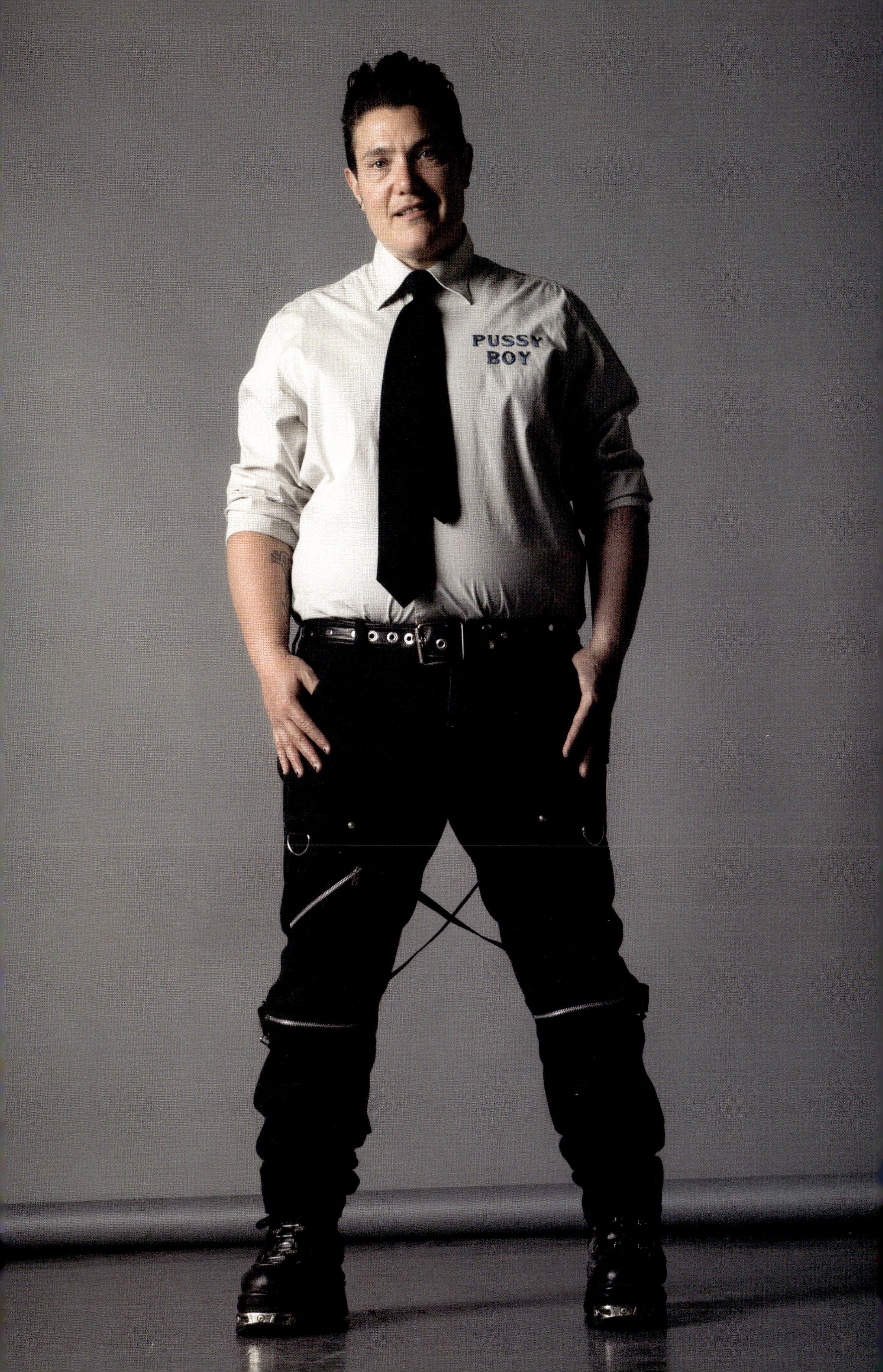
PUSSY
BOY

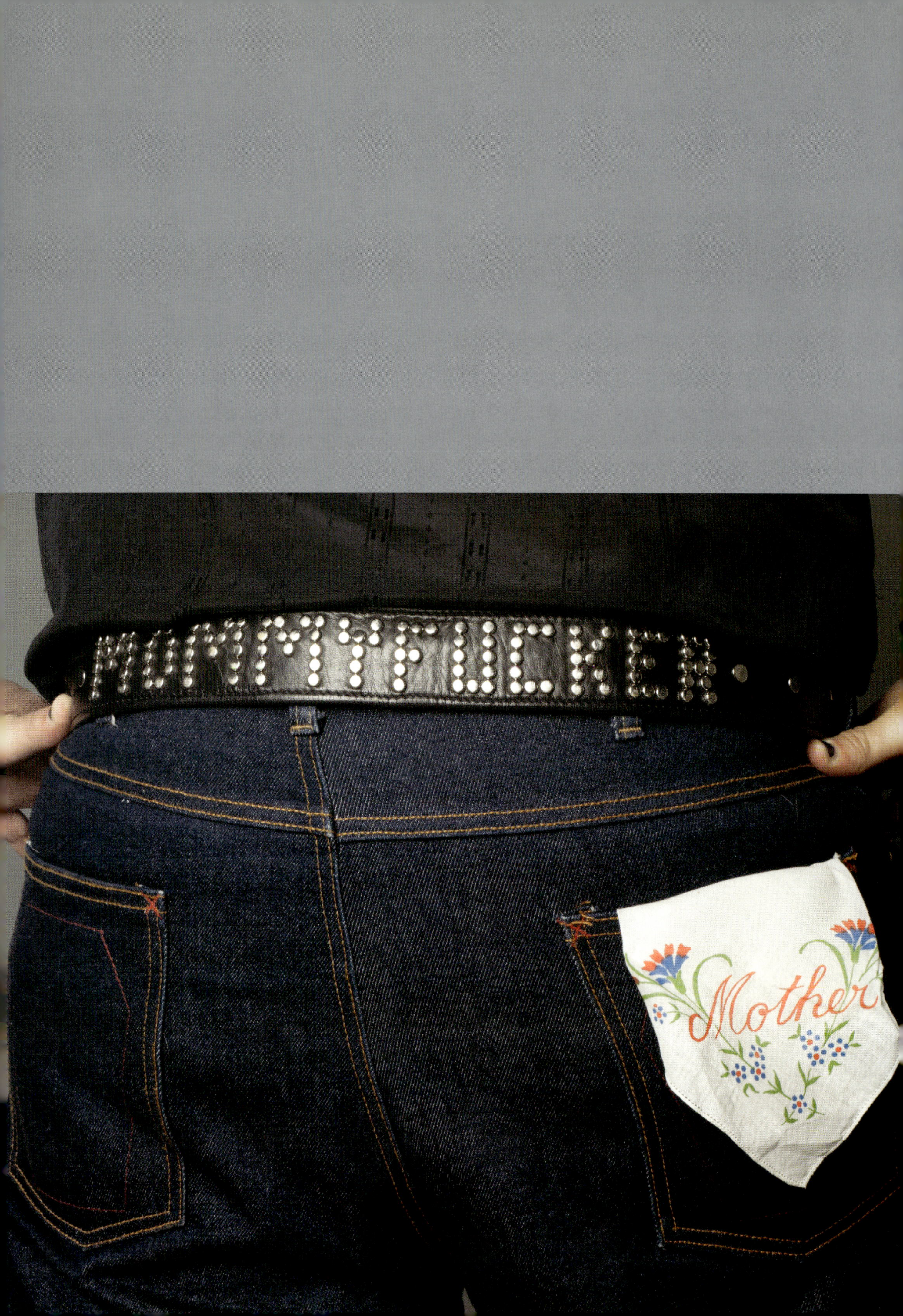
MOMMYFUCKER
Mother

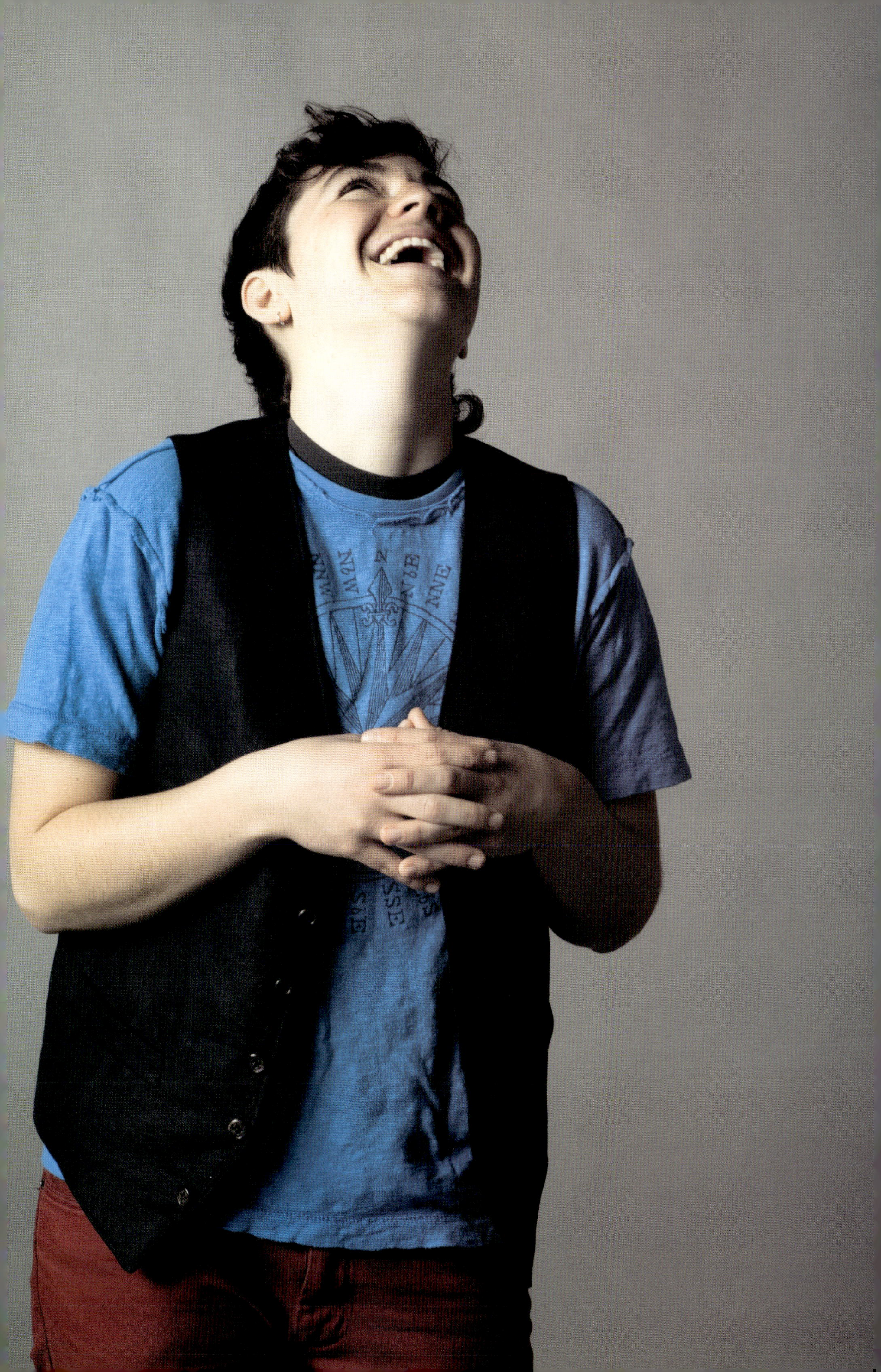
N
NNE
SSE

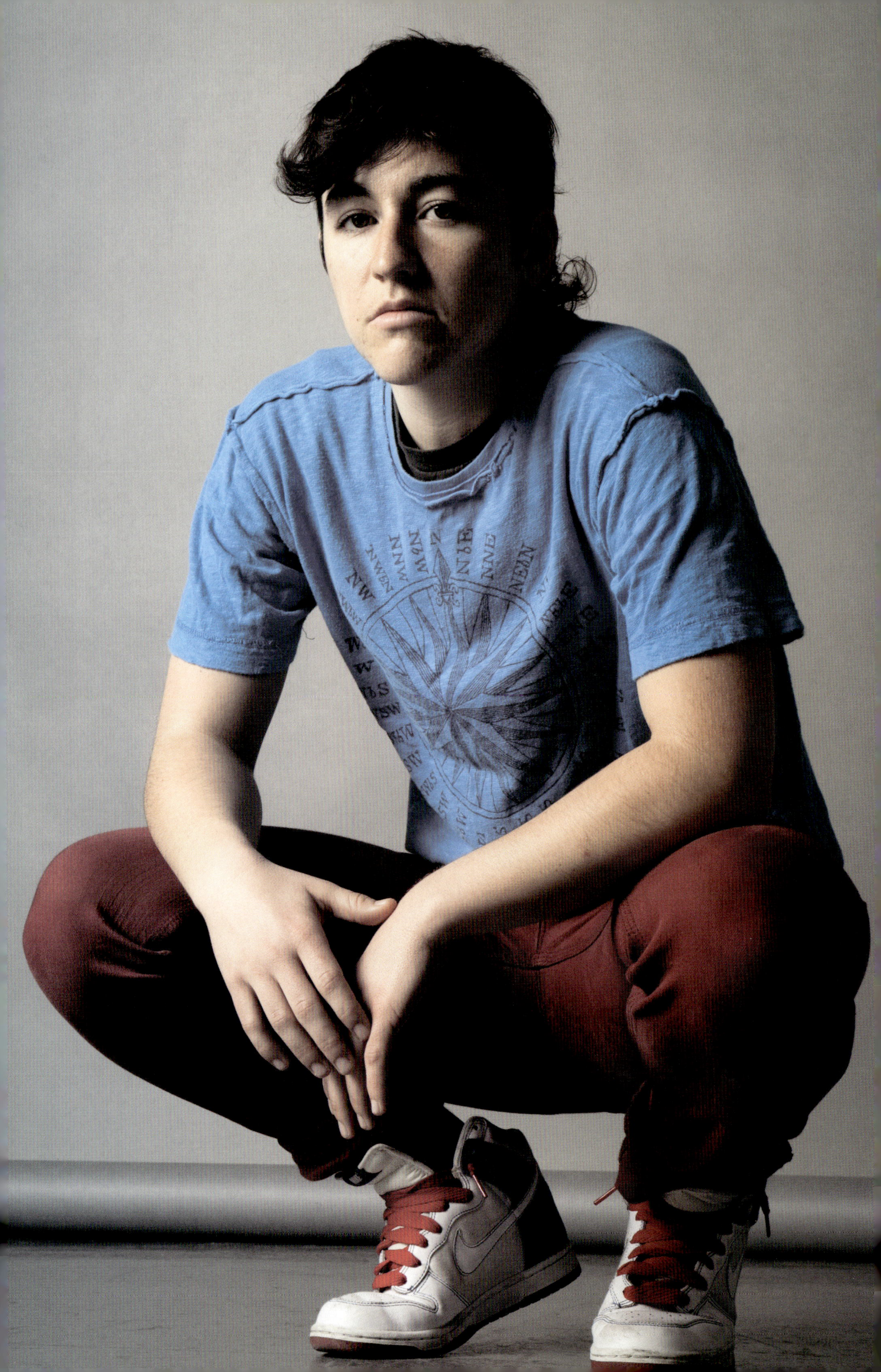

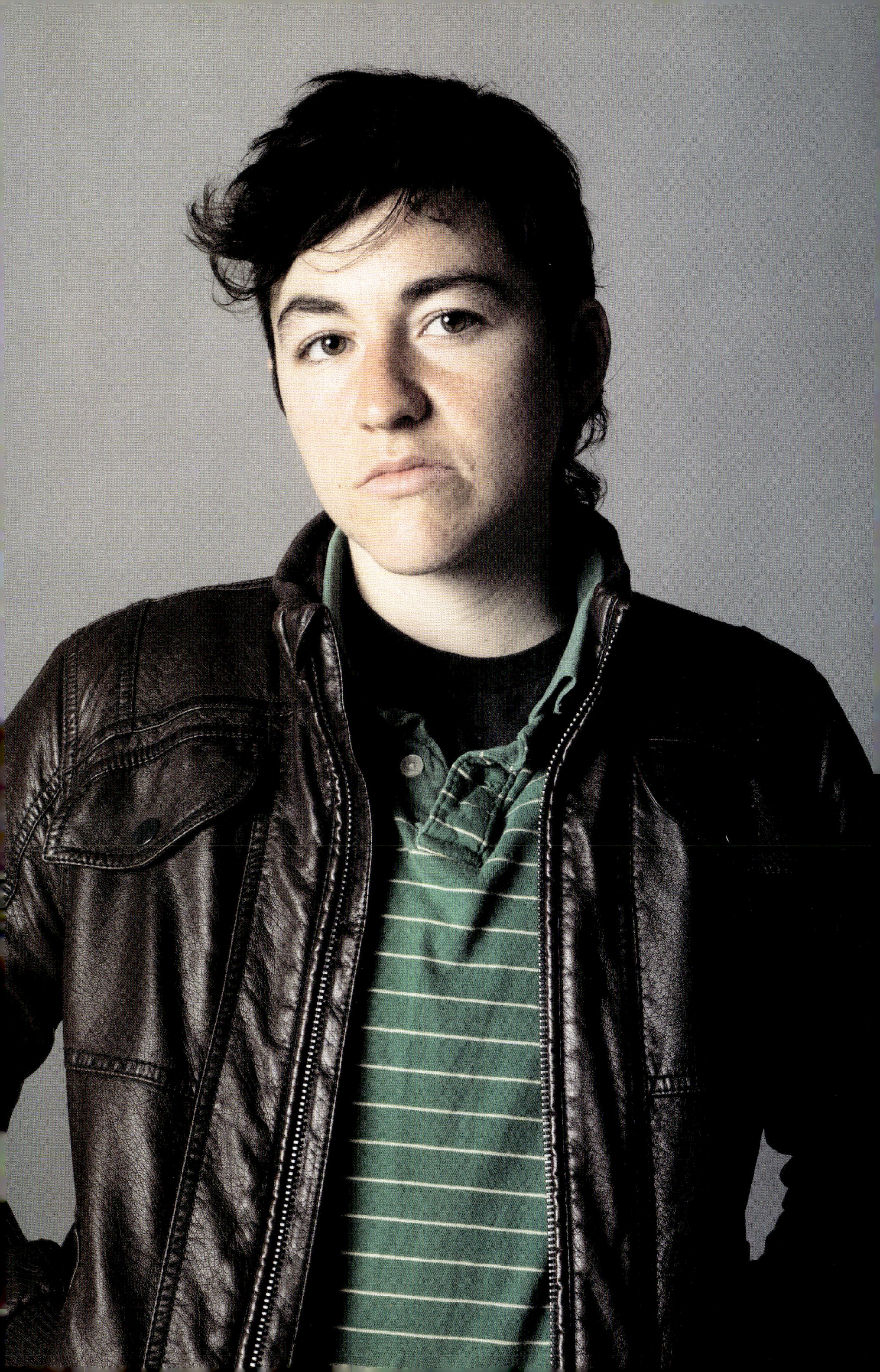

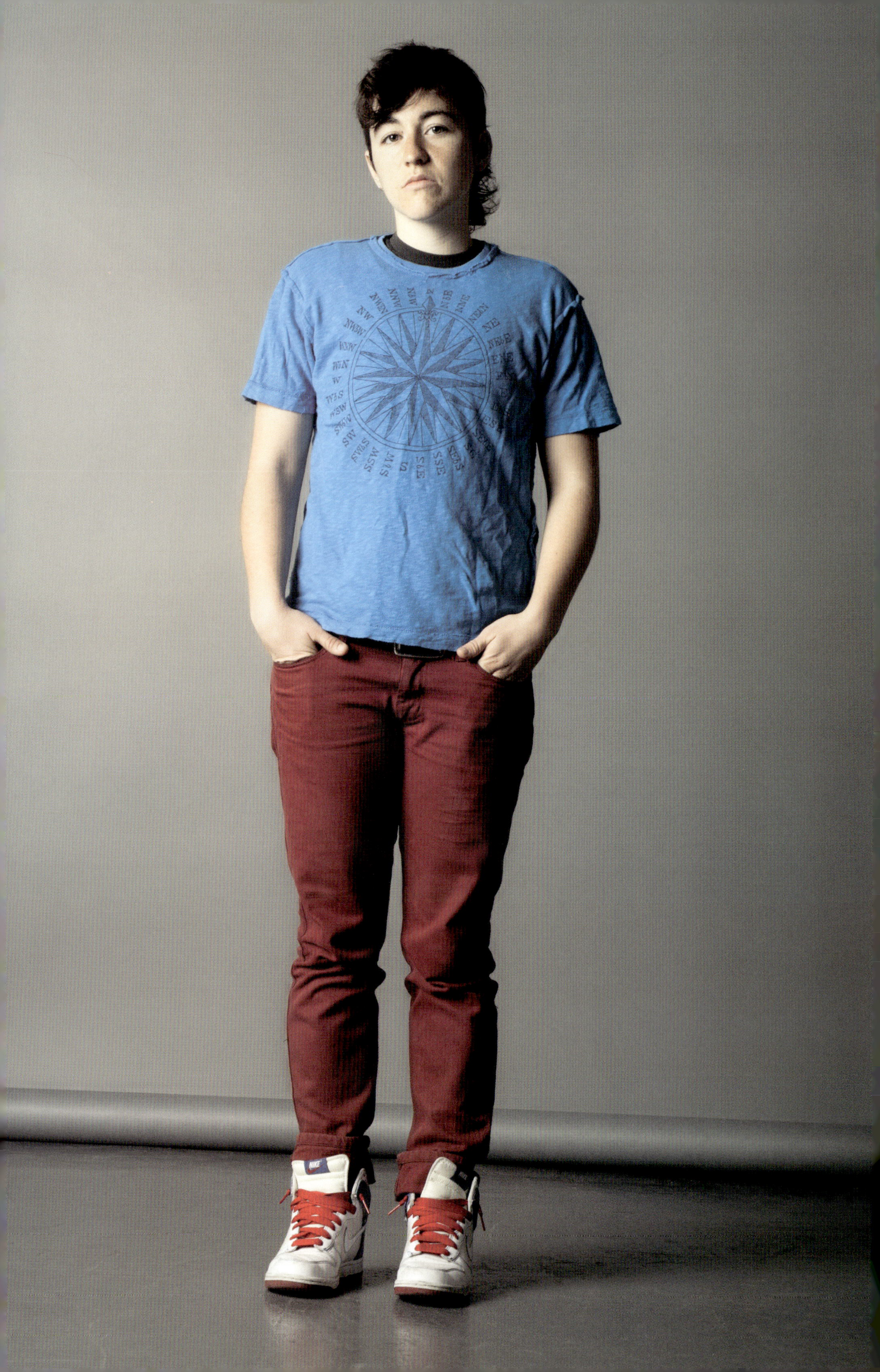

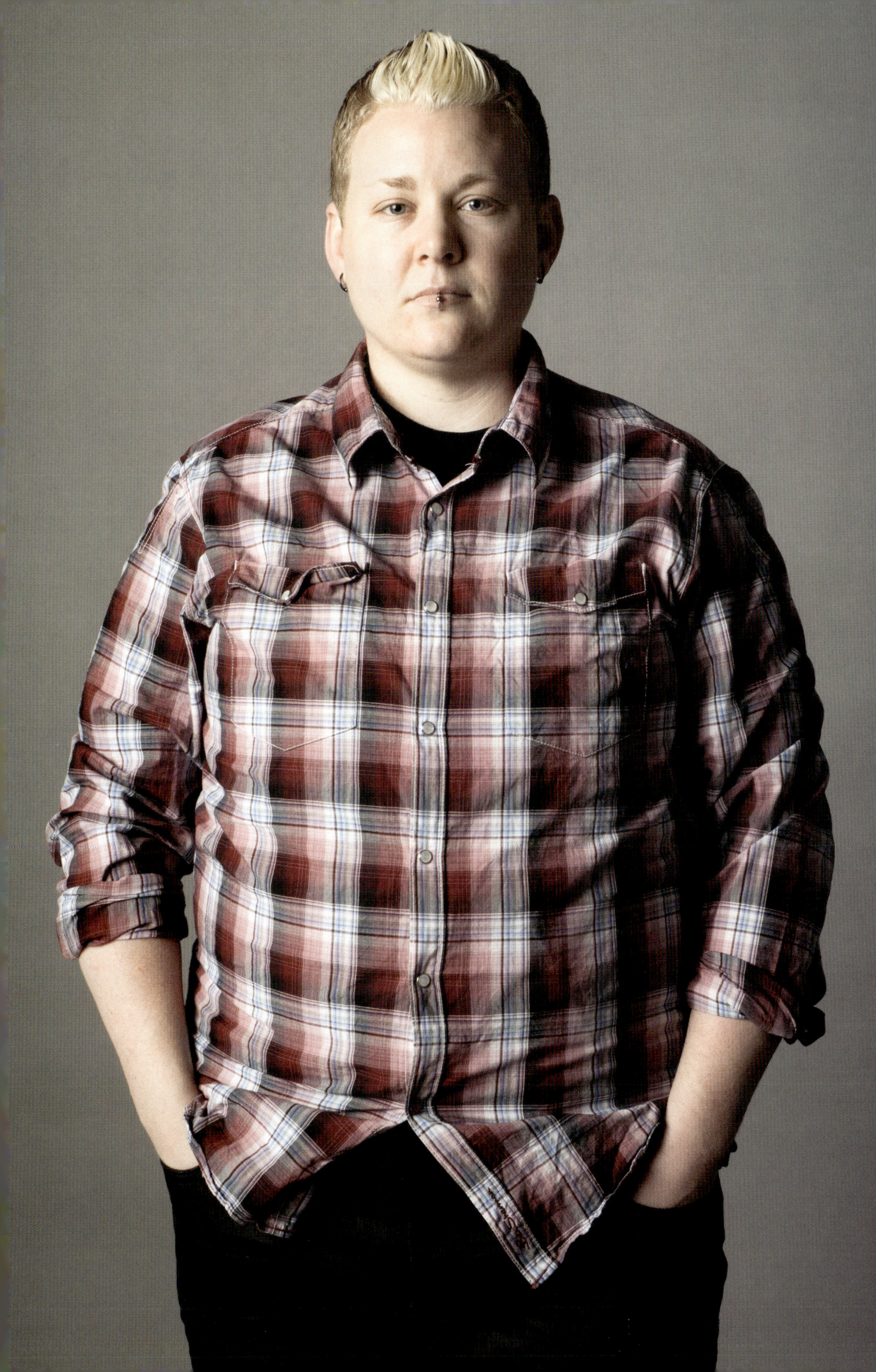

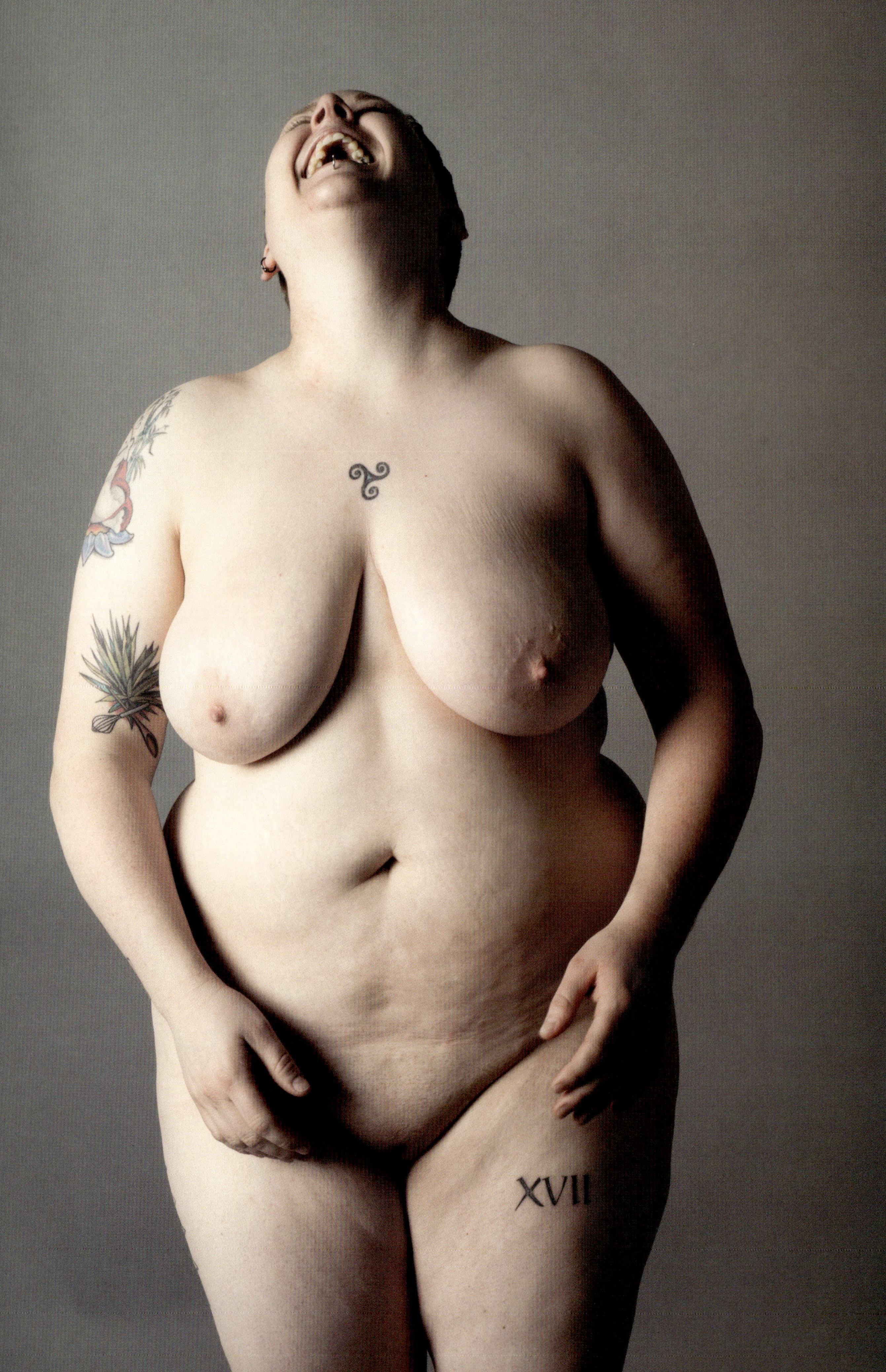
XVII

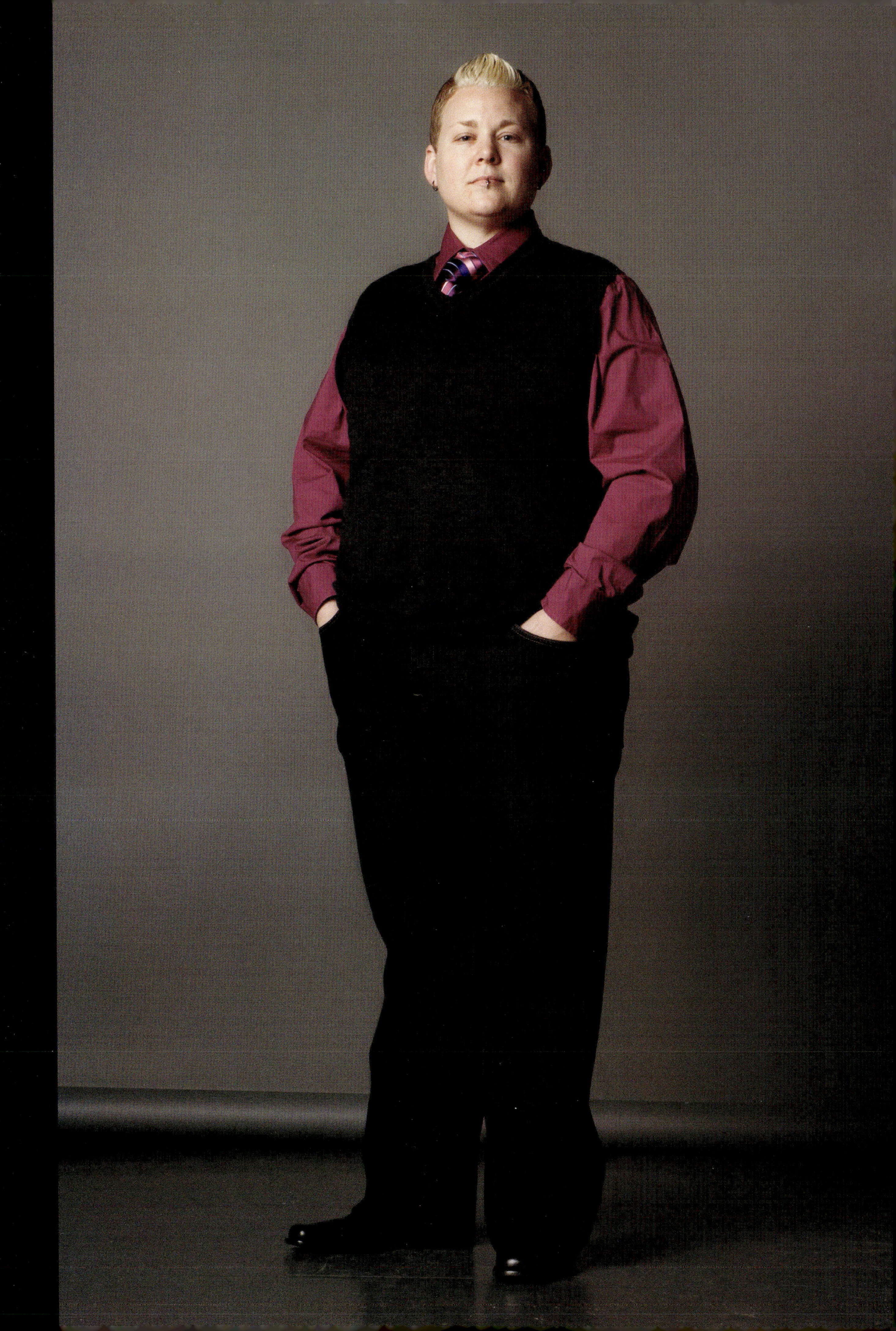

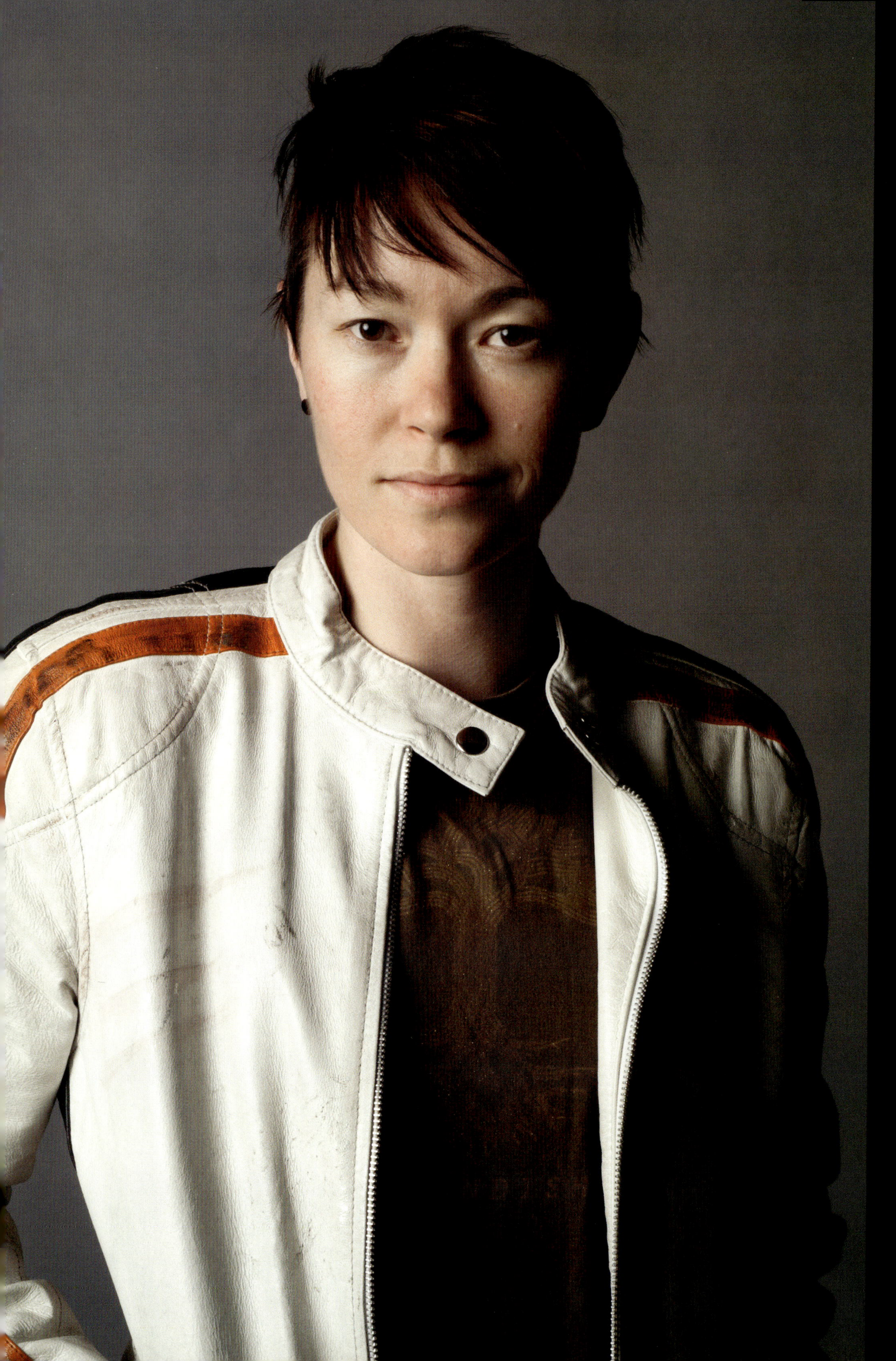

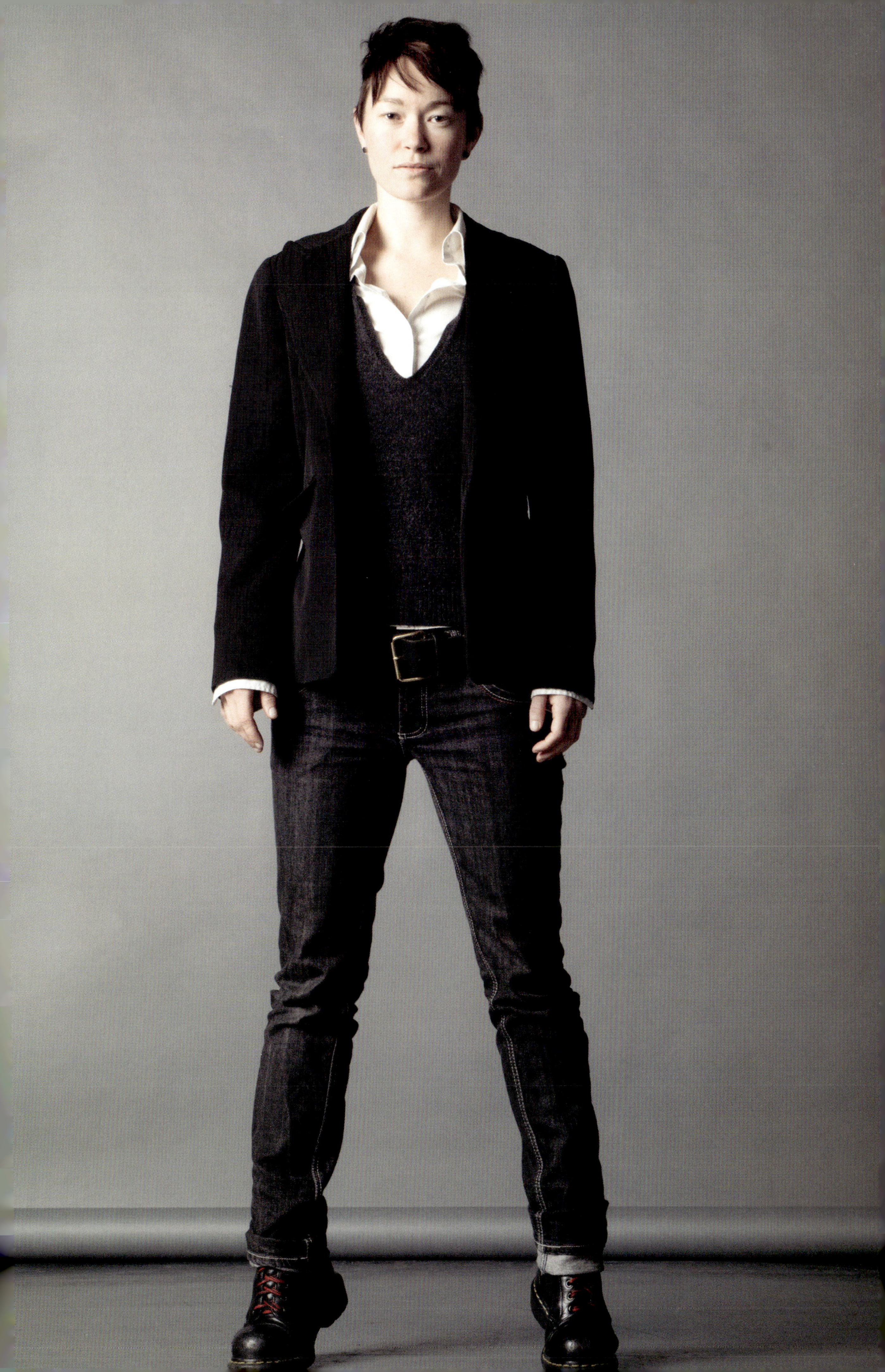

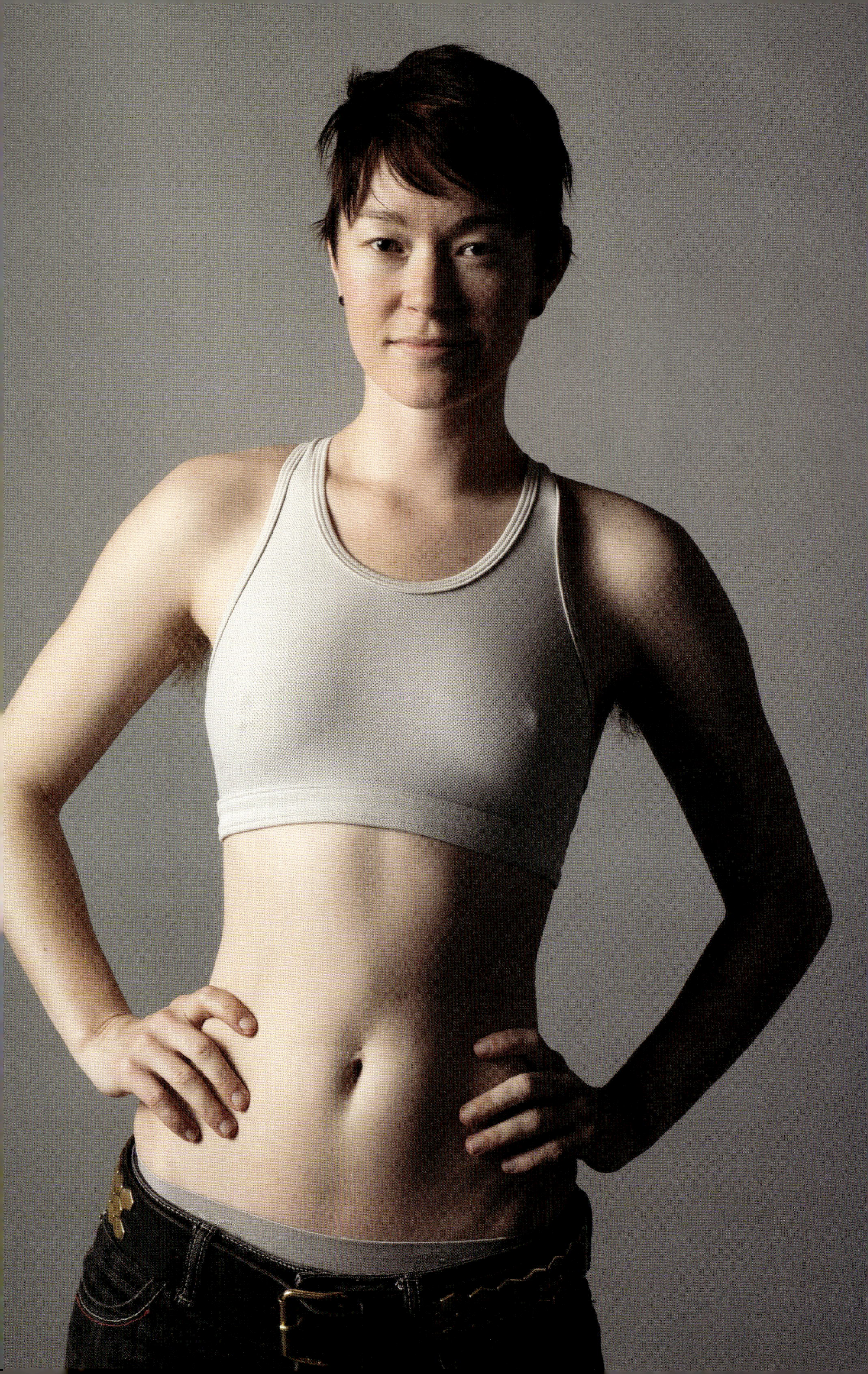

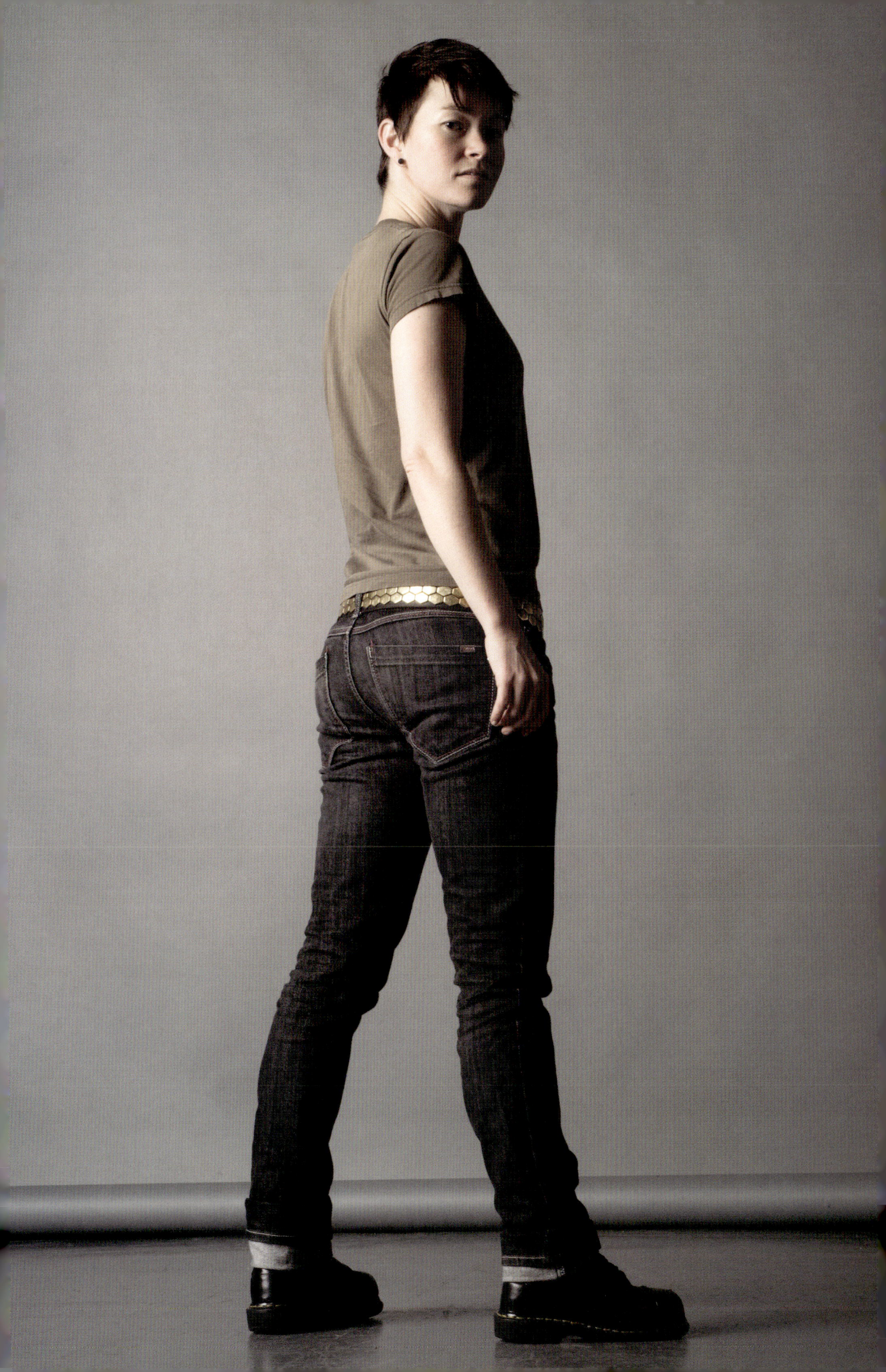

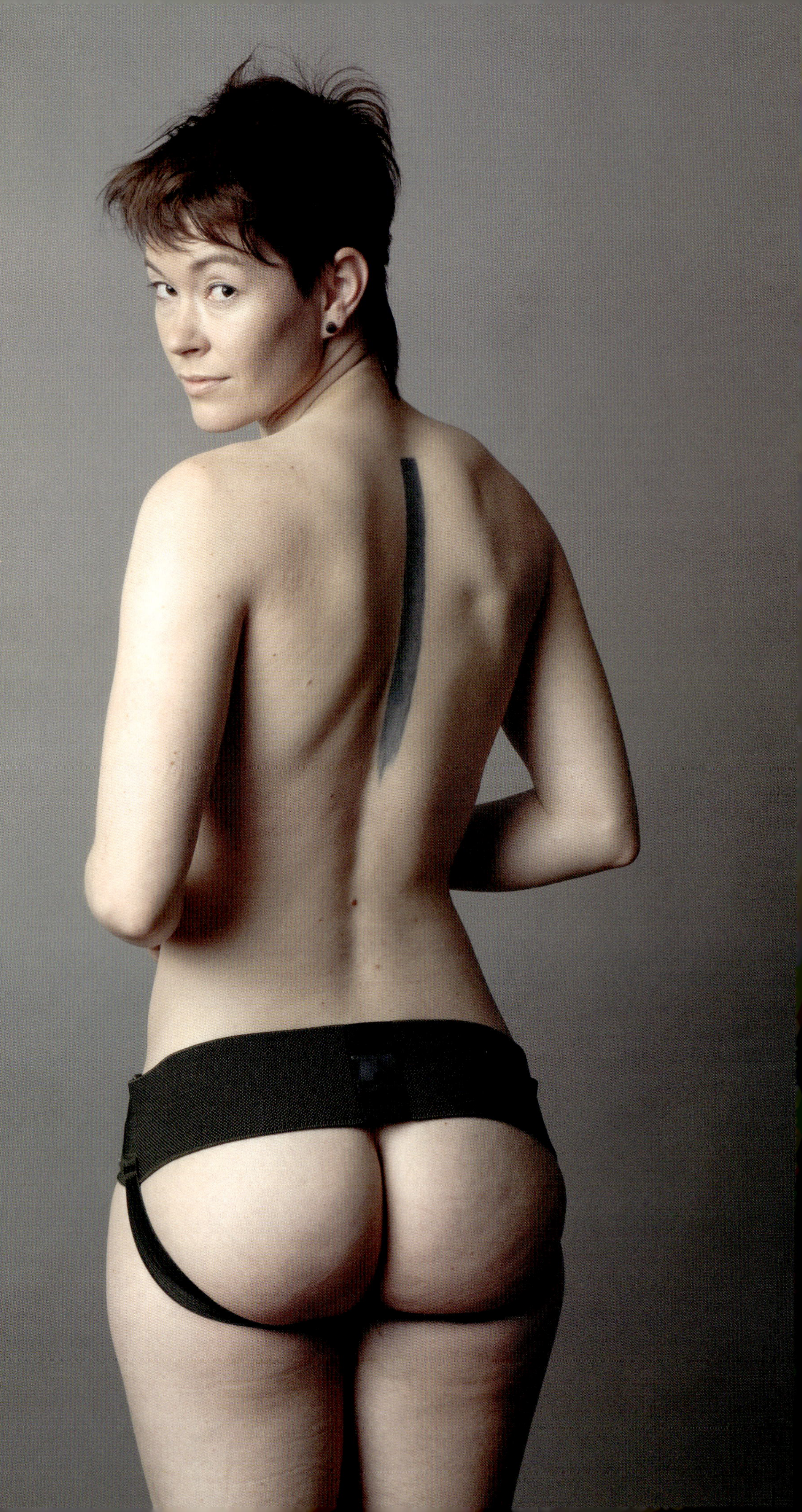

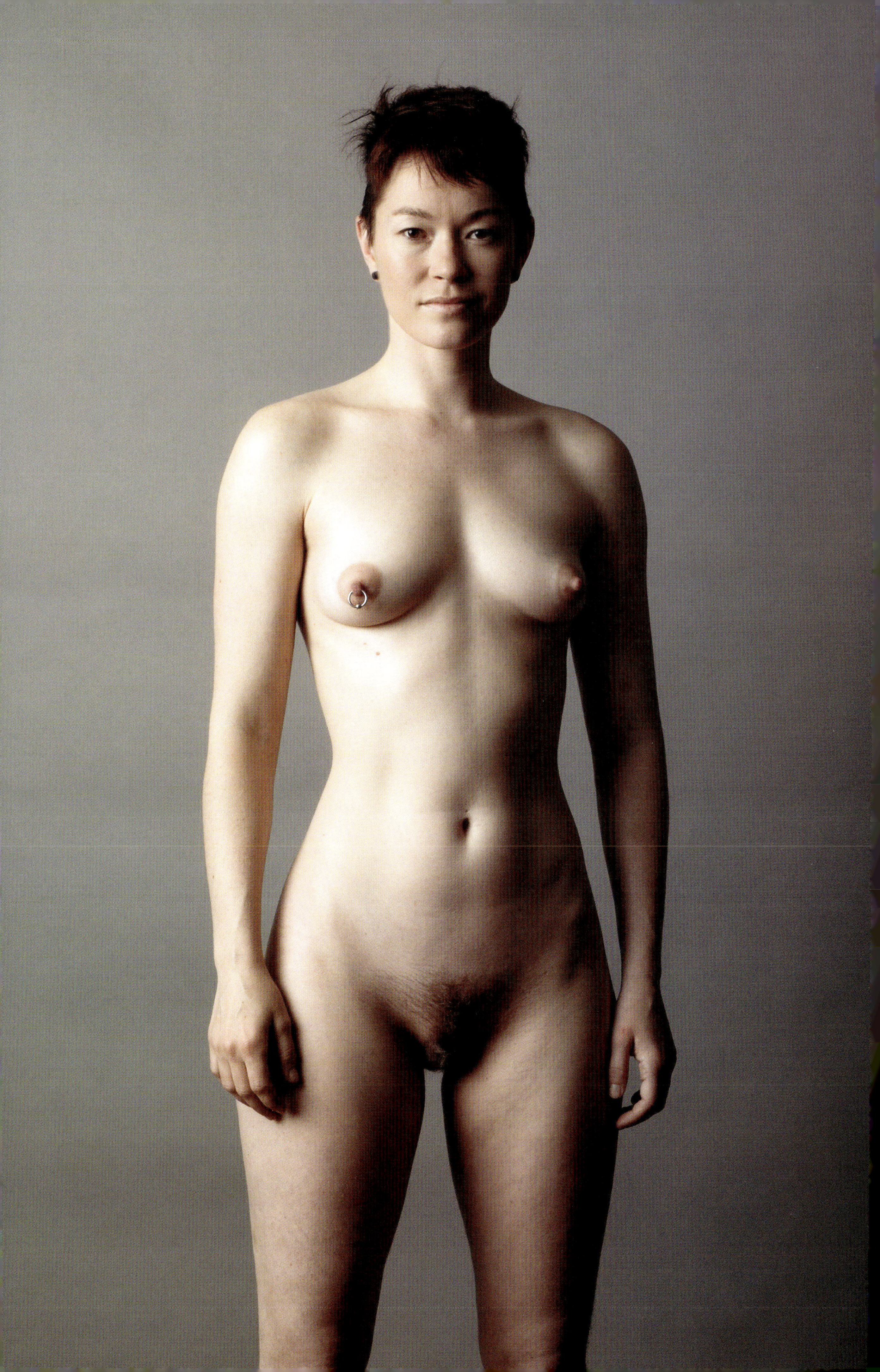

TOYING WITH PLEASURE: CAN GENDER BE A SEX TOY?

Gender describes a broad range of physical, mental, and even behavioral characteristics that distinguish between masculinity and femininity. Gender can be one's identity or self-expression, it can be a part of exploration and play, and it can be extremely erotic.

But how can gender be used in sex, as someone might use a sex toy? My experiences in pornography are shaped by an exploration of using my gender on camera as a tool for arousal and pleasure.

First, some background: I did my first porn in 2005. Before this, I was indifferent towards pornography. Of the porn I had seen, none of the performers looked like me. I assumed that if I were to do porn, I'd have to look more like a girl. While I appreciate feminine performers and those who dress the part for their job, I wasn't interested in what felt like forced feminization. I abandoned the thought, concluding that porn just wasn't for me.

Then I saw queer porn screened in a small theater in San Francisco, and I found my niche.

Some of the first films I saw that featured performers who were androgynous and trans were Christopher Lee's *Sex Flesh in Blood*, Morty Diamond's *Valley of the Tranny Fags*, Sex-Positive Production's *Please Don't Stop*, and SIR's *Sugar High Glitter City* and *How to Fuck in High Heels*. It was upon seeing the performers in these works that I knew porn had a place for me. I could do porn without having to change who I was.

Enter *The Crash Pad*. I performed with my lover at the time, a pivotal moment in my life and what launched my adventures in porn. Our scene was called Boi on Boi. We matched in gender and appeared in our everyday clothing: jeans, sneakers, shirts, boy briefs. The scene began with a wrestling match, an homage to gay porn that determined which of us would be top or bottom. (I lost: bottom.) Our verdant performance was a turn on then and now.

The film accurately portrayed my gender, and I rejoiced in finding a place where I could be sexy by being myself. I felt comfortable and found porn to be a safe space. In later productions, I began to toy with the use of drag.

My genderqueer identity is one of neutrality. Whether I dress up in suits or a skirt, either direction on the gender spectrum feels like performing in drag. I use drag to explore my interactions with others based on my perceived gender. When I use it in sex, it's a visual, physical, and emotional adventure.

The second film I did was one in which I was cast as femme. I created a character, Vasa, named after the Chicks on Speed song "Kaltes Klares Wasser"—meaning cold hard water. (Appropriate for both my love of female ejaculation and because the sex scene was in a kitchen, involving a spray nozzle from the sink faucet.) Vasa is a sassy punk chick and a sexual switch. Not wanting to wait in line for the bathroom at a house party, she pisses in the sink where she is approached by her costar. Midscene, her choppy blue/black wig is removed to reveal a boyish crew cut with the same dye job. A gender twist ensues as the sex is flipped and she attacks her costar with a blast of cold water.

Doing femme drag felt comfortable to me in the context of queer porn. In preparation for the scene, I decided to get waxed for the first time. Most of my life, I've been au naturel. Suddenly bare, I was surprised to find smooth skin so arousing. I was constantly aware of my labia and was reminded about my naked vulva was every time I took a step. It felt dirty, like it was my little secret. I couldn't wait to show it off on camera.

Interestingly, packing a flaccid cock has a similar feeling for me. Wearing a soft-pack in public adds a new awareness to my pelvis, a secret realistic bulge waiting to be discovered. Once, after shooting with Belladonna in *Strapped Dykes*, I gifted her one and she surprised us all by packing when we went out that evening. "I'm wearing it," she grinned as we ordered dinner. I recognized her coy smile; it's one I share when I'm out on a date and my partner discovers I'm packing. It's an arousing example of gender play.

Playing with gender can dismantle sexual stereotypes. For example, many believe that being feminine means being submissive and masculinity equals dominance. While this can describe some, it's not true of everyone. Femme can be submissive just as easily as it can be dominant. And male sexuality can certainly be submissive. I've found that my femme drag is often toppy, controlling the scene regardless if I'm the one being fucked or not. With masculinity, I've discovered that my boi is often a bottom, or if I'm the one fucking, a service top. The pleasure I give or receive is one of emotional lust, visceral physicality, and a conscious aesthetic. Visual display is a big part in my arousal when I use gender in sex.

In *Justify My Jiz*, my costar, Wolf Hudson, and I took inspiration from *Vogue* fashion. We wore fishnets, heels, jockstraps, and eyeliner. Our naked chests and entwined legs gave the appearance of two effeminate men in bed. Sometimes it was difficult to tell whose legs were whose. I pulled aside my jockstrap and Wolf took my flaccid cock into his mouth, sucking and pulling on the shaft with his full lips. I imagine a gay sex scene as he's blowing me. In the shot, the camera pans to also reveal my small breasts. Here the scene morphs; at a glance, I look like a trans woman. Then, my cock is cast aside as Wolf laps at my clit, his head nuzzled between my thigh-high fishnets. Now is it a straight scene? Later, Wolf's on his back. My realistic strap-on cock is about the same color and size as his flesh penis. I slide in his ass, stroking his penis in sync with my thrusts. From my point of view, it looks like his cock is an extension of my own. An M. C. Escher dick of surreal proportions. My sex became his, and we end in mutual ejaculatory orgasms.

Playing with gender can explore sexuality and desire. Gender can be a prop for sexual escapades, and a useful device to break down stereotypes and find liberation in sexuality. Much like vibrators, dildos, and other sex toys can be used for foreplay, arousal, and self-discovery, gender can provide an erotic experience in toying with pleasure. Can gender be a sex toy? You bet your vibrating, silicone balls it can.

JIZ LEE

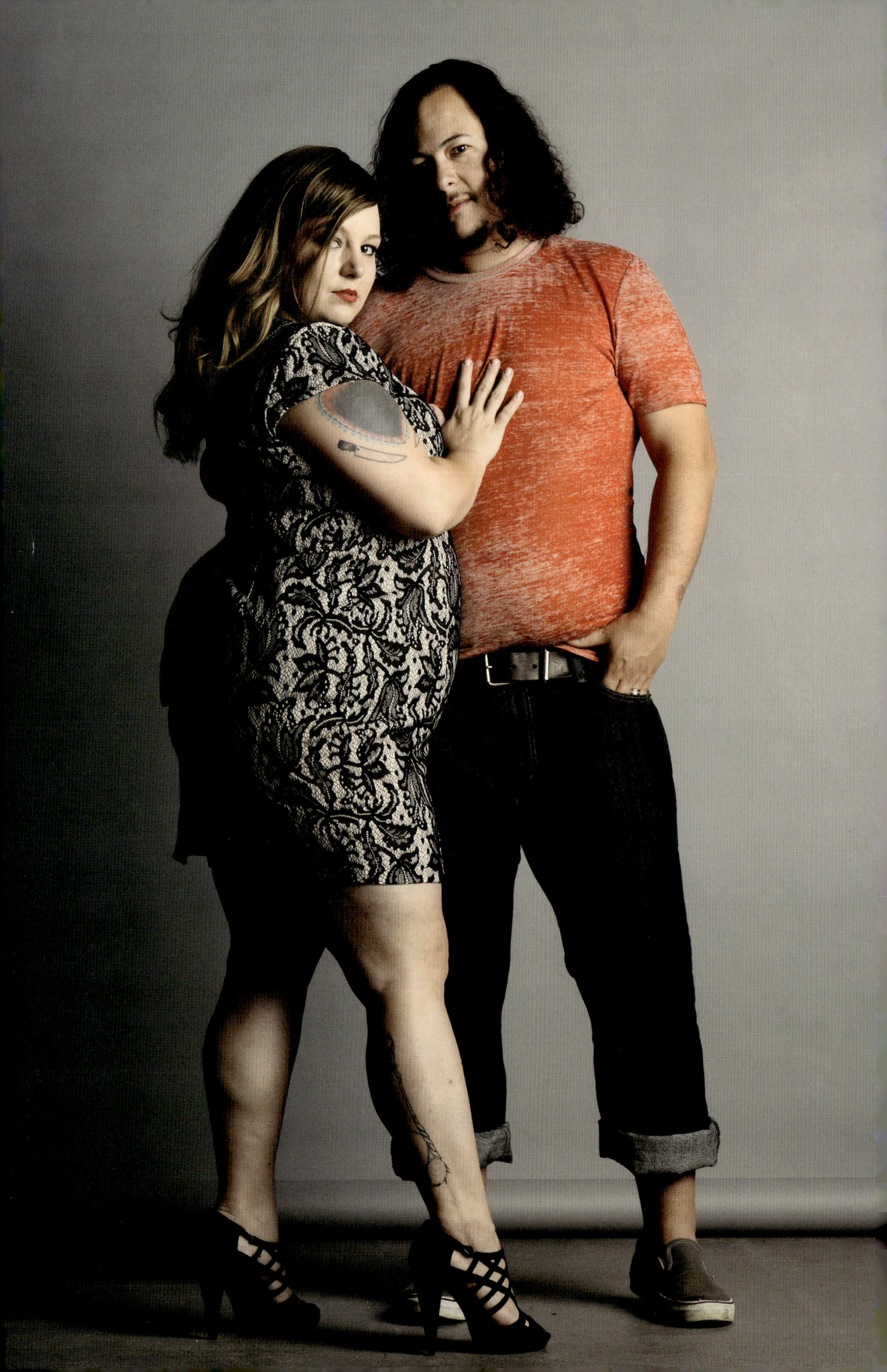

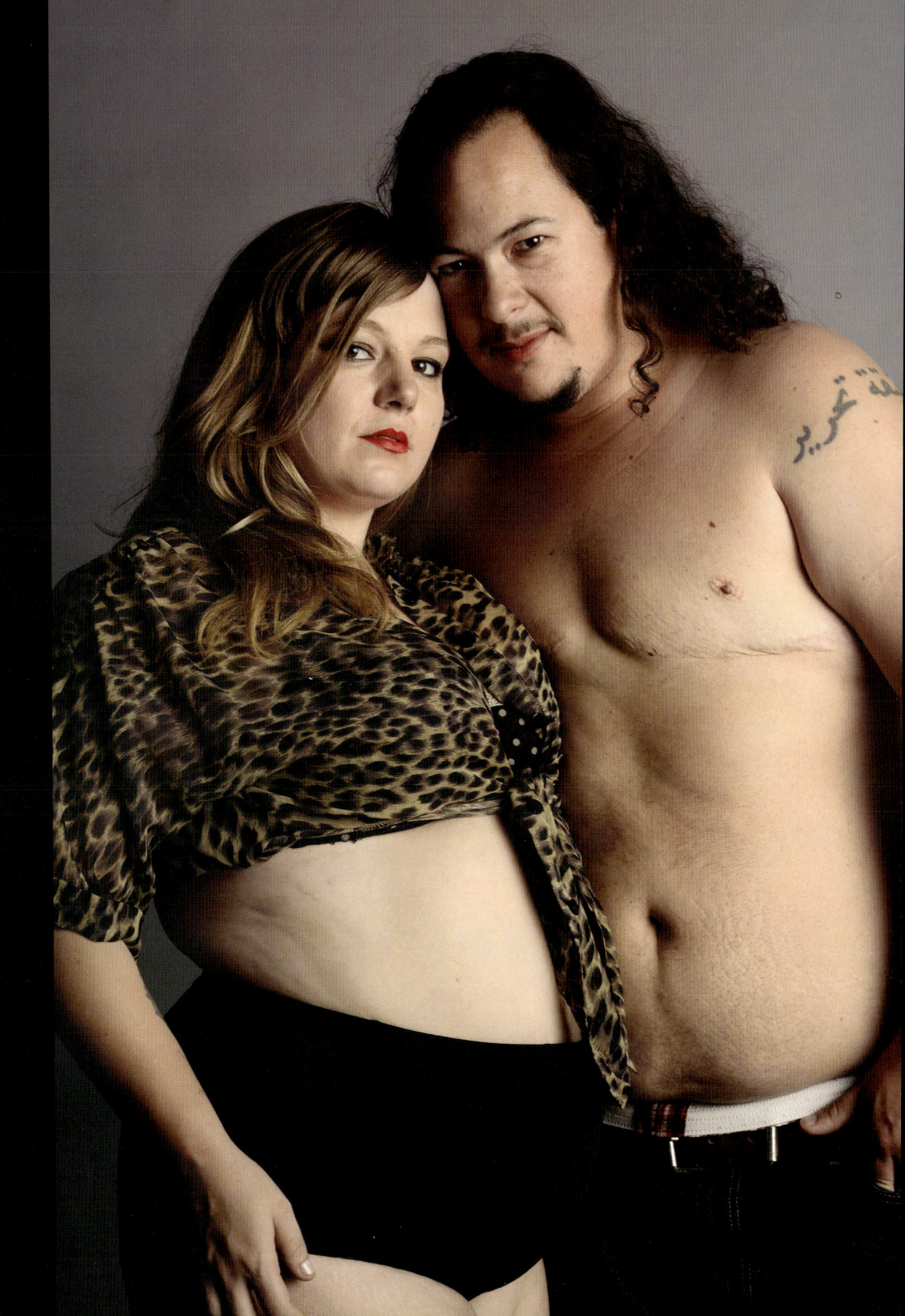

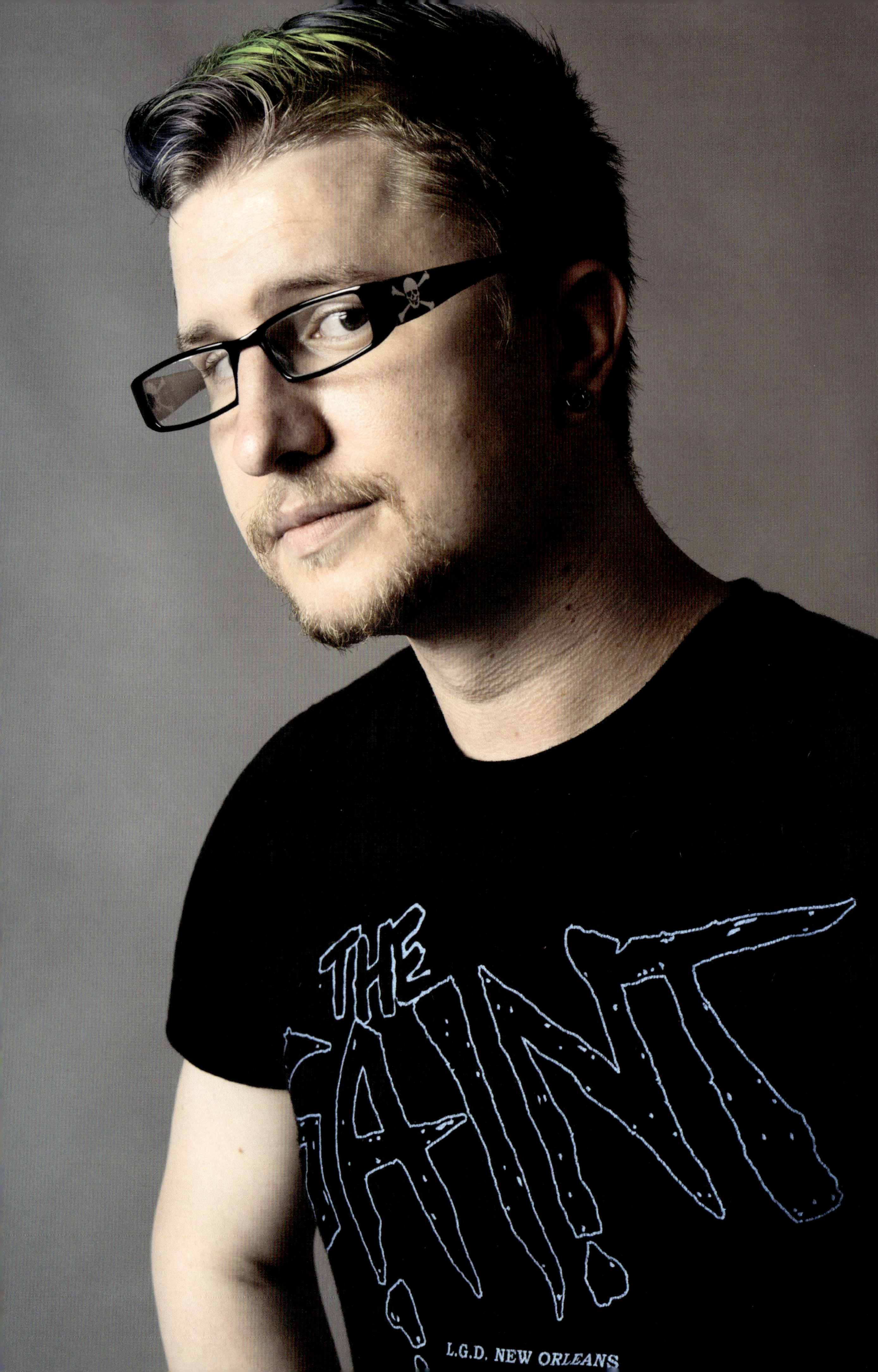
THE FAINT
L.G.D. NEW ORLEANS

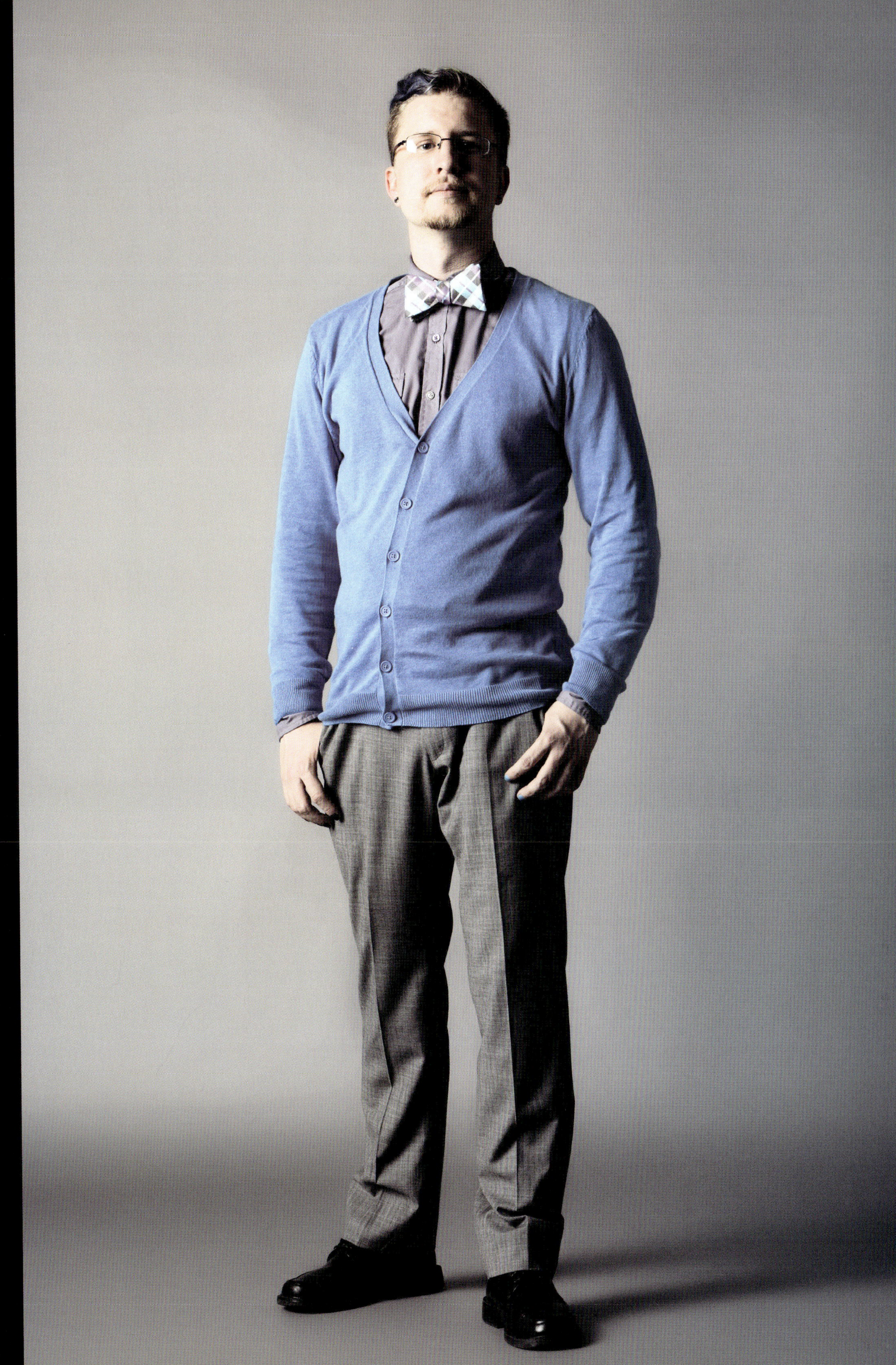

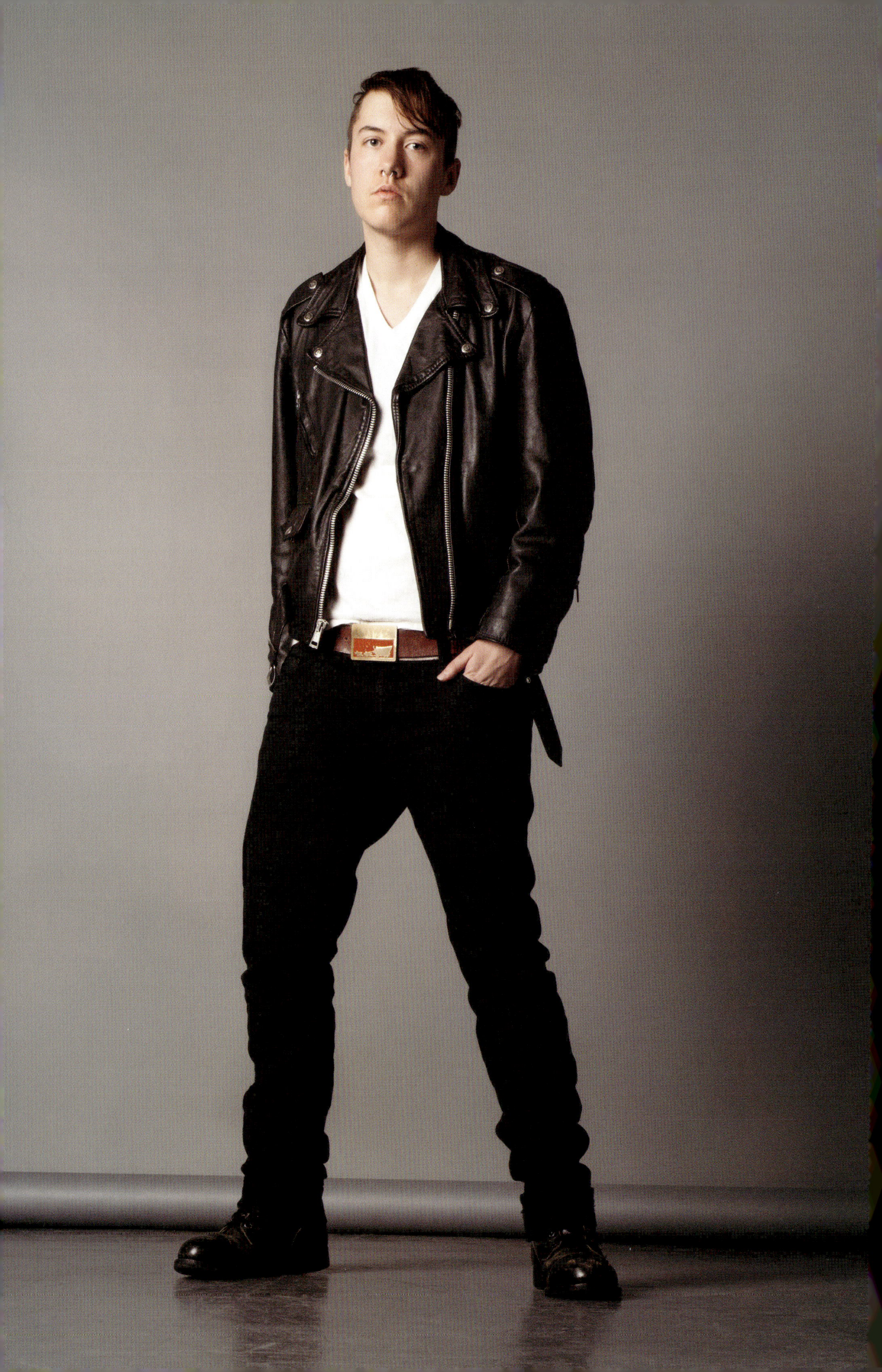

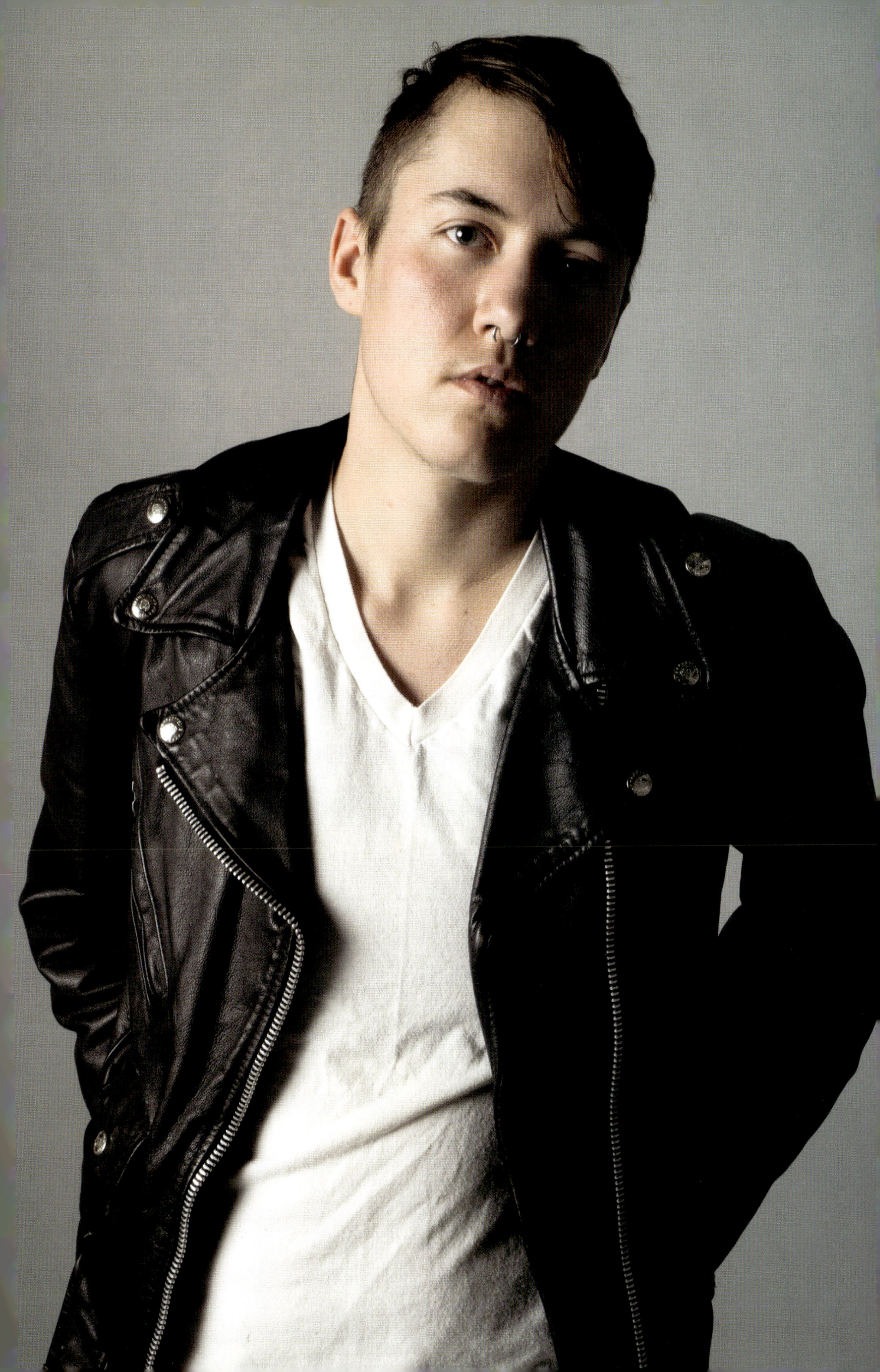

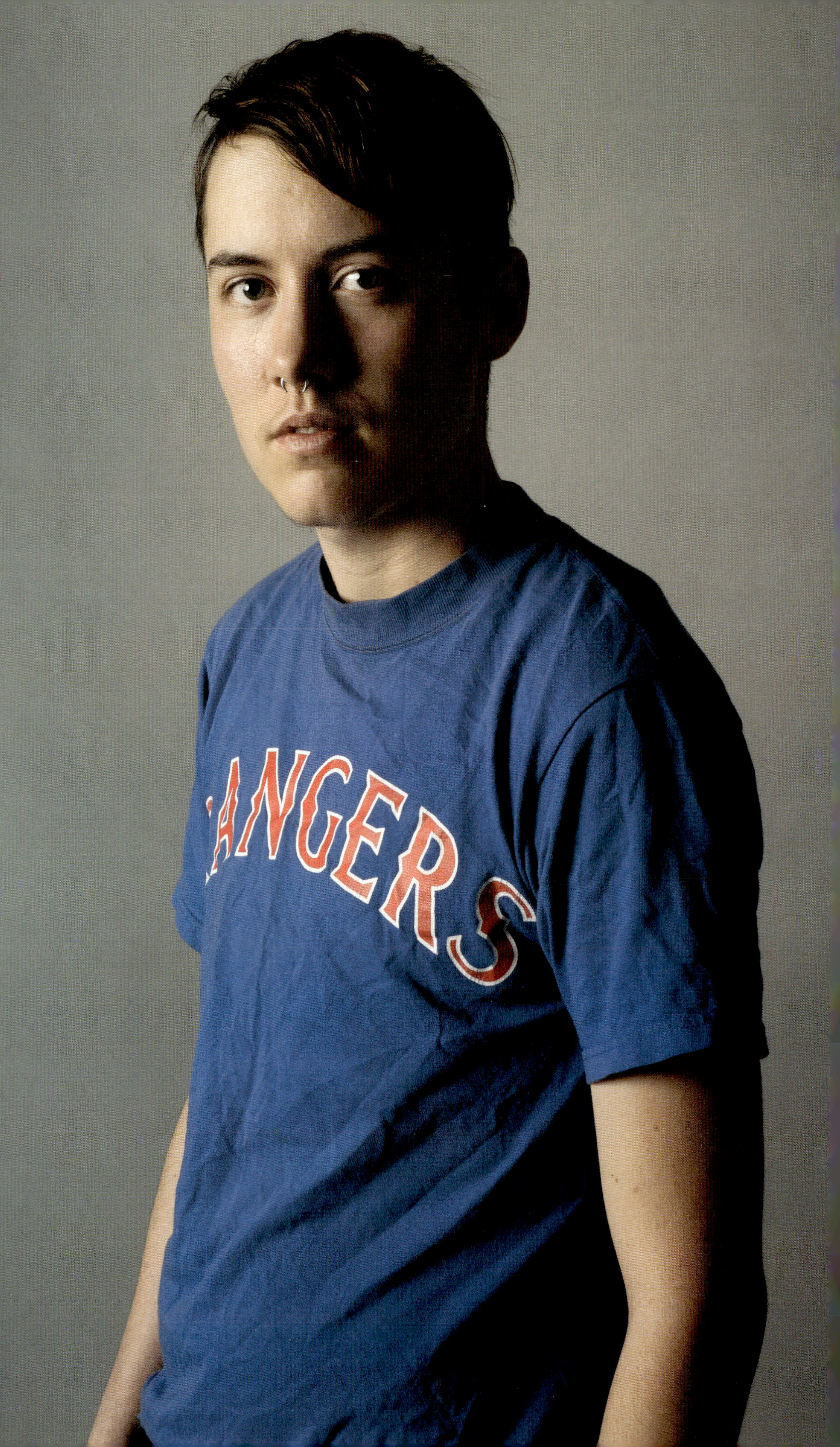

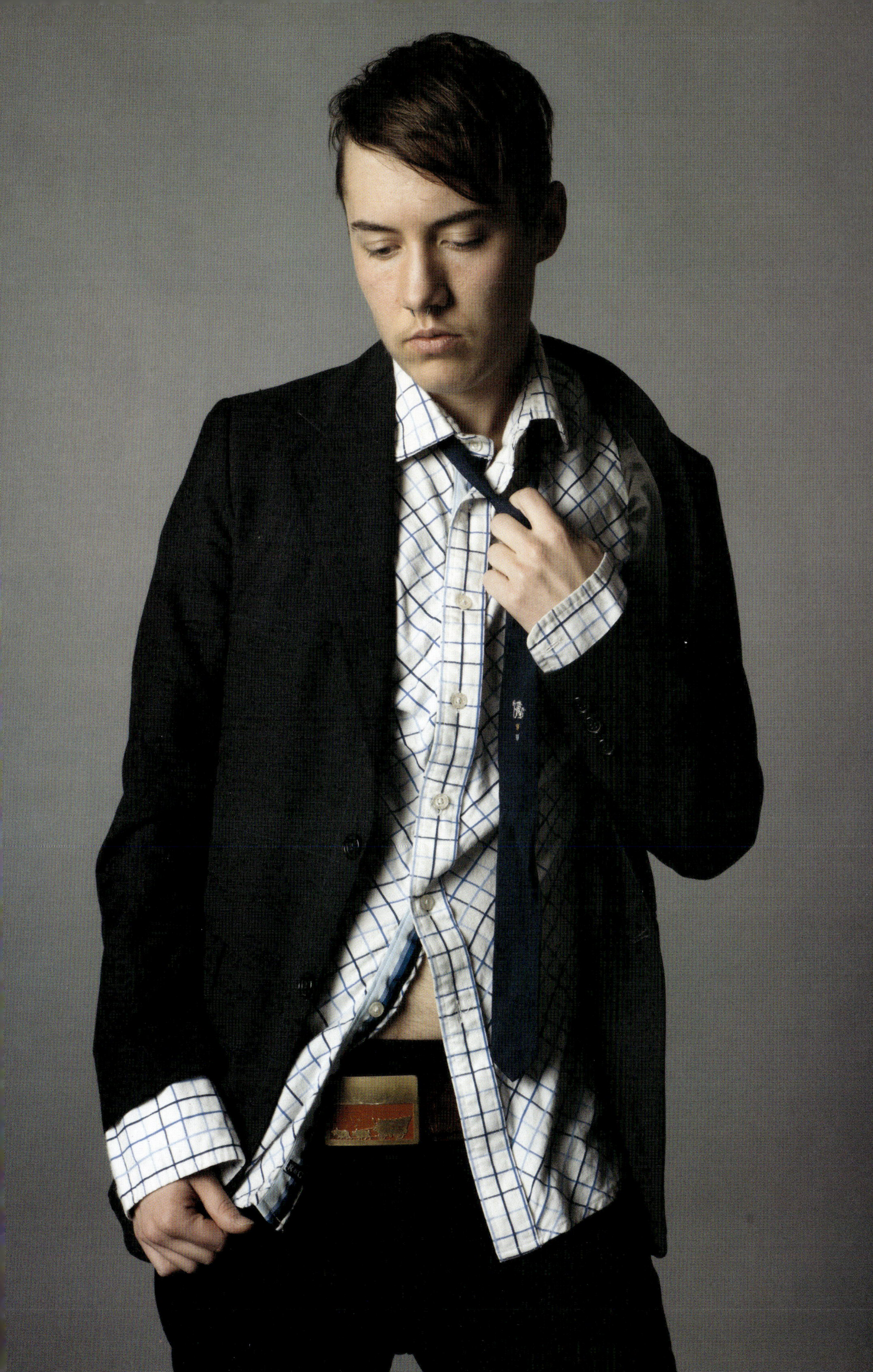

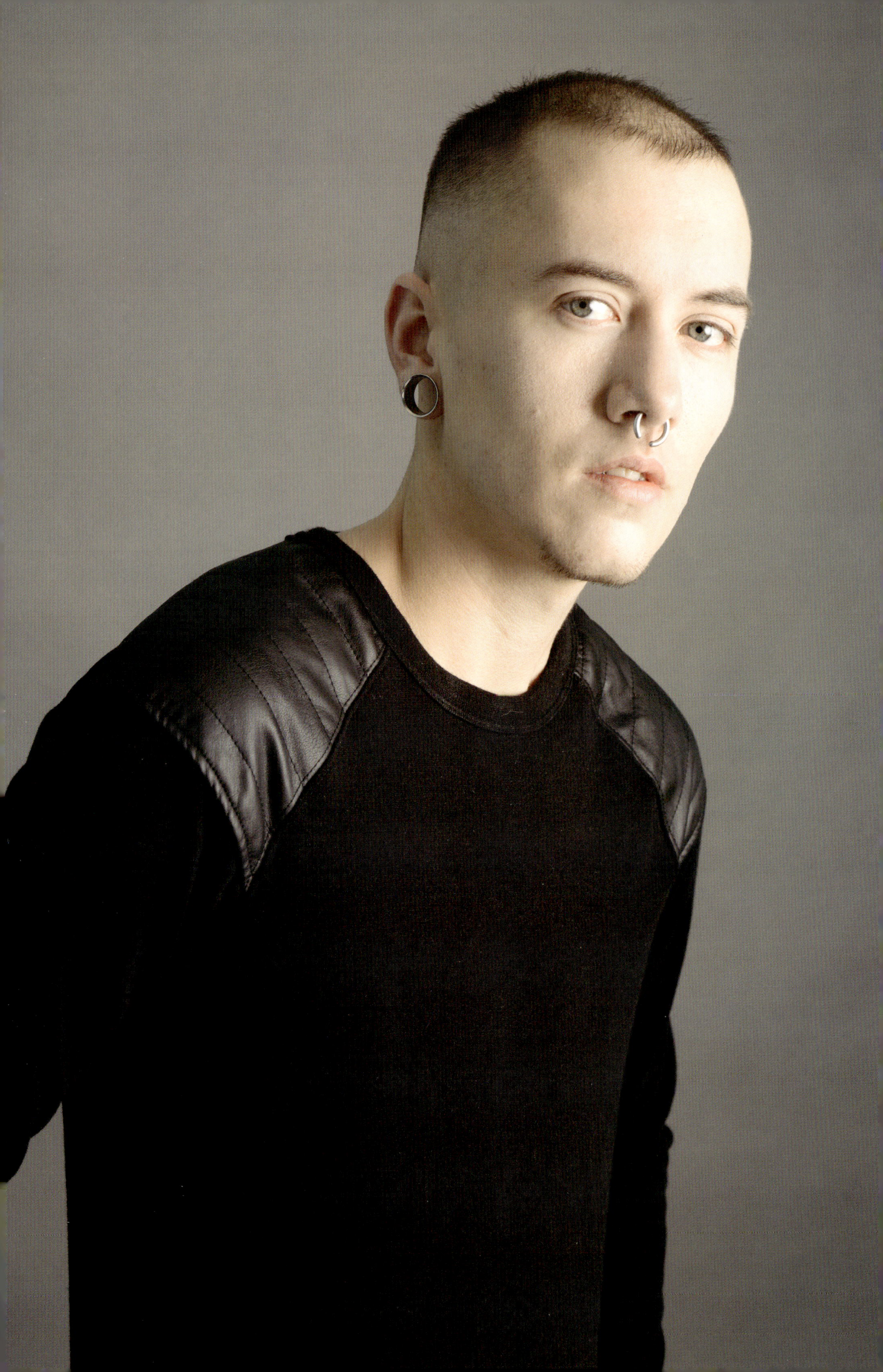

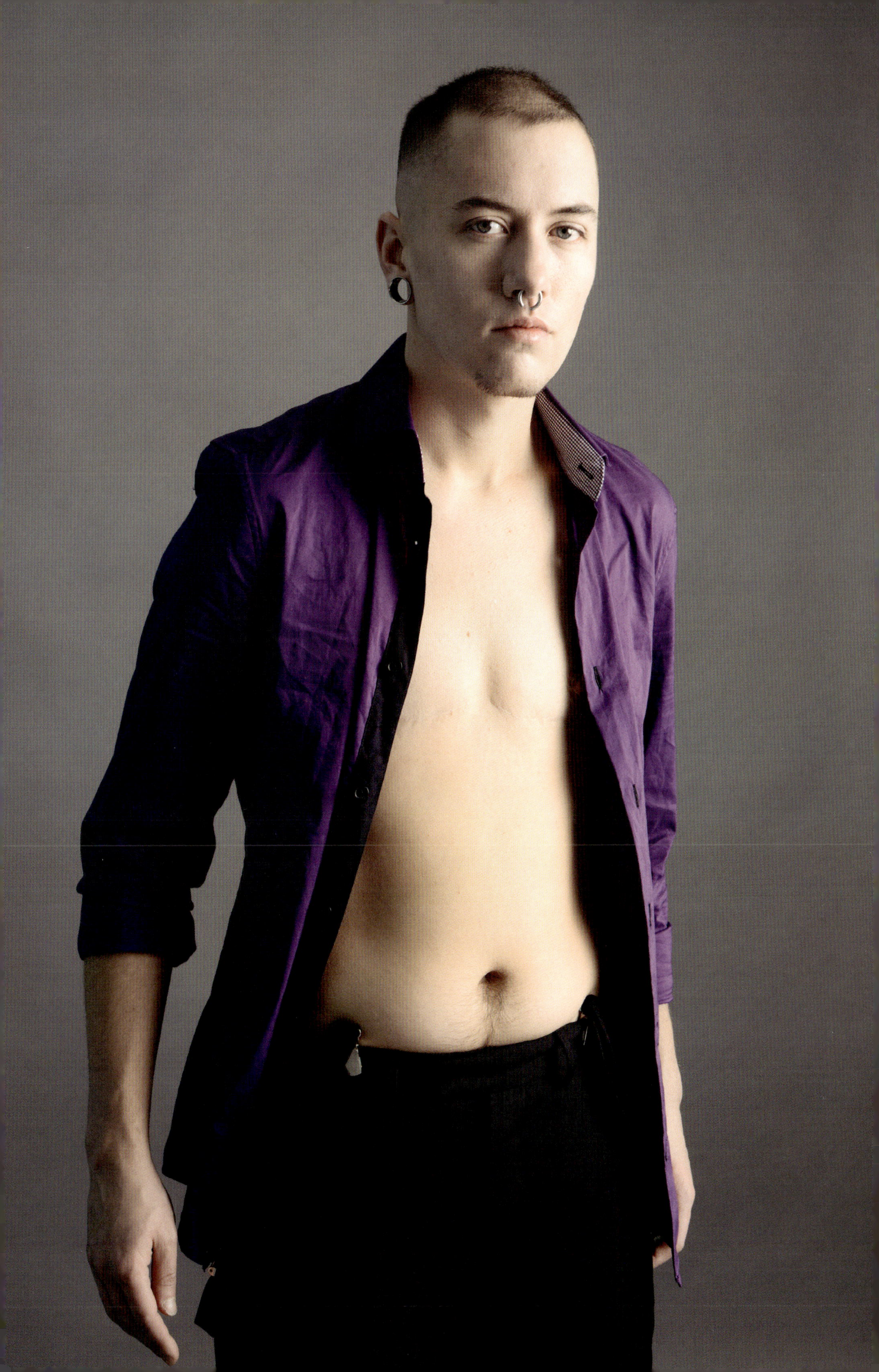

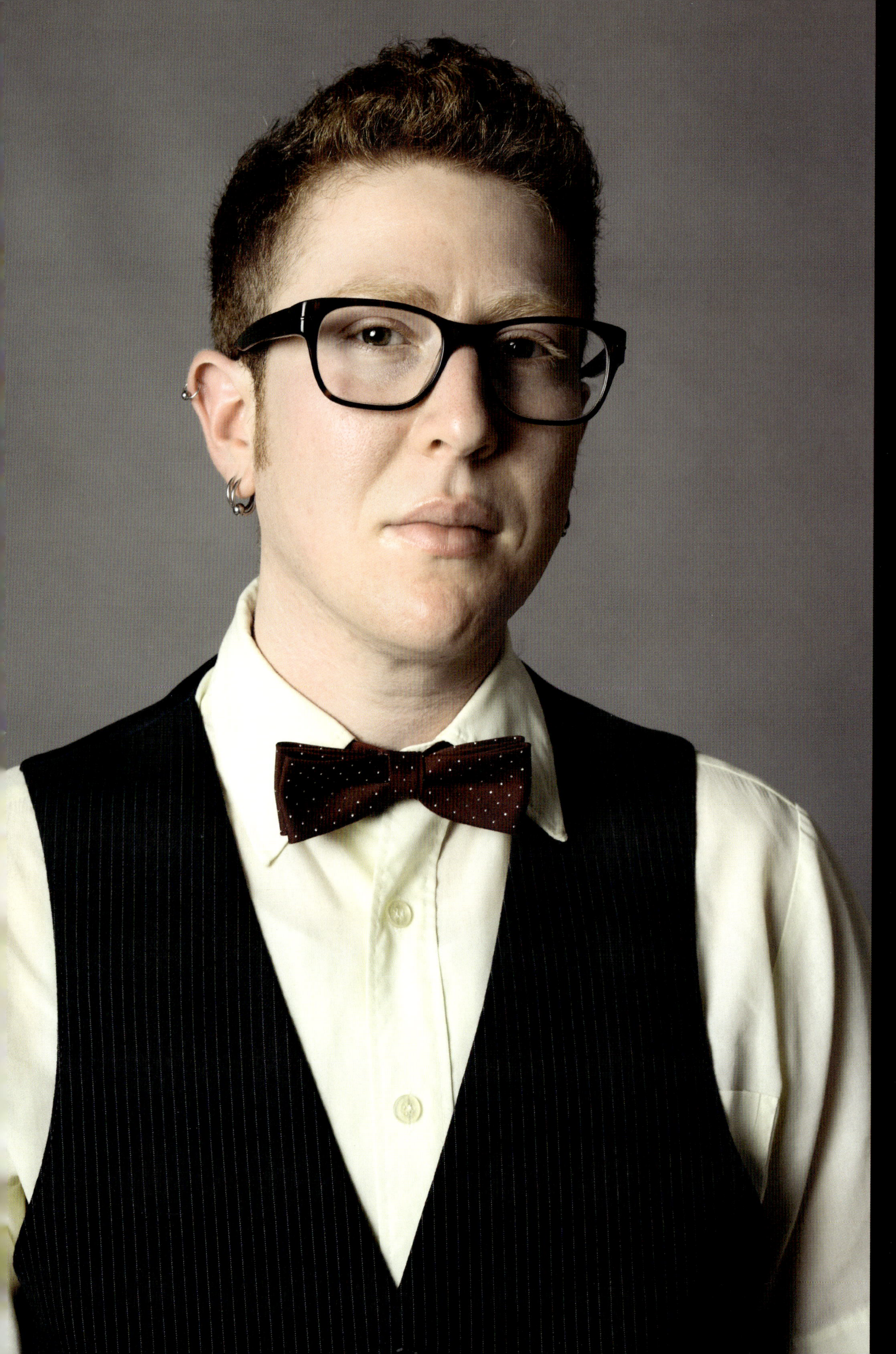

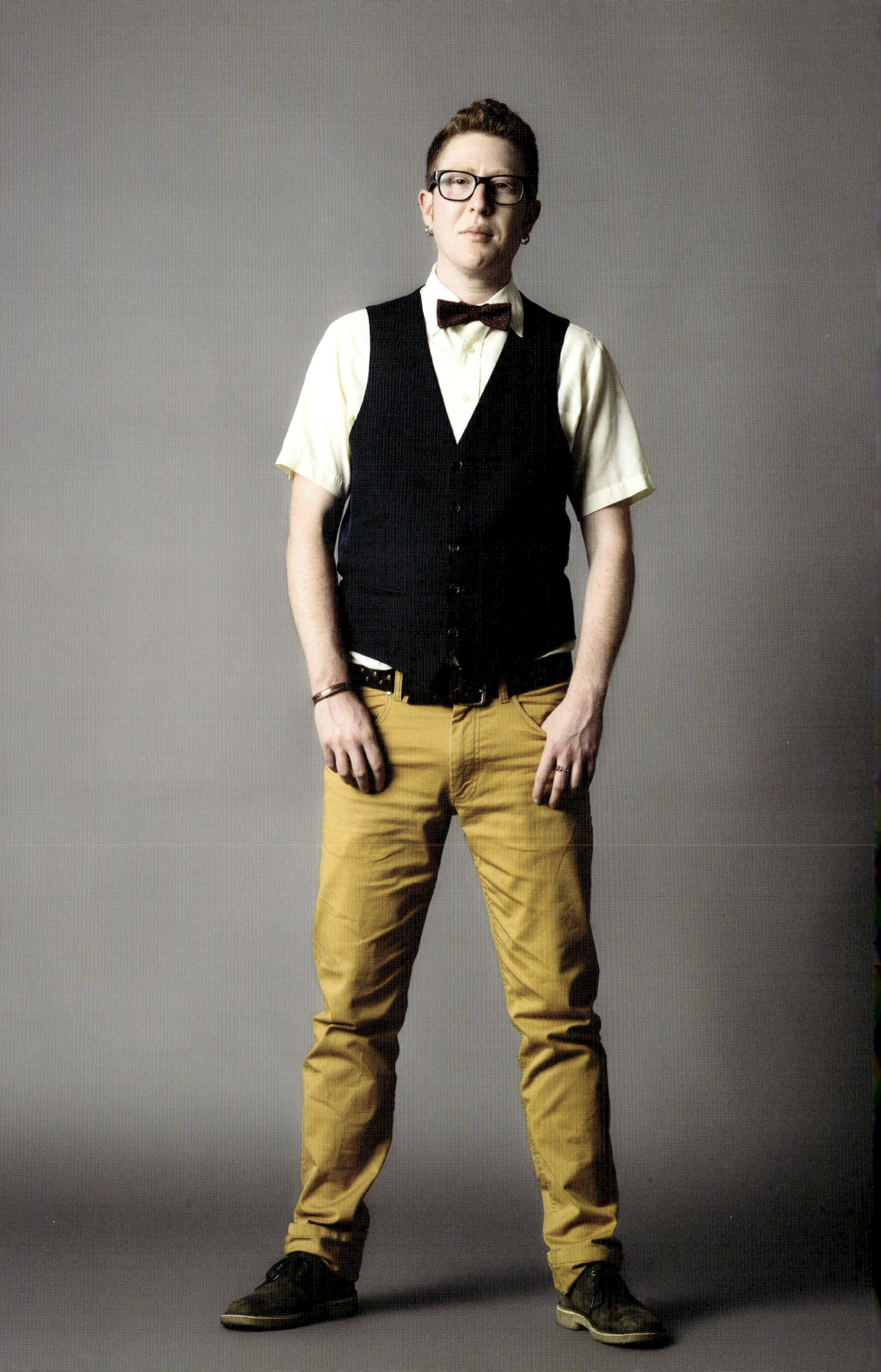

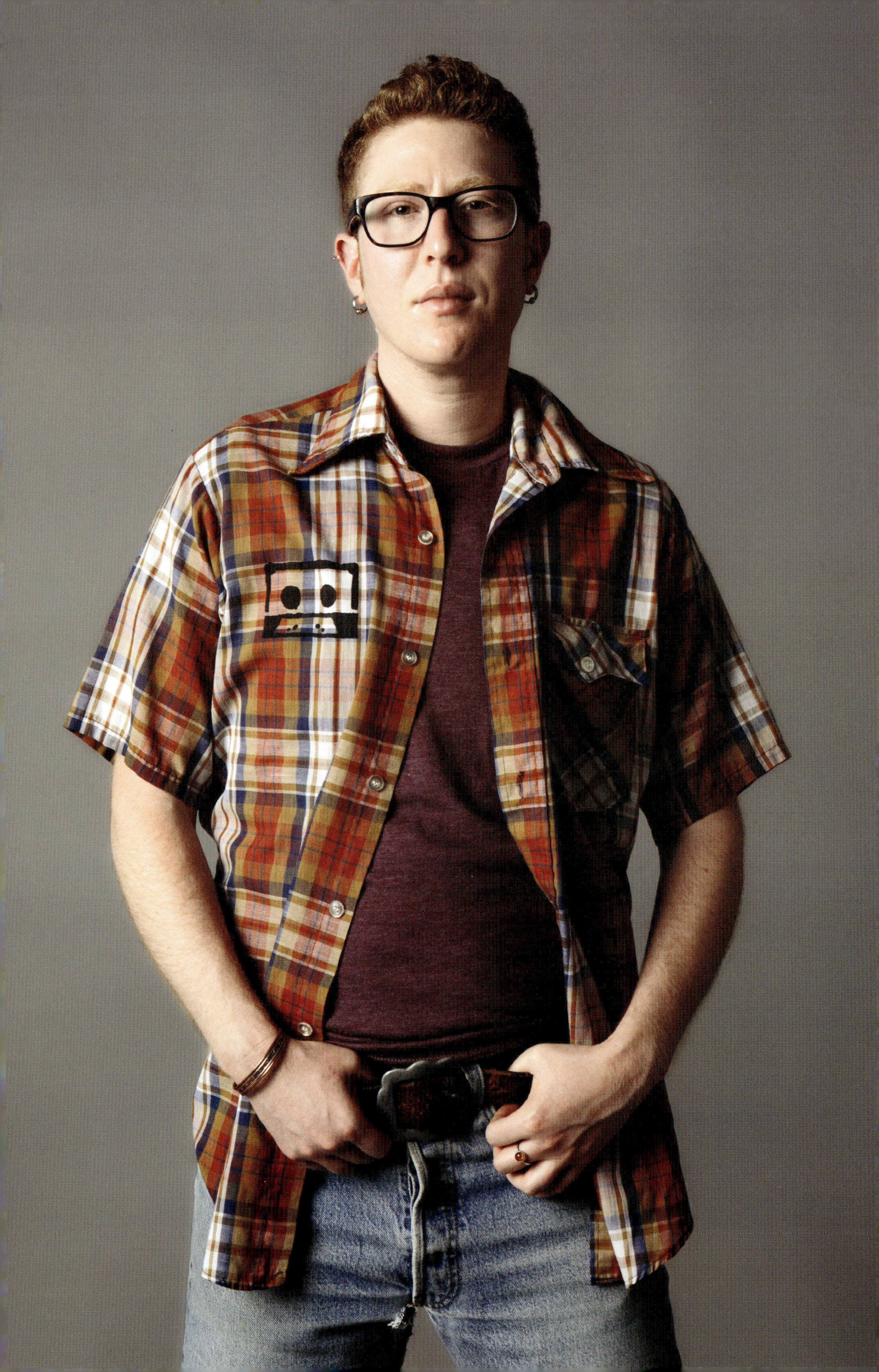

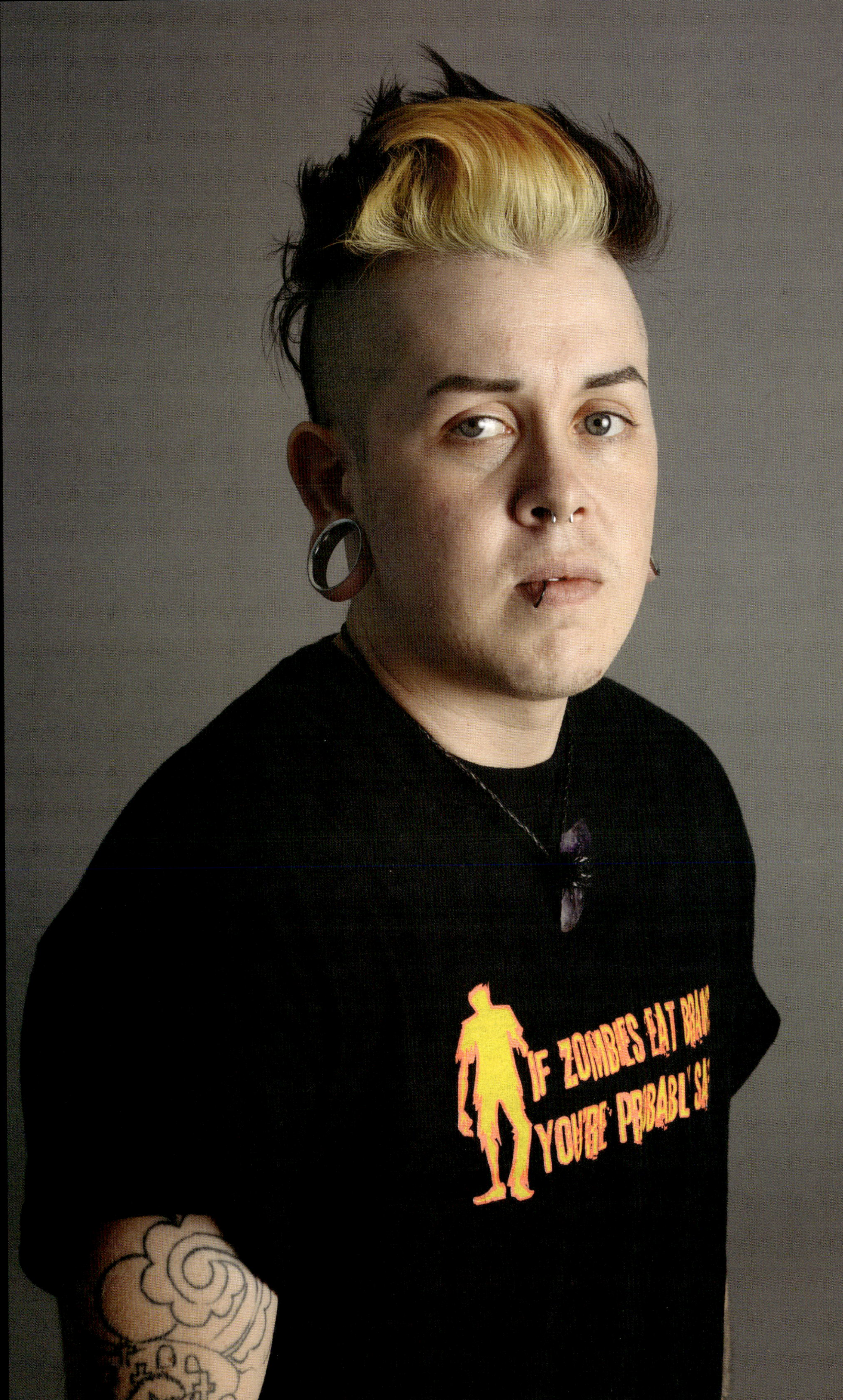
IF ZOMBIES EAT
YOU'RE

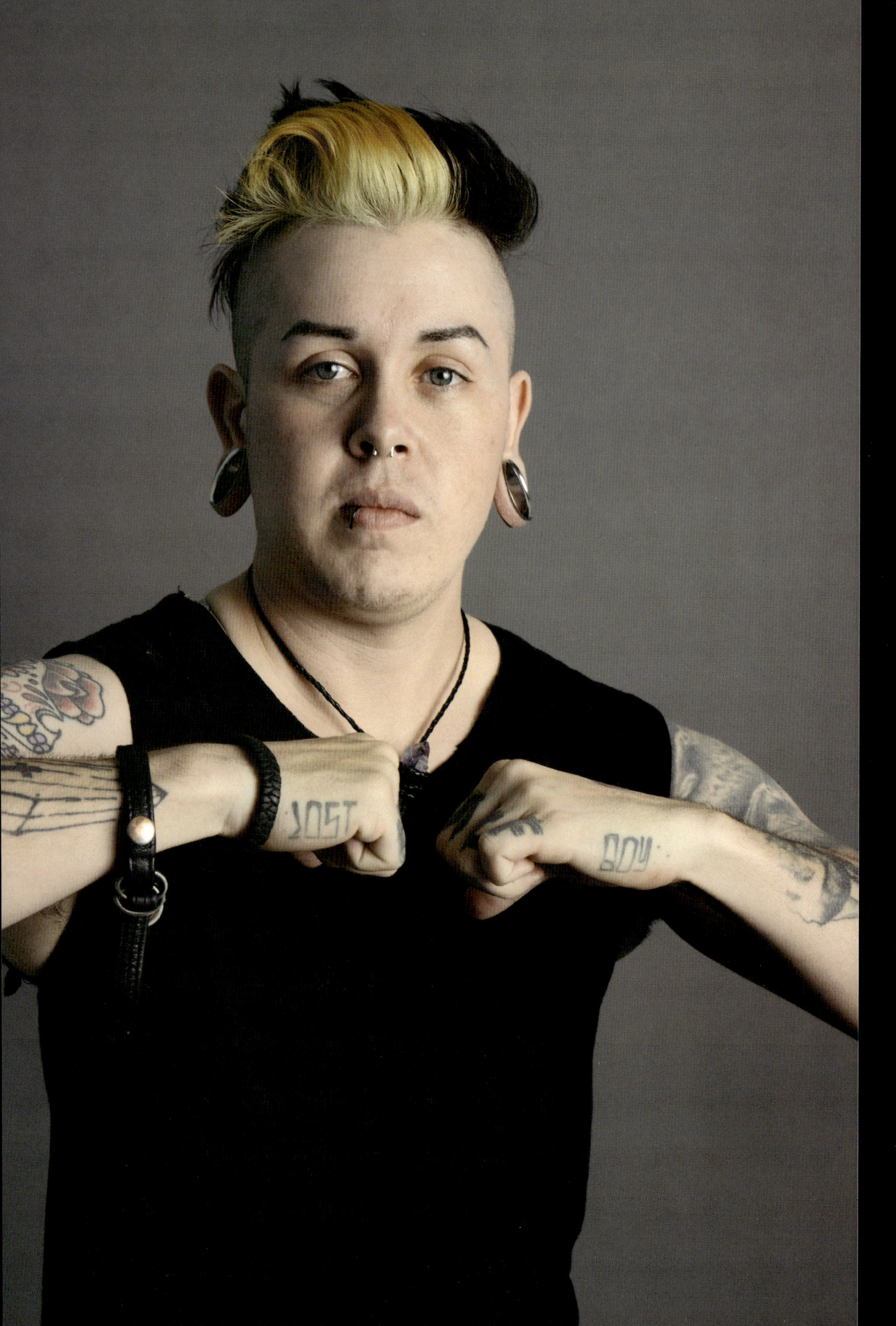
LOST
BOY

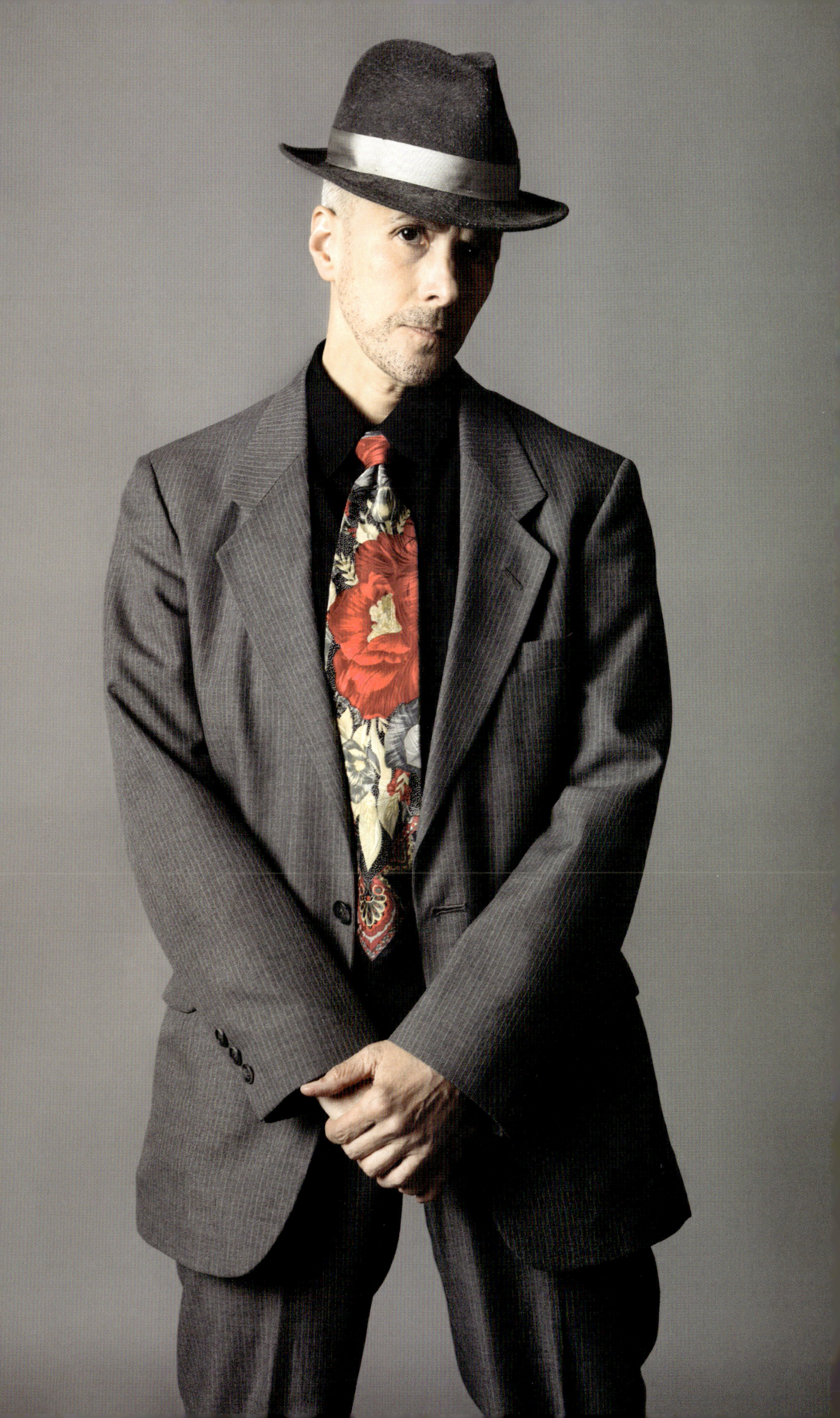

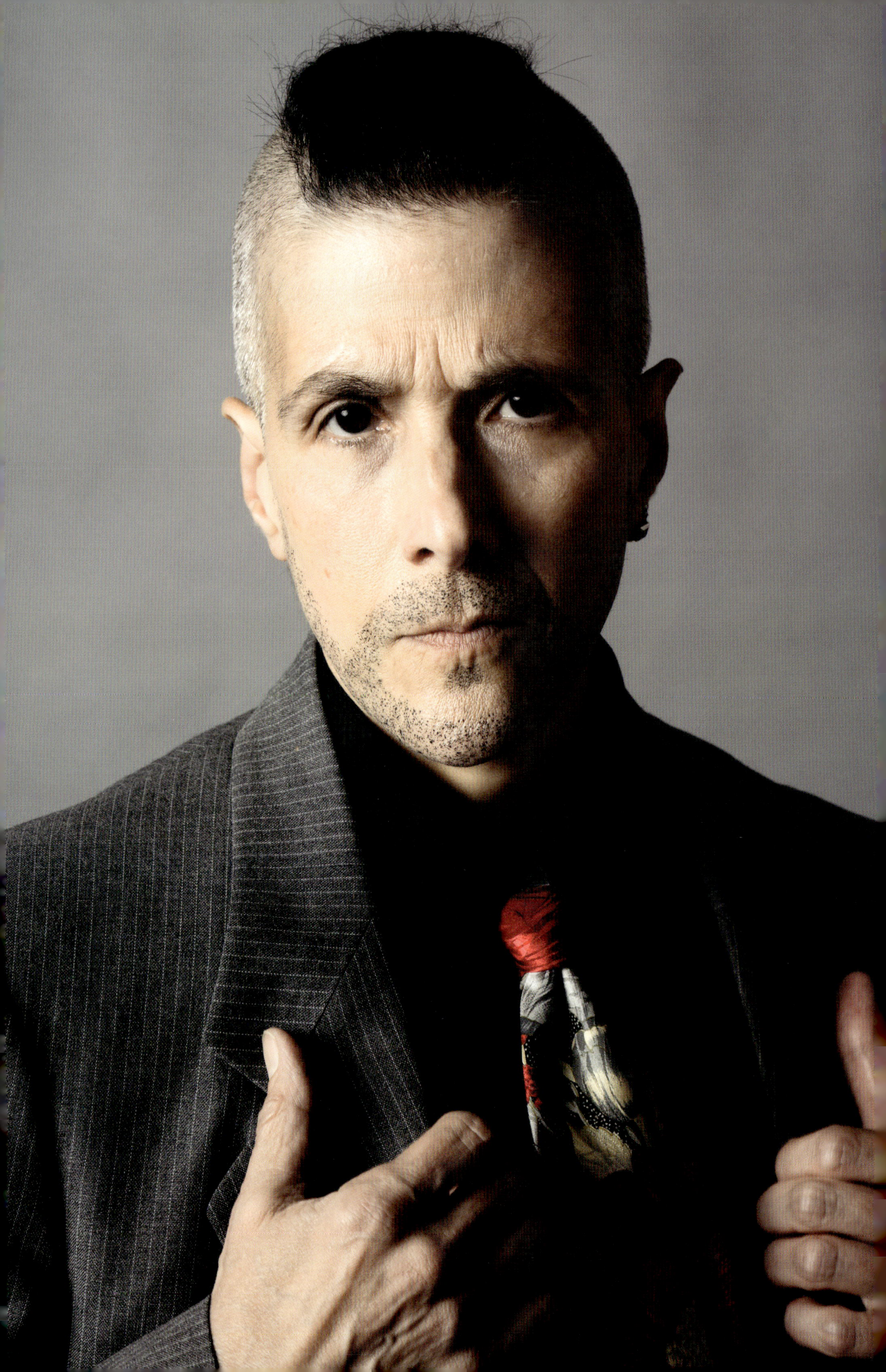

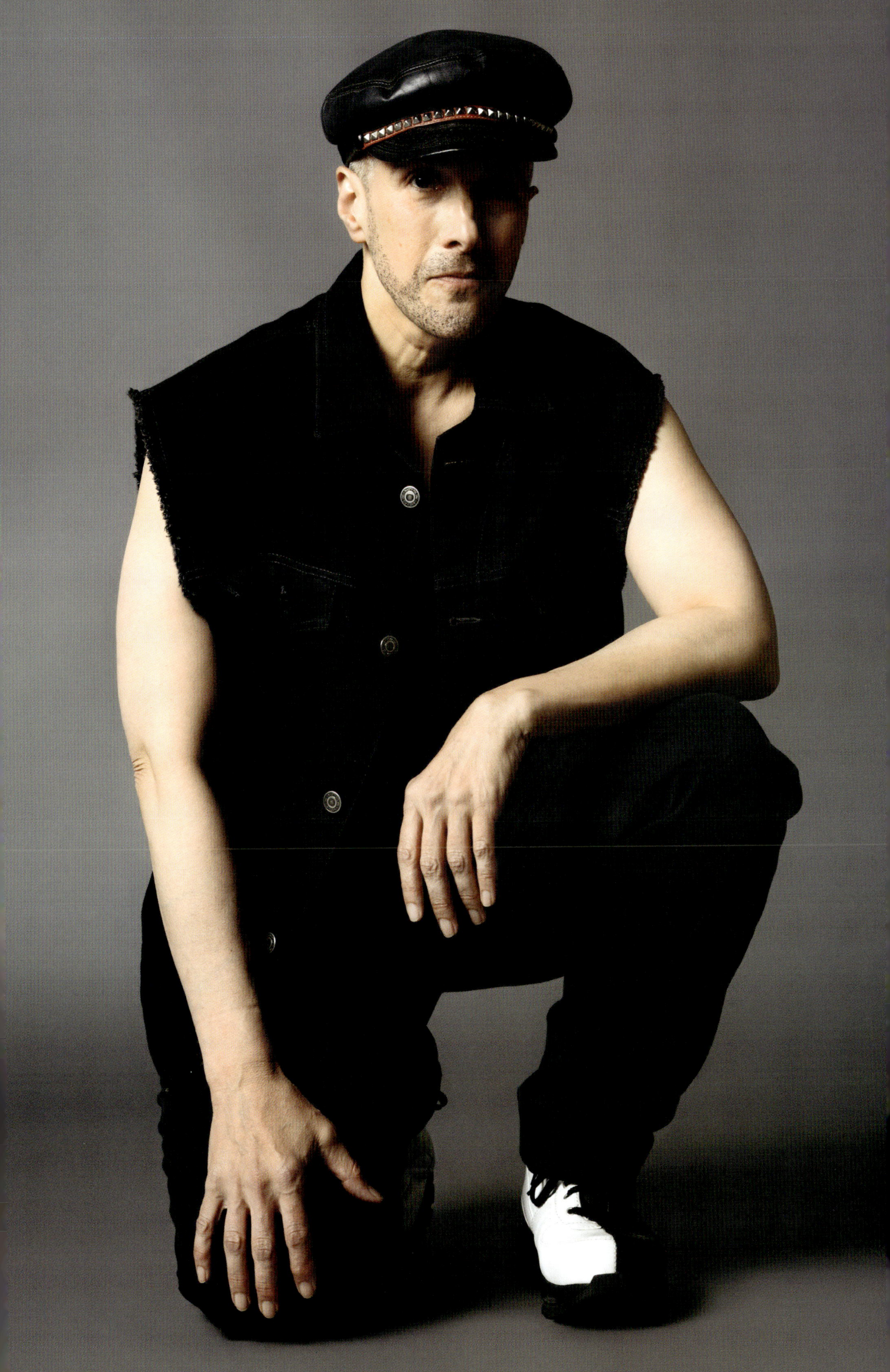

GENDER IN STEREOGRAM

Do you remember stereogram images? Think back to when it seemed like everyone was standing in front of one of these multidimensional graphic images, head cocked to the side, brows arrowing downward, intense looks adorning faces. People would stare and wait in anticipation until that moment happened—the moment when an embedded image was revealed to them within the original image. I remember people being excited about these magical pictures that seemed to be everywhere at some point. Some people had the ability to see the inner image immediately, others took some time, and yet others weren't able to quite see what everyone else could. This is what I feel when people look at me. I am a stereogram waiting for people to see beyond the initial image of "female body" and into the other dimensions of my identity. The initial stare is quite the tell. Depending on how their eyes penetrate me, I know if they can or cannot see. The stare can be the vehicle of seeing or surveying me.

The idea of stereograms blew our minds at one juncture, but with new graphic technology now it seems so simple. The concept of seeing what is beneath the surface is not so complicated after all—once you understand it. Some of the simplest ideas seem to be complicated beyond belief, making them impossible to see, comprehend, or accept. These simplicities become unrecognizable in their true form, thereby rendering them false or nonexistent. For those who couldn't see beyond the top layer, the image was broken. The dimensionality did not exist.

This sounds very familiar to me. My gender identity is complicated and simultaneously simple. When one cannot go deep to view with an open mind, I am rendered null and void.

There are many layers that form who I am, personally and in the world. My internal sense of self, my culture, history, spirituality, and my politics inform who I am. I am a queer trans Black-Boricua Taíno. Queerness is almost always equated with whiteness, Blackness with homo/transphobia, and the Boricua Taíno is dead, I'm told. My identity is challenged on several core fronts. I must prove my existence. This is fueled by systematic oppression that enforces the denial of me and helps to fuel my own internalized oppression. Language betrays me as well. As I reteach myself the language that was taken by colonizers, I hope to rediscover the Taíno language that tells the story of me. Images of Boricuas and the racist, regurgitated idea of machismo delete our history and belief in dualism. My people believed in the union of male and female, mother and father, thus depicted in aspect of daily work, deities, and art. The Spanish language, handed down from colonizers, doesn't allow for my pronoun, neither does the English language, even though I stay firm that it is correct. They is denied and put on a platform to be argued. I concede the argument. It is irrelevant. My pronoun is they and therefore I am. In Spanish my pronoun is not ella or el but elli—deal with it.

I am a mujerista (Spanish for womanist, aka feminism without the racism) but identifying as trans, for some, is seen as a hatred of all that is female, the feminine and woman. Historically, I have known firsthand socially constructed ways of what it means to be a girl, a young lady, and a woman. This is my vessel. I will honor my history. It will forever be a part of me. The thing that dwells within my core tells a broader story, though. I am not a man, nor do I want to be. I have dreamt about transitioning is some way in hopes that I would be seen, but that desire isn't strong enough and it is not who I am. I understand my privilege within my no operation/no hormone aka no-op/no-ho identity. Privileged to some extent because at times, I can be seen as a woman, thereby passing. Others don't have that luxury. I'd rather provoke confusion, but confusion begets discomfort, begets anger and violence. I don't want to pass as a woman but sometimes this gender attribution saves my ass. Every day is unpredictable in how I am viewed, treated, and catcalled, and although passing as a woman in many ways is safer than being viewed as a man in a dress, or an imposter, being deemed a woman, and being a person of color within that, brings about its mix of misogyny and my sexual self as public domain. The violence perpetrated onto us rears its ugly head via sexual violence or physical hatred and overkill. People don't know if they want to fuck me or punch me.

There are many words one could use to identify my gender variance—trans, genderqueer, gender fluid, trans-entity, gender fucker, trans-former and/or gender nonconforming. Complexities emerge within the trans community in regards to trans enough. Am I trans enough if I do not intend on taking hormones or having surgery? Do I need to choose and fully transition to earn the right to be trans? In comparing invisibilities of sexual orientations, this idea of choosing a side is not so unfamiliar with what bisexuals have been up against for so long. Bisexuality is seen as a pit stop to gayness. Within itself, it is not acknowledged. We can see the unseeing of the femme queer woman, and the masculine gay man. They don't look queer, the inner image not viewable, thereby feeding into the notion of cookie-cutter queer models. These ideas limit us greatly.

The way I am viewed or not viewed affects every aspect of my life. It affects how I show my emotions, if I decide to bind or pack, and how I have negotiated sex. Since certain attributes are associated with feminine or masculine traits, at times it aids in altering my behavior. If I'm meeting someone for the first time, I butch it up a bit. I help their process in this initial viewing, hoping they can see what lies beneath. Within my genderqueer community, I'm comfortable in all my manifestations. I'm comfortable limp wristed, leg crossed, high pitched, and unbinded. They get me. Outside of that, I am careful.

The first impressions will either allow for the realization of the imbedded or it will never happen. I shift between femininity and masculinity, but at times I stay close to the shores of one until it is safe to test the rest of the waters. When negotiating sex with cis men or women, I am guarded. Deciding to keep my binder on, only topping, or only doing anal. This isn't always the case but the internal process is there. The fear of invisibility stays.

My identity, in its many facets, continues to be complicated by the state and other institutions. The state created and society maintains the exclusivity of the gender binary. It is maintained by the binary heteronormative forms we fill out, by doctors we visit, social services we seek, by our employers, our religious institutions, and our support networks. For many years, I have worked as an artist, an activist, and an educator using this privilege as a tool for change, education, and my sanity. I've been able to cut out a piece of solace for me and do great work. I've had a platform that allowed me to talk about my gender. Leaving this bubble of comfort has been terrifying to me. I've worked so hard to crush the surveillance gaze and be seen. Depending on where I am, who I'm hanging out with, and what I'm doing, the stare shifts. The way I'm perceived in the world is in constant flux. I hate this and understand it. I only wish that society had broader visions of gender identity and expression. I wish they weren't so afraid of it. I wish that they'd understand that historically, gender variance has always existed.

My gender identity is multidimensional. I am deep. Penetrate me with your eyes passionately. View me. See me. I am gender in stereograms.

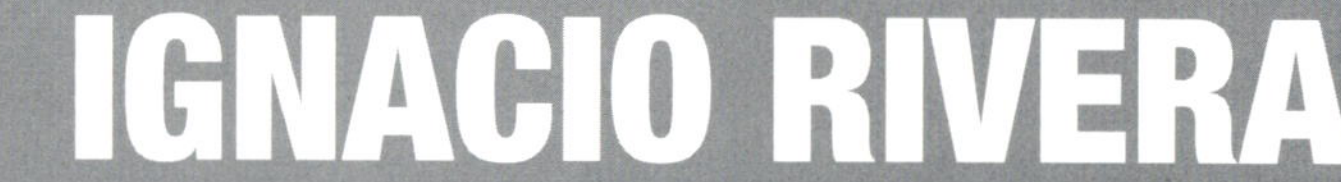

IGNACIO RIVERA

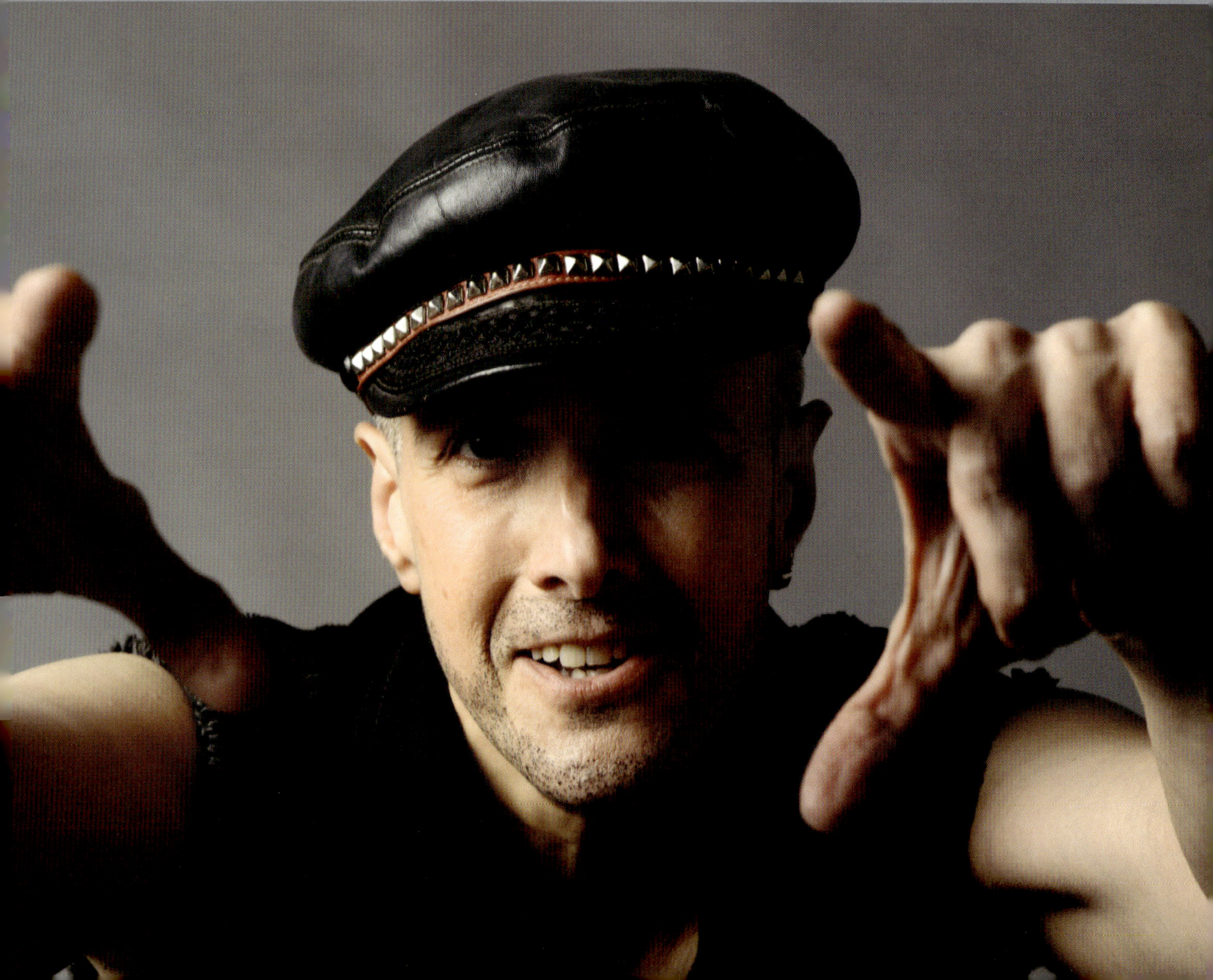

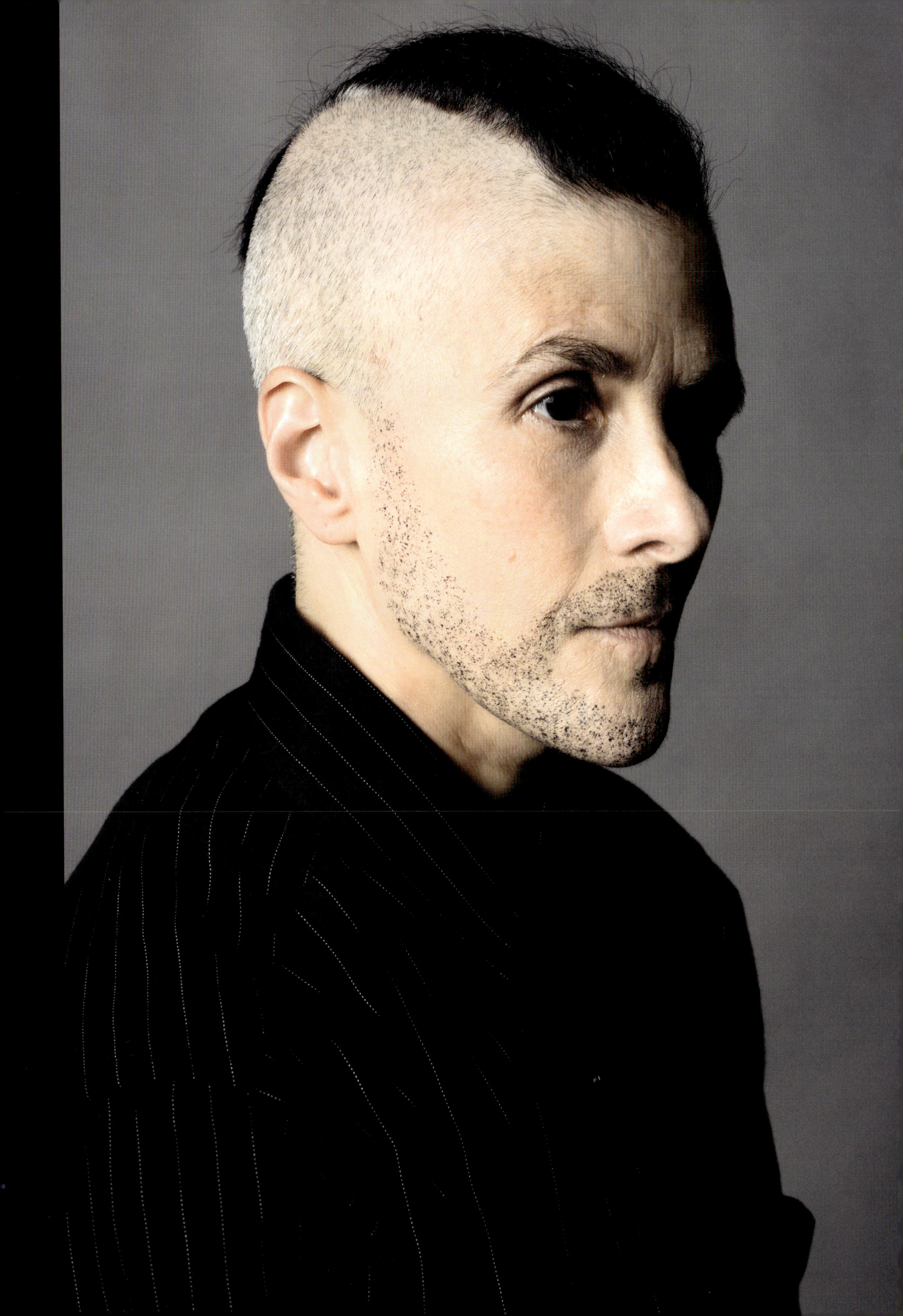

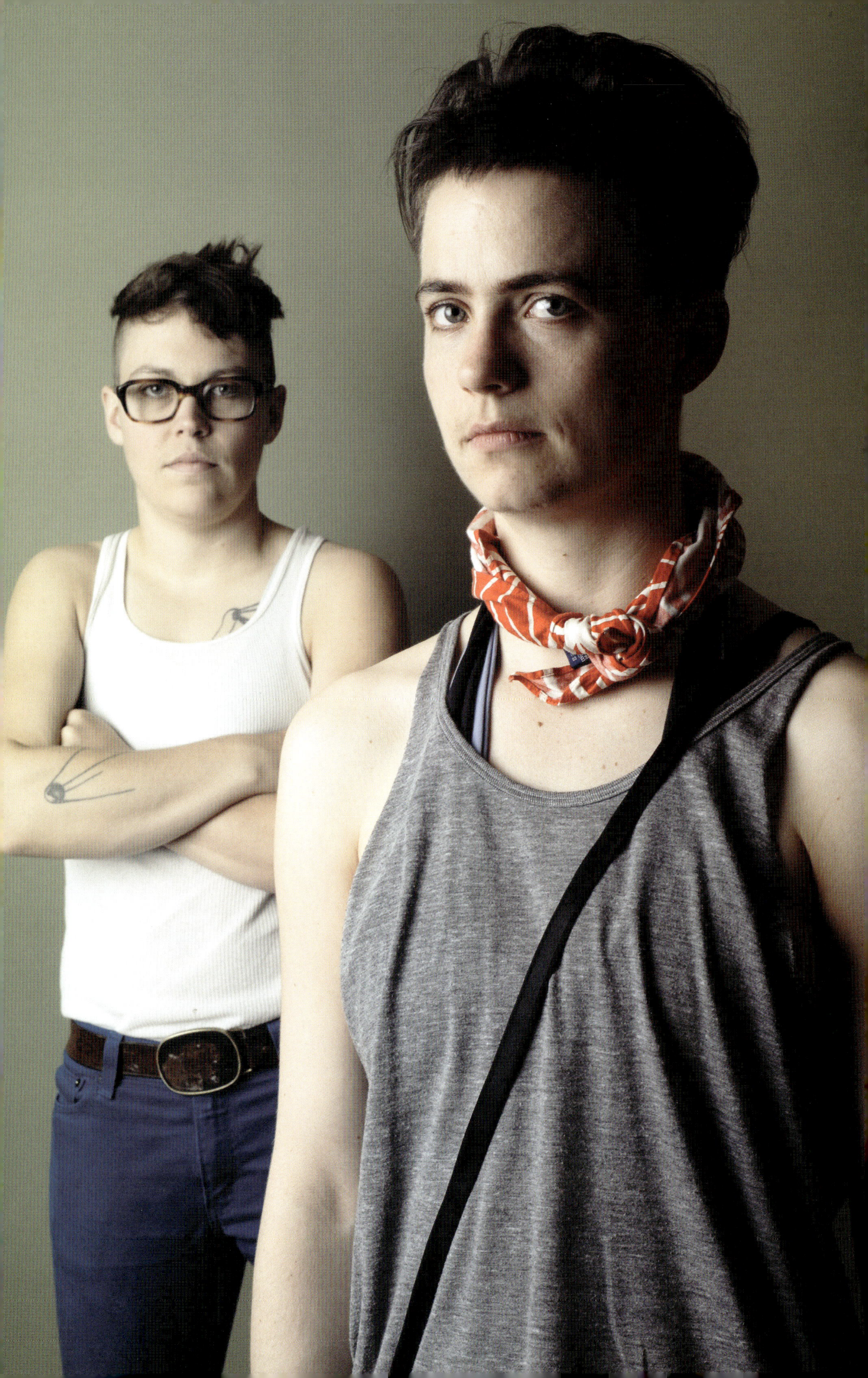

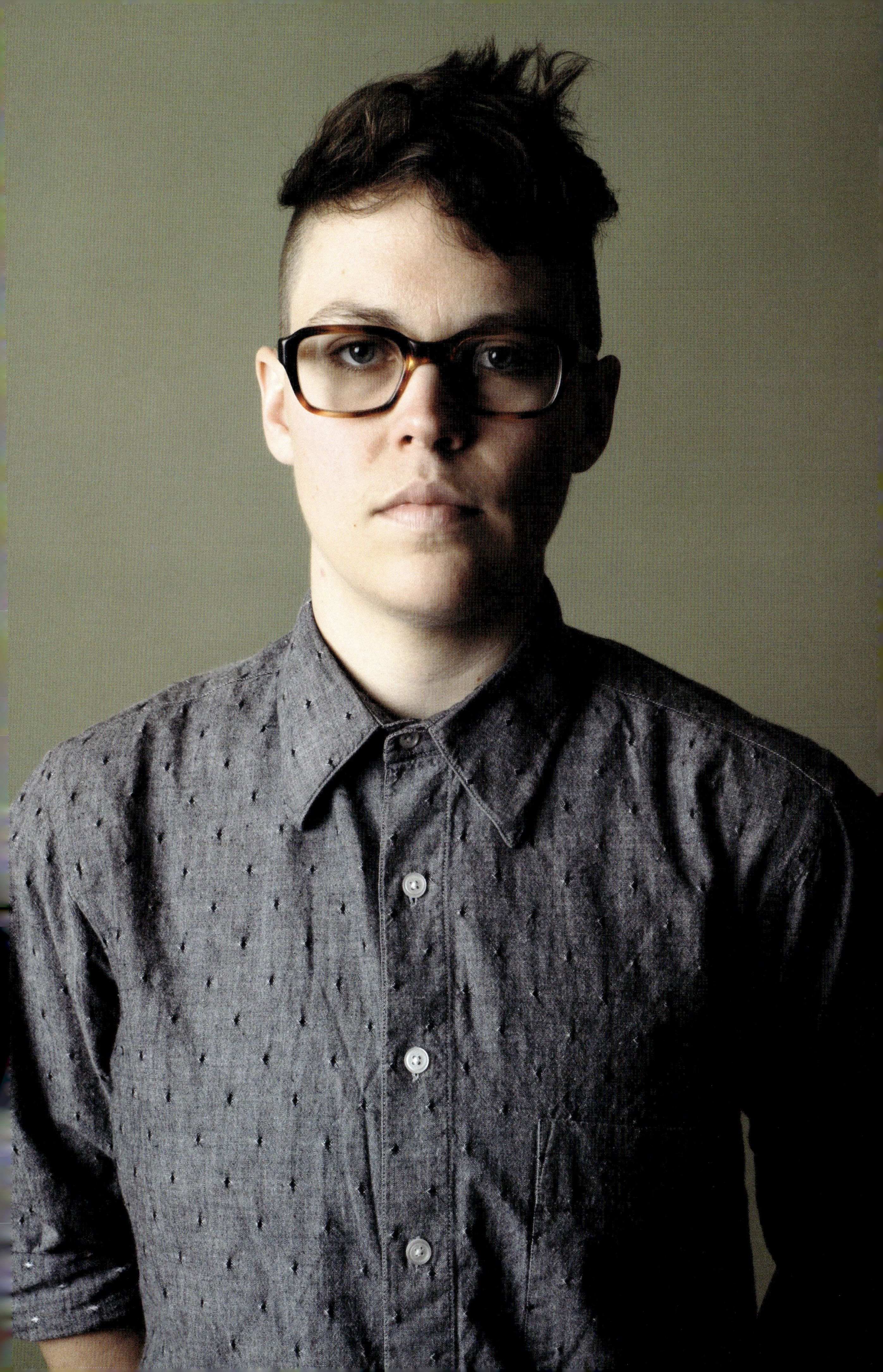

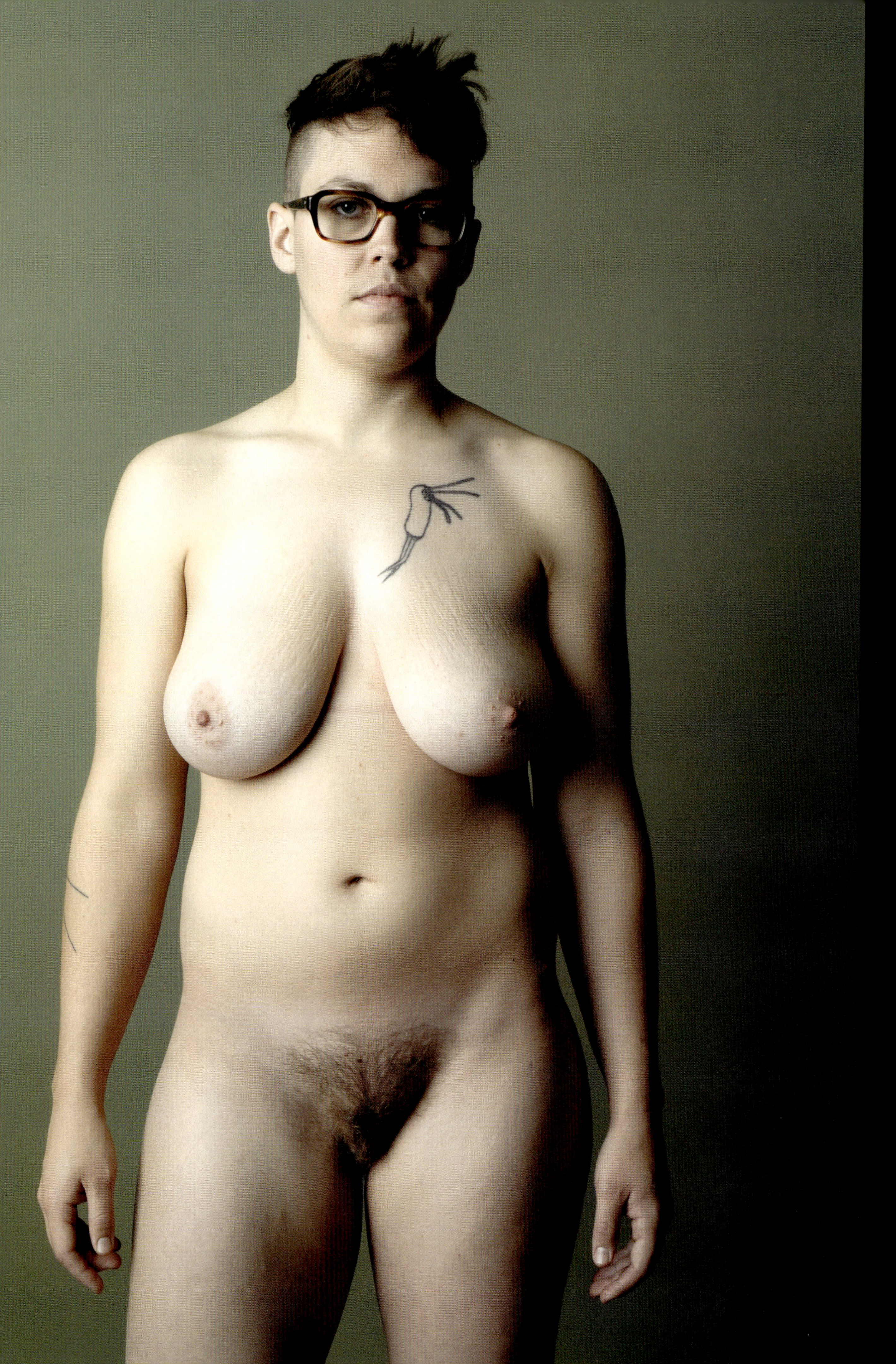

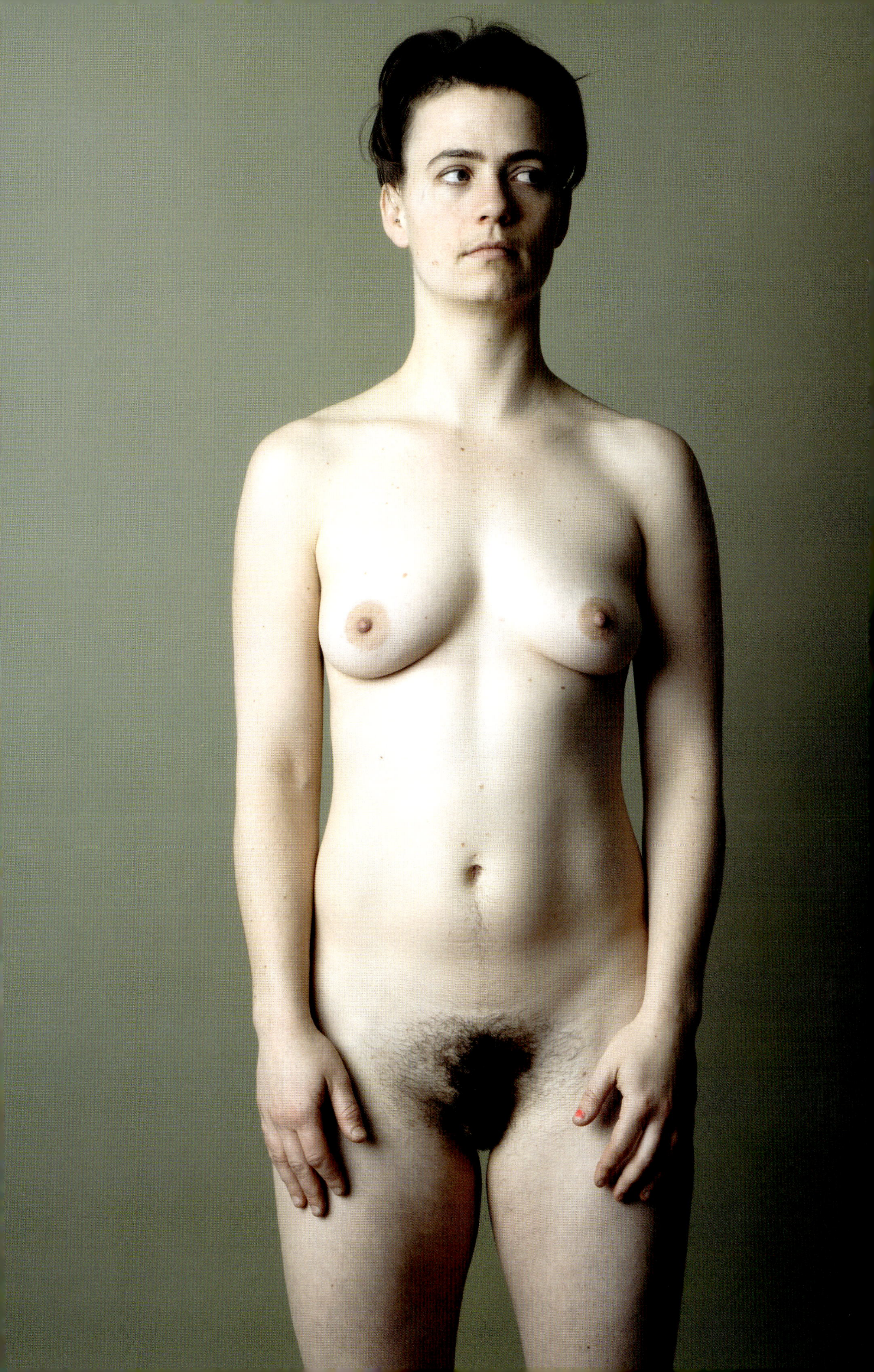

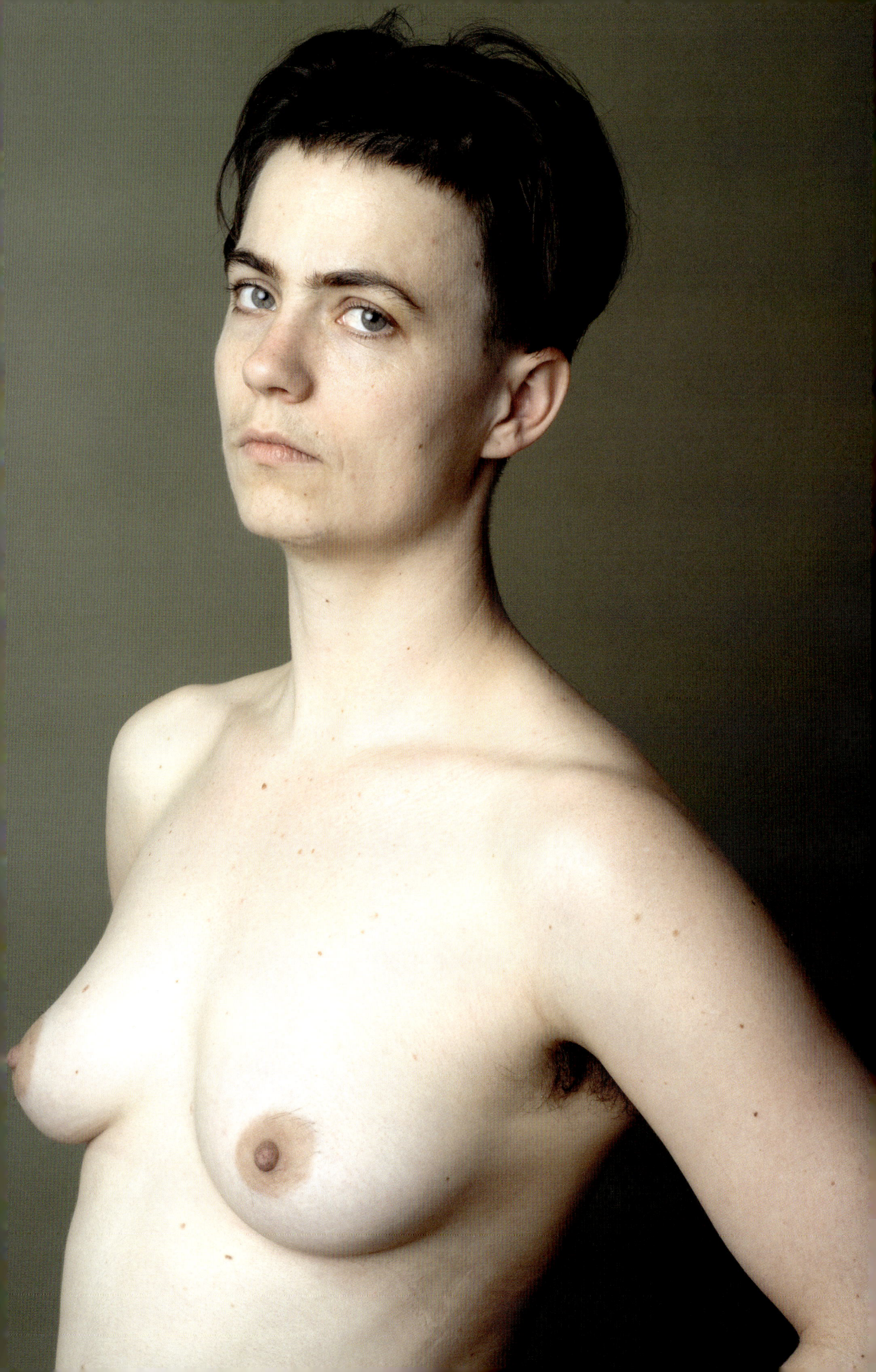

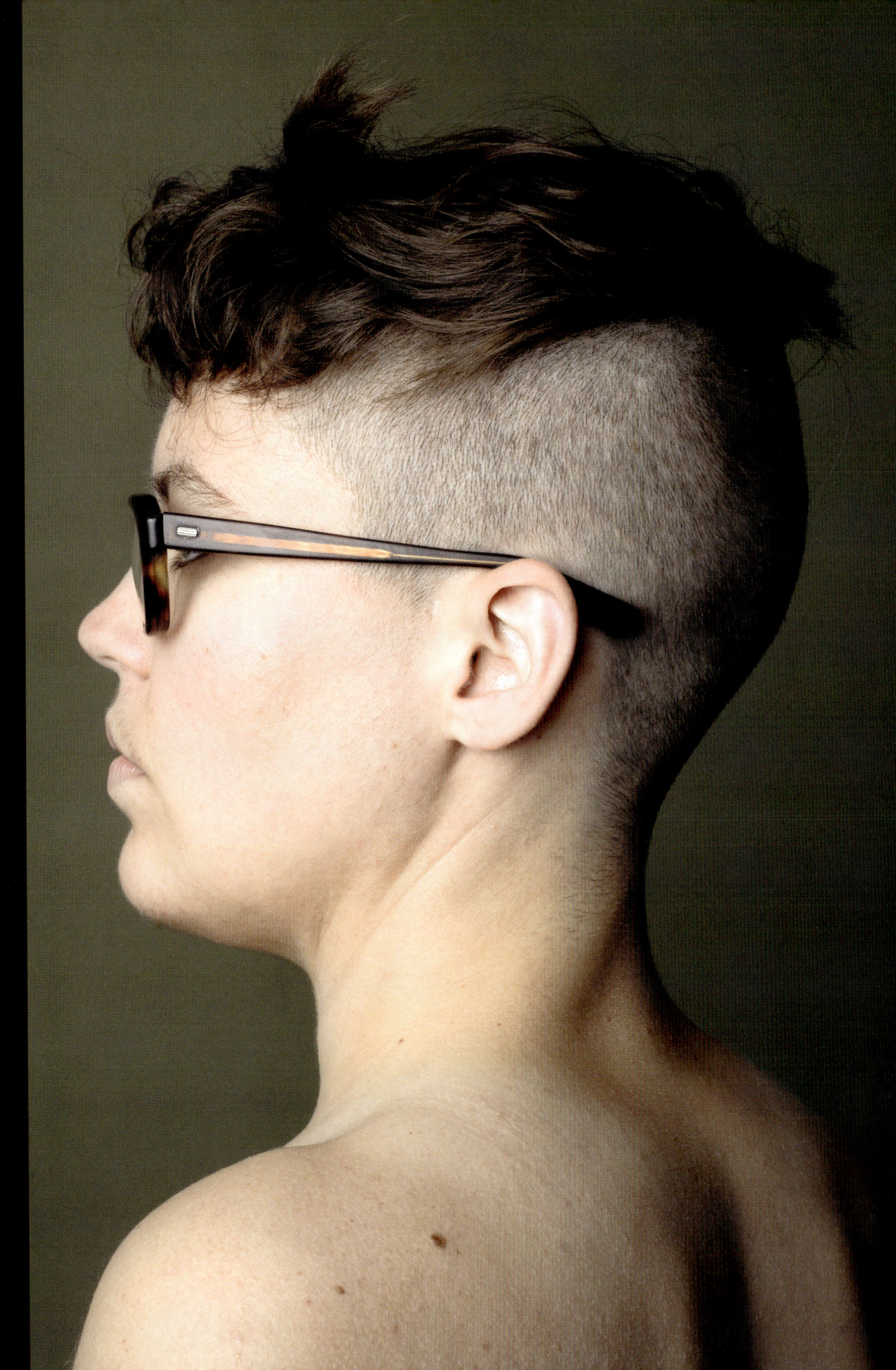

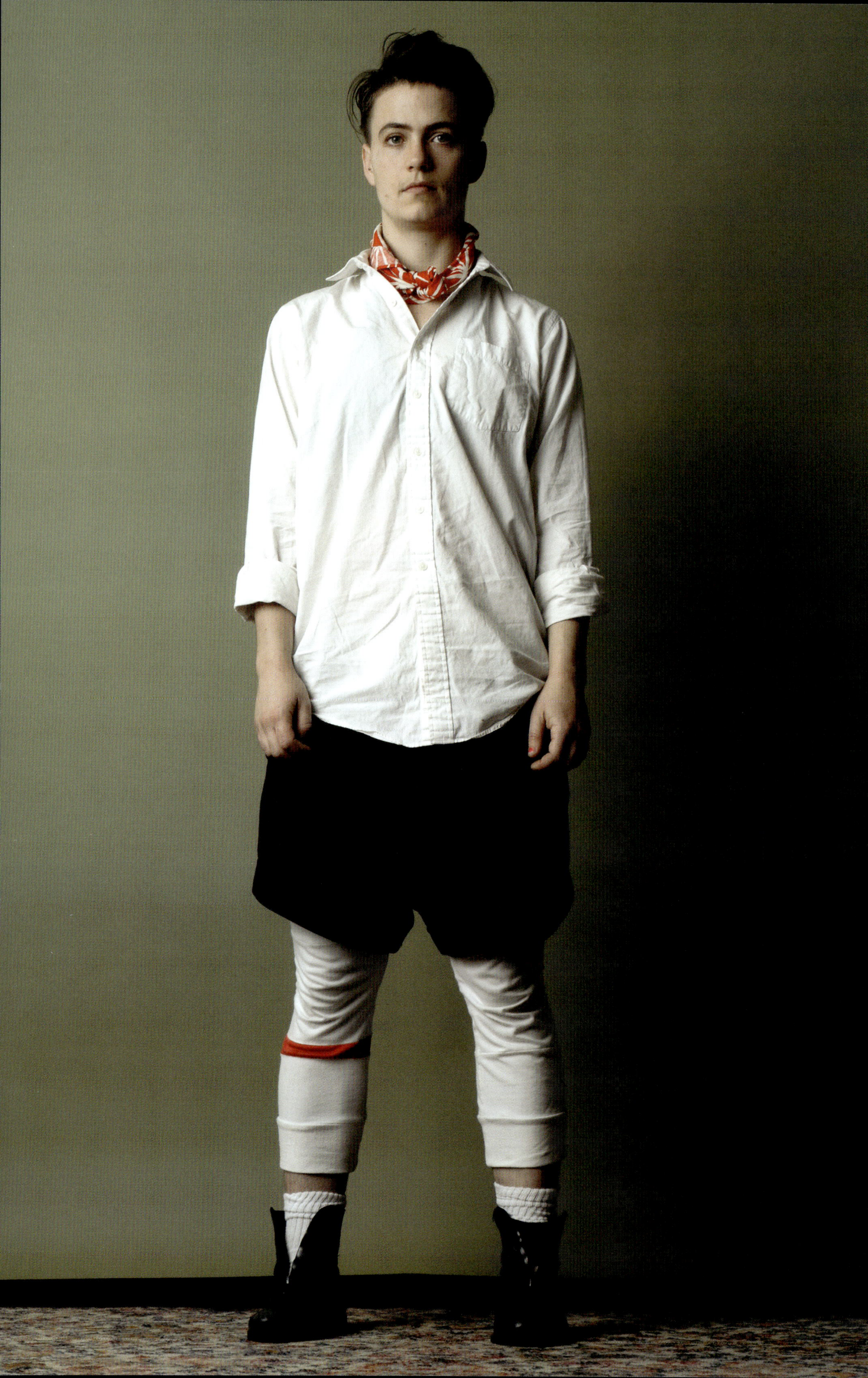

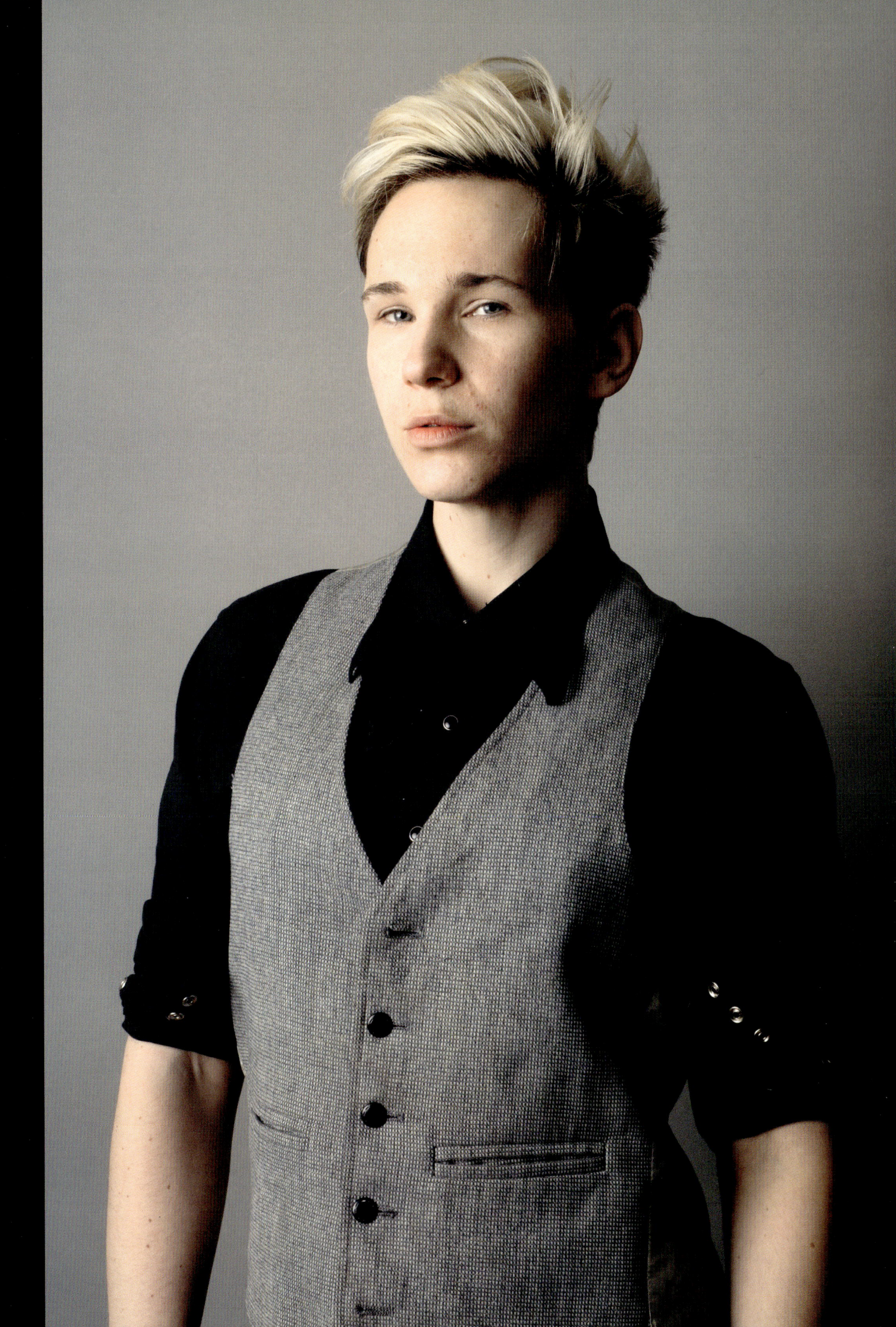

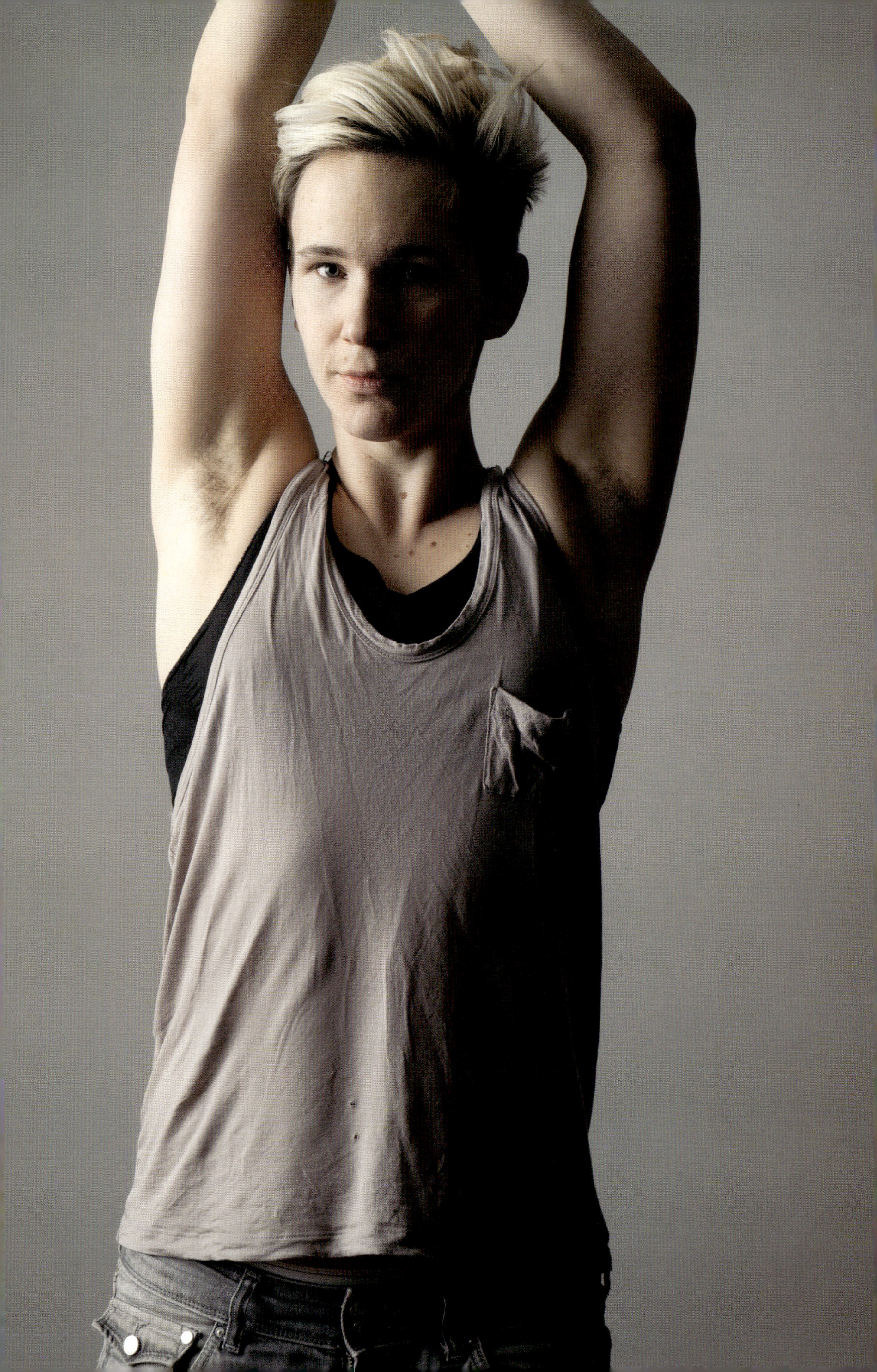

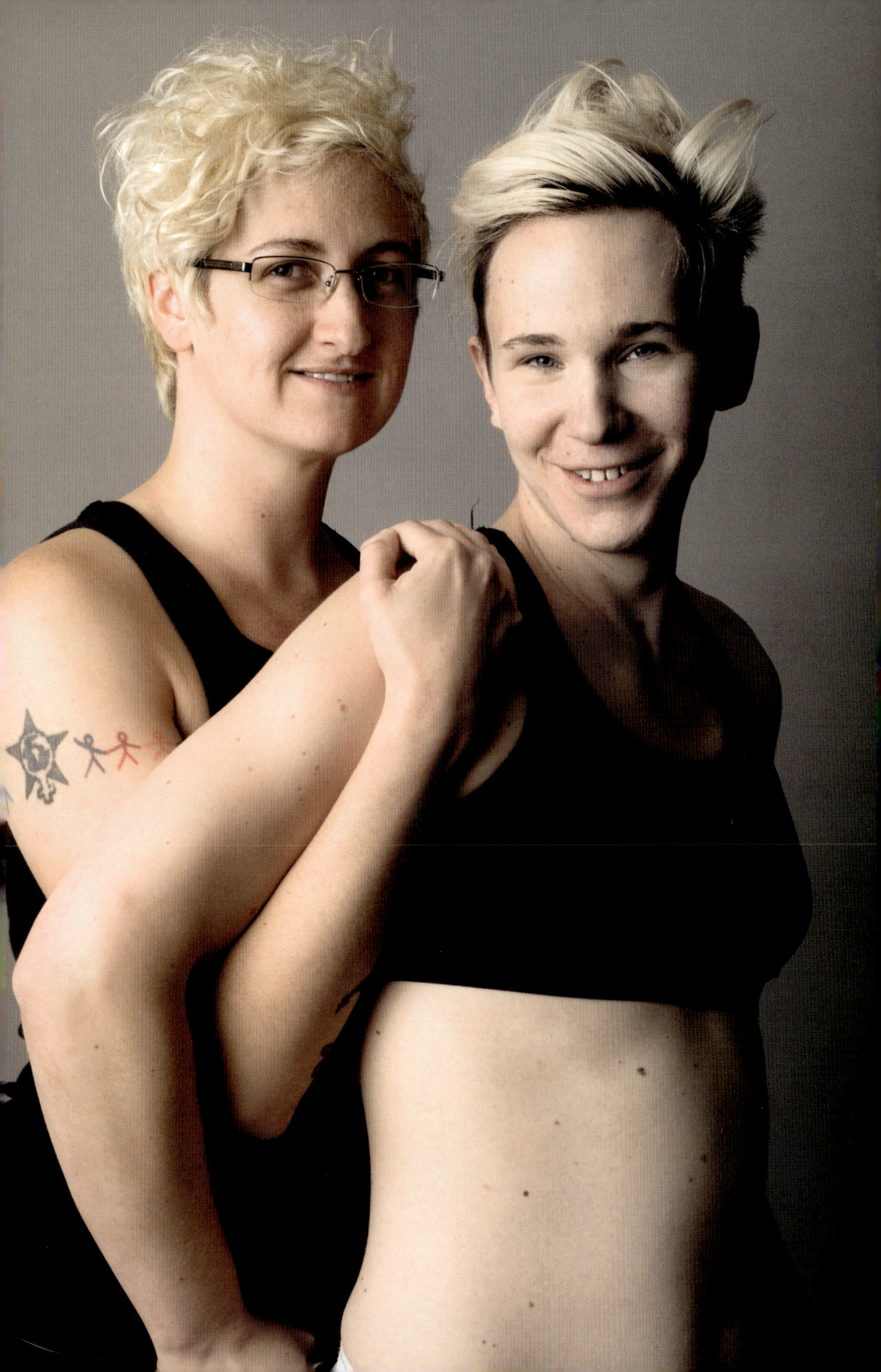

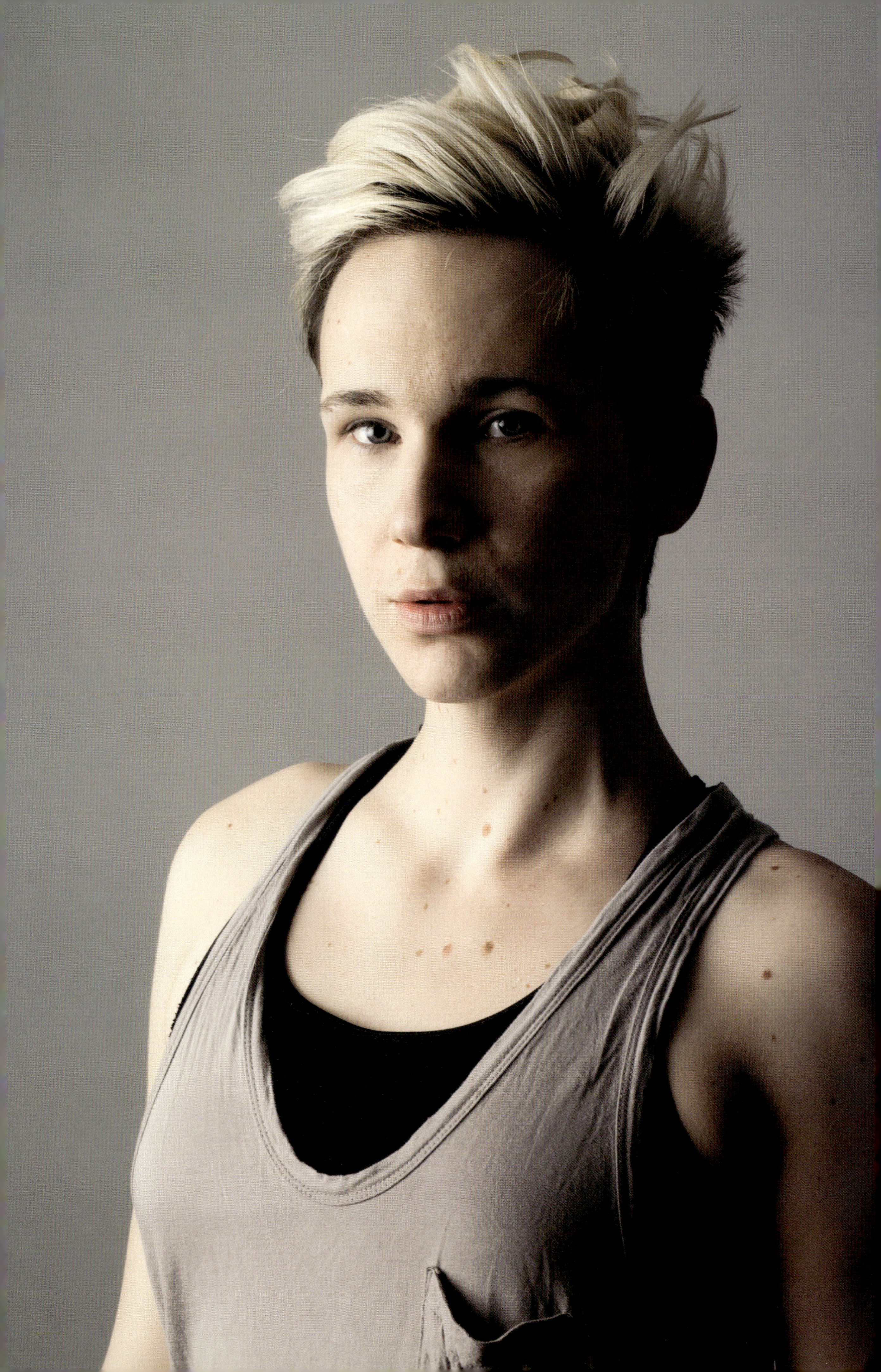

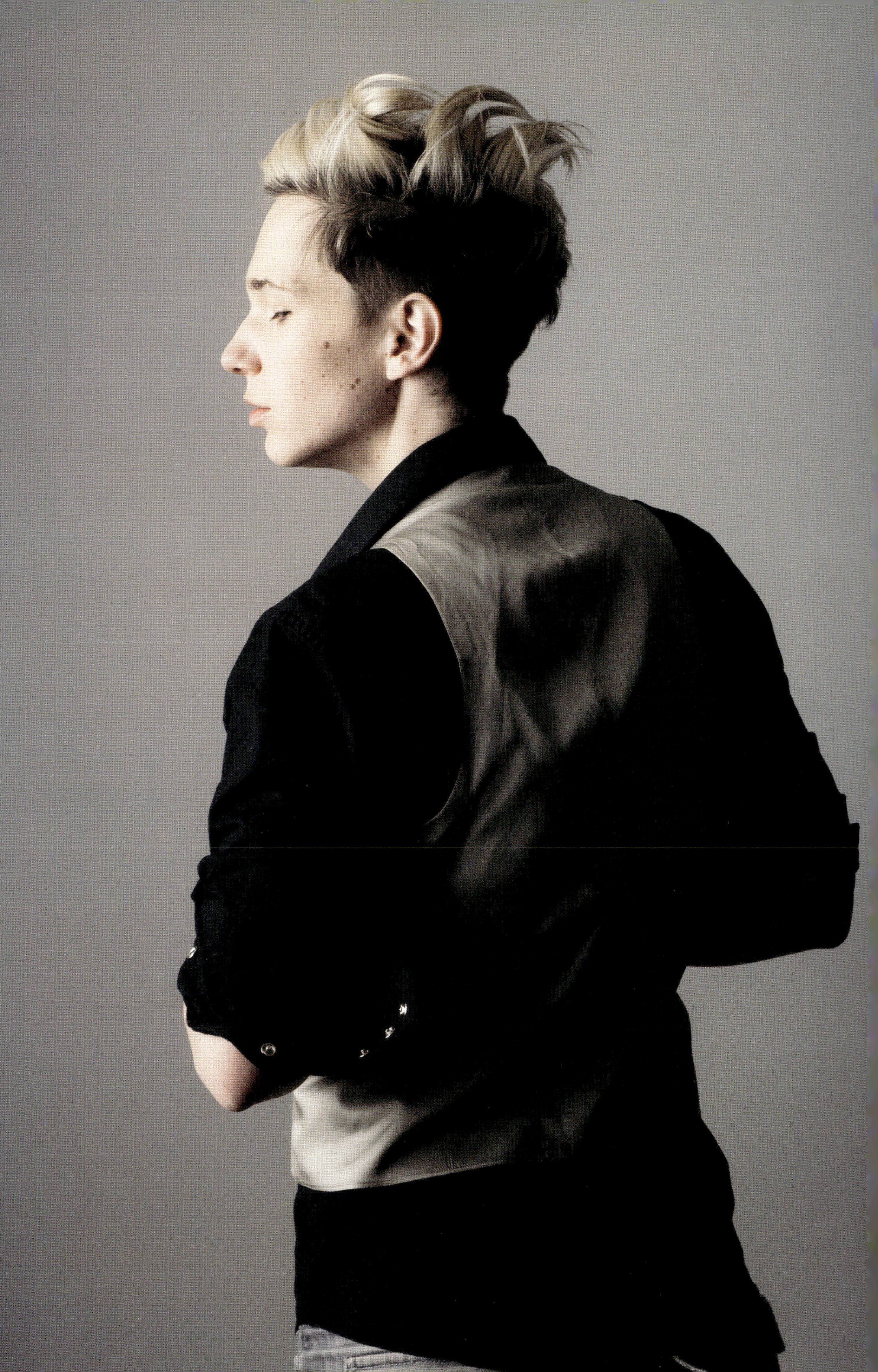

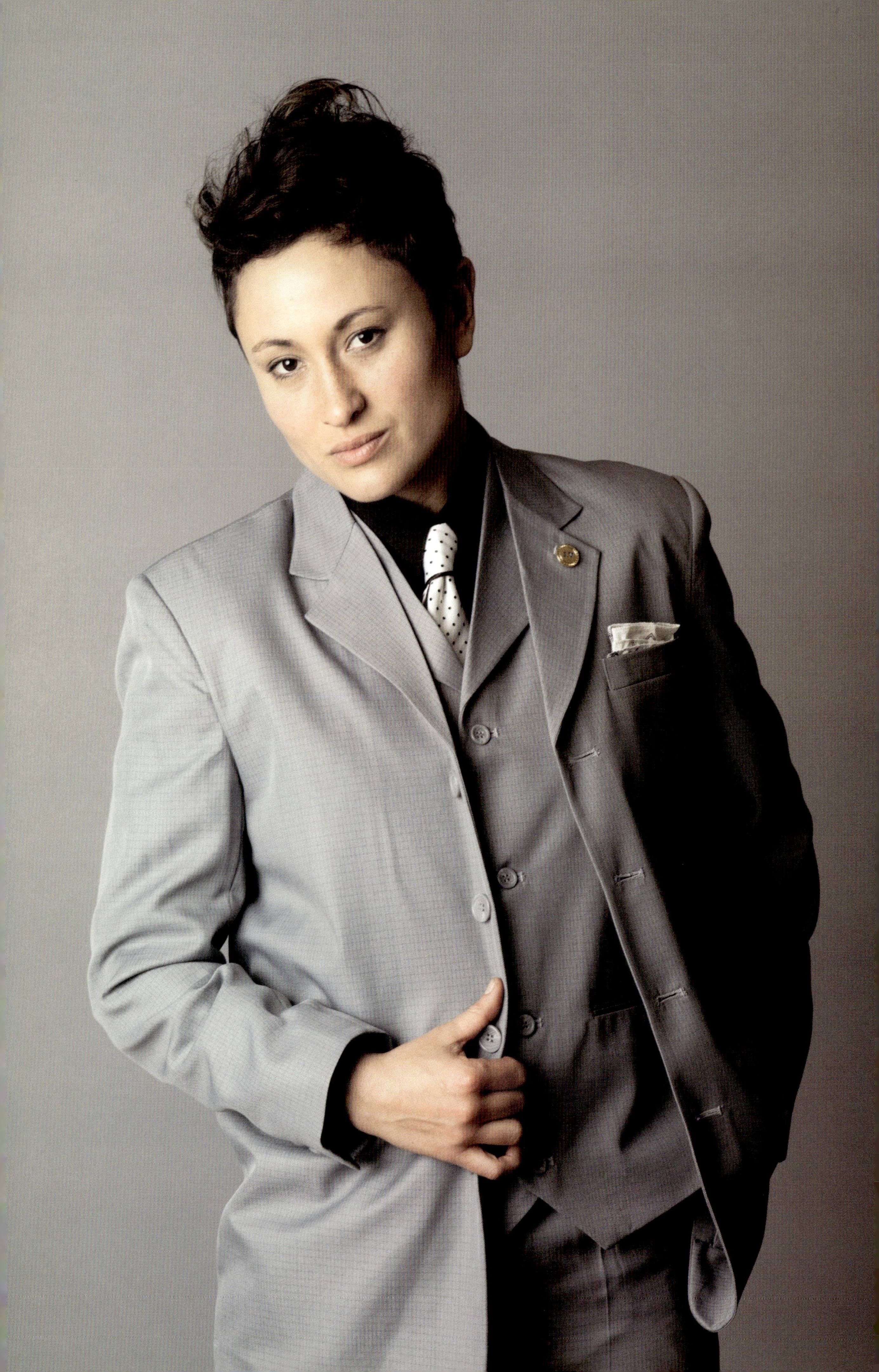

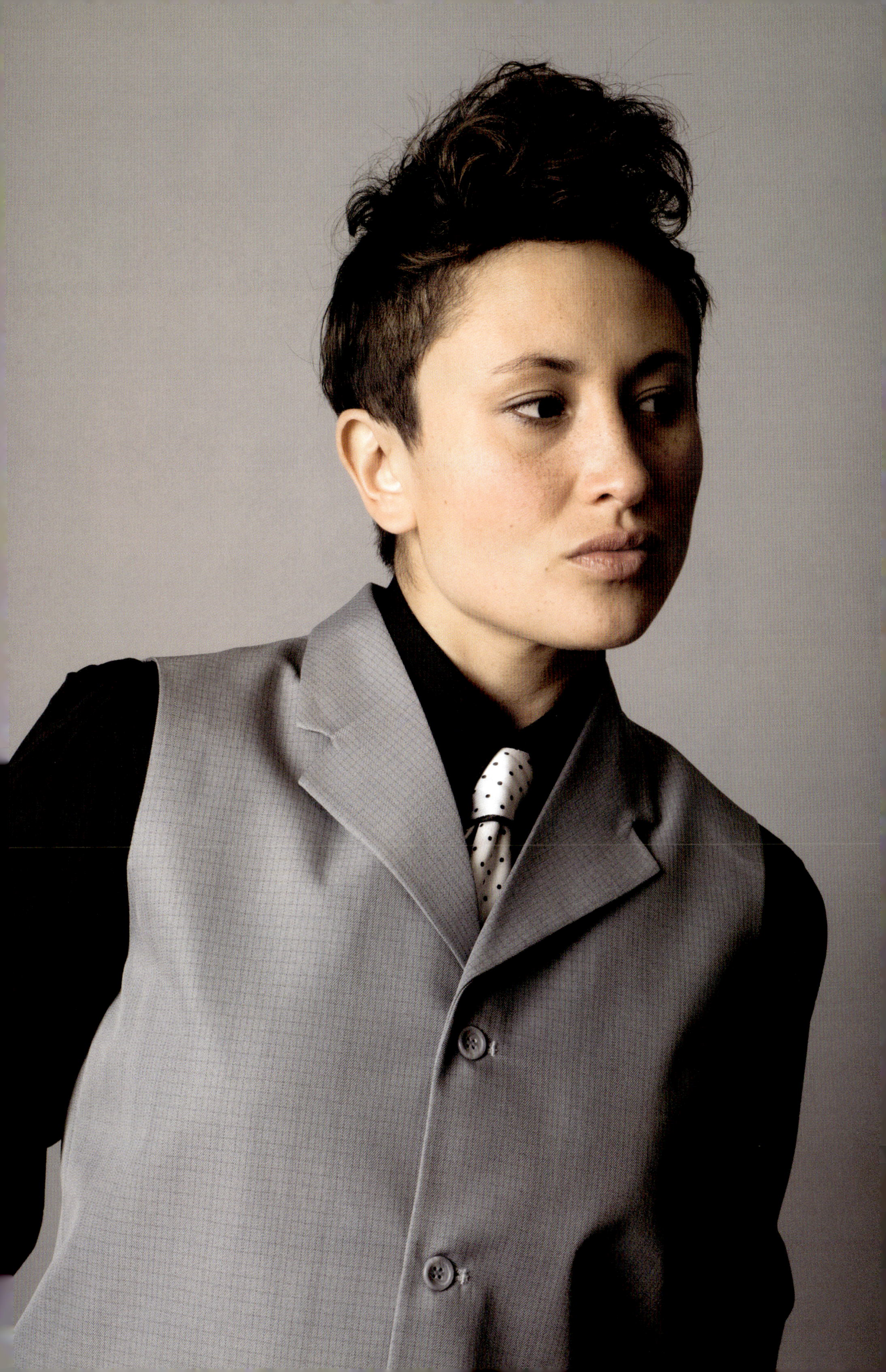

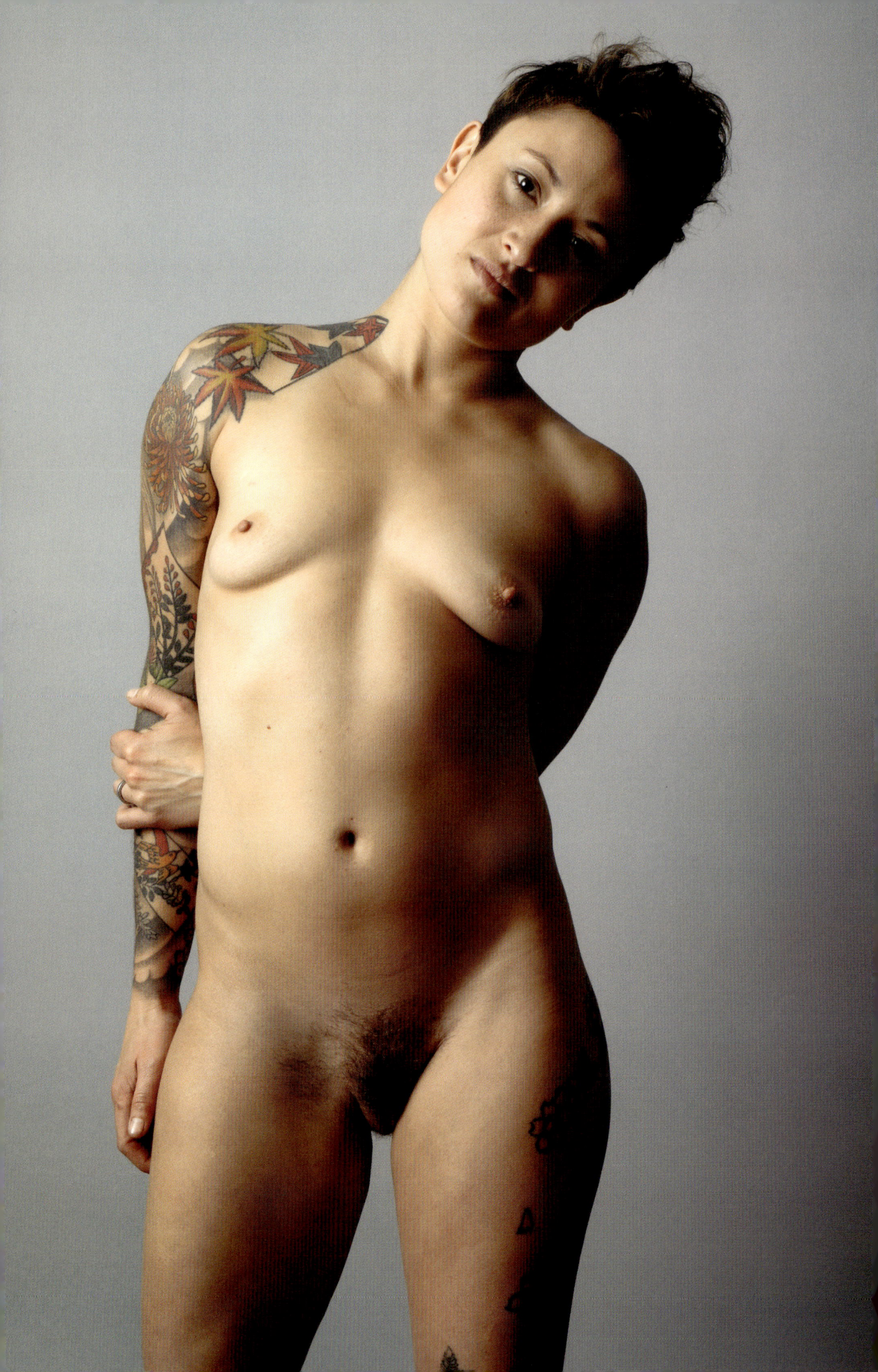

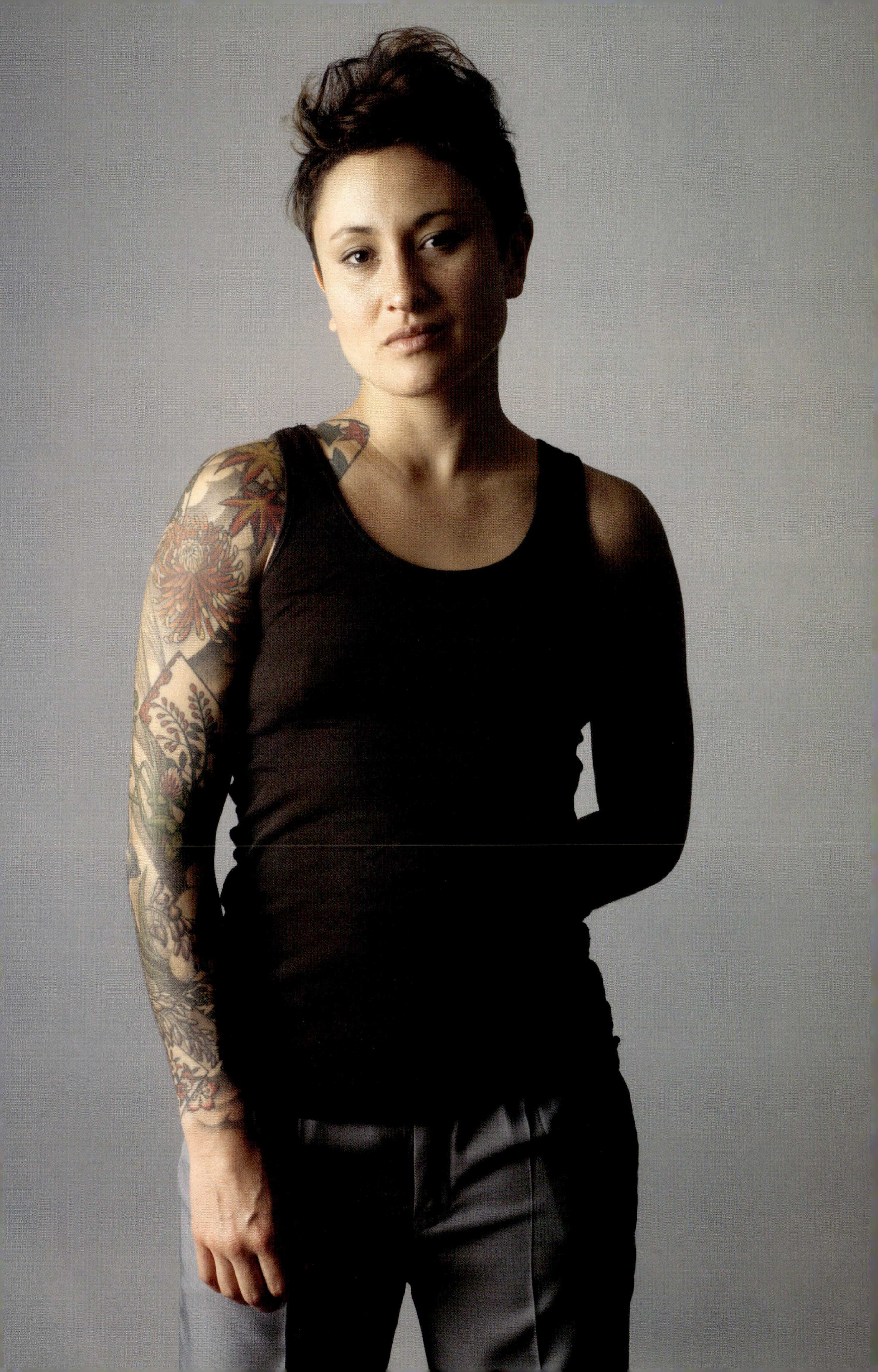

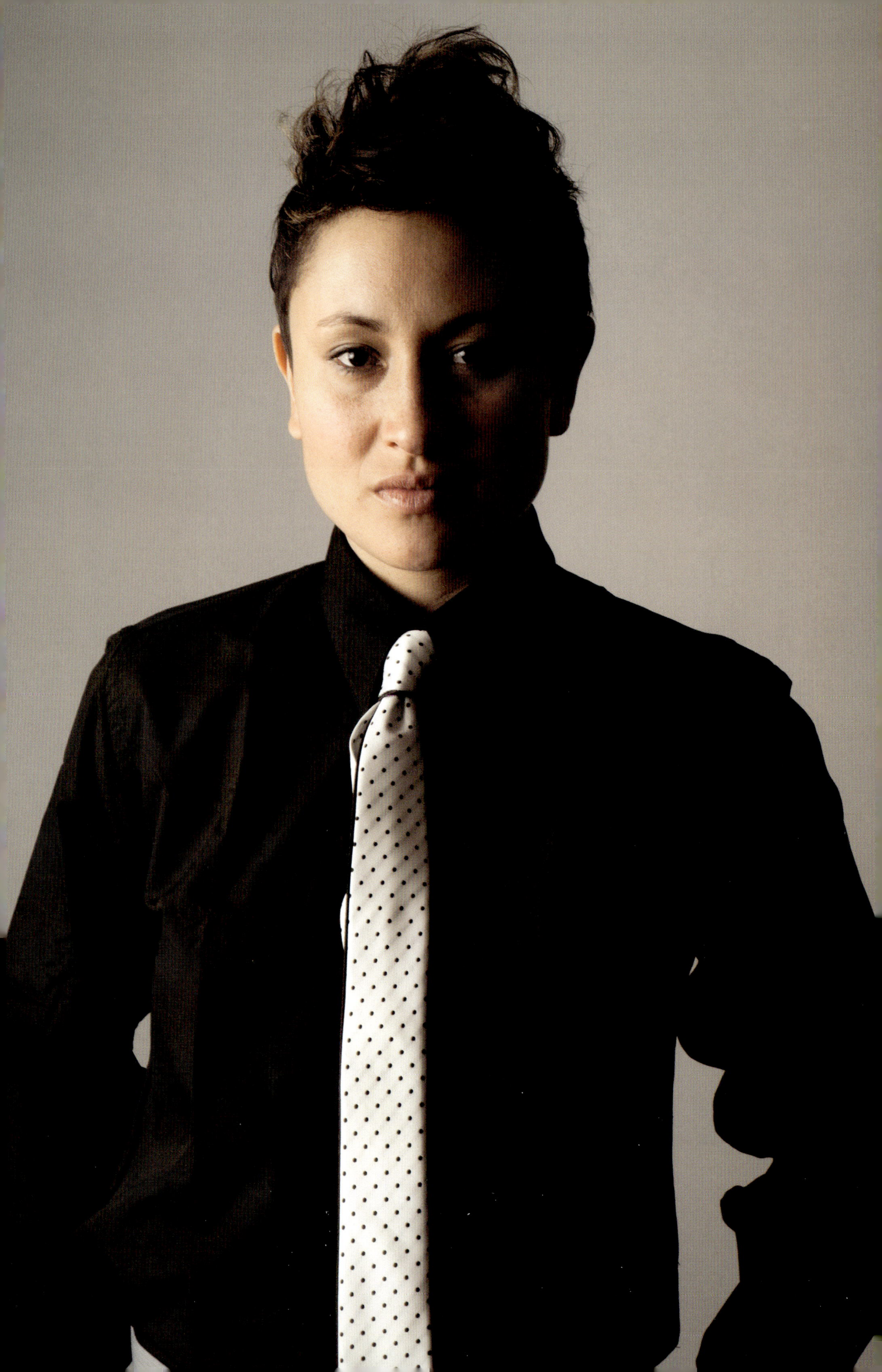

A NINE GENDER VALENTINE

In 2002, a five-hundred question gender quiz out of Australia lit up social media.

My ex-husband took this quiz, and sent me his answers. I took it. My girlfriend (now my partner of thirteen years) took it. Imagine my amazement...my ex-husband and my current partner scored almost exactly the same gender identity number. These numbers partitioned, named, and arranged gender into nine bins, not determined by body type. Did this mean that my differently-bodied partners carried very similar genders? What did that say about who I am and how I love?

I don't know the answer to those questions. I do know my own subjective impressions. For instance: To me, he does not seem like a soft man, nor she a butch woman.

He has the lithe frame of Fred Astaire with the angled determined face of Clark Gable. She is all high cheekbones and tawny, a sort of cool drink-of-water, tall but taproot, with her feet flat on the ground. In traits of mind, they've each complemented my chattery fluster. Good insightful listeners, they both hold their privacies. They're both good at taking apart a washing machine with a combination of analytic insight and a tinkering spirit. Deeply caring, participatory humans, they each do compassionate inconvenient things for other people—less for moral justice and more out of a sense of enmeshed empathic connection.

I'm not sure these are truly gendered traits of mind—calm, quiet toughness, rational tinkering analysis, emotion-based compassion—but we tell ourselves they are.

By now it seems self evident that the lived kinesthetic experience of gender is a spectrum, or perhaps more like a fabulous five-year-old's finger painting done by a grown-up corporeal human that farts and fucks and colors its way all red and orange on a sheet of neatly entrusted gender lore.

Stand somewhere with mile high movie posters or marketing ads for peanut butter and you'll see it—a binary. Male-seeming men. Female-presenting women. All that depth and shadow forced into invisibility via the conflating, misnamed, body-rigid demarcations: male and female. But quiet the mind. Feel the body, its organs, its gentle knowing of itself—and who knows? Gender starts to ooze and shine all over the place, three-dimensional, animal, and real, telling (or rather whispering) its own quiet lived experience.

There are great scholars writing about gender today—trying to name and even map the not yet nameable planet. Fantabulous words spring to mind: cis, hir, hen, genderqueer, trans, ftm, mtf, boi.

These scholars are bringing us all a language of belonging; engaging in the power that comes from naming. Saying there's a there there and helping, perhaps, to pick apart the places where sex-identity-based gender identification is broken, distorted, misnamed, mismarked, crass, and even (yes) damaging to all of us.

Scholars like these, and artists/models/thinkers who are living a genderqueer reality have a right to a write an essay like this one.

Me? I'm not qualified. I'm more of a lover than a scholar. And this? This is only a valentine.

For the fuzz-capped, teddy bear-bearded scholar who once sat with me in a writing class. For the handsome, small-boned man, just my size, who carries my sixty pound bag of organic grain-free dog food to the car at my favorite homeopathic pet store. For the strapping cowgirl of a former football player, who is one of my dearest friends (still) from college, and once had to come out to me simultaneously as both a woman and a lesbian. For the poet who once reminded me that if I wanted to teach at a college that engages with issues of social justice, I shouldn't take self-presentation for granted, and should invite each participant in my workshop to identify the gender pronoun they prefer to think of when they think of themselves.

I'm qualified to tell you one true thing: That my heart skips a beat every time we speak; every time I have the opportunity to relate body-to-body, mind-to-mind, with someone who carries a space not marked by conventionally body-conforming gender, whether we're remembering our frosh dorms over coffee, or dishing for ten seconds about a new wound-care cream for dogs.

I get that deep-in-the-body mental sexual fluster.

So why? Are these friends courageous? Do I see what's real or only what I imagine is?

Here's the nearest I can get to an answer. In my distorted way, I see a deep presence (my imagining that there's more human parts authentically showing up for the conversation here) and the pain of lack (ugh…I imagine lack). Lack we all have, of course. But the lack I imagine seeing is for what isn't possible (an opportunity to wake up every day and go out in the world with perfect socially-conforming, body-sex-type-conforming gender). But I'm not sure that's really so different from the courage every one of us has when we wake up still in this human coil, with our real needy selves, morning after morning to rent and bills and jobs and shame and desire and joy and coffee.

So my fluster—I think it's less about the Other, and more about Me.

When I am with my friends whose conscious experience of gender has been forced by circumstance or self-awareness to become complex (genderqueer, gender-sex nonconforming, trans-identified), I finally live in a world with room enough for me.

My gender, which is, by luck and accident and unluck and accident, apparently conforming, is a lie some of the time. In fact, virtually every human, sexually-dismorphic binary gender seems to be some part a lie.

Fuck the scripts. Fuck the peanut butter commercials. Fuck the Hollywood films.

Heterosexual marriages need a more complex truth about gender. Queer friendships need a more complex truth about gender. Schools do. Homes do. Children do. We all do.

And so we need complexity.

We need our authentic and seeking people.

We need people's real parts to show up when we level with one another.

If we are ever going to see one another—or ourselves—without distortion. If we are ever going to connect, not by cultural script, but true self to true self.

On this burning planet. While we're all still here. While we still can.

JENNY FACTOR

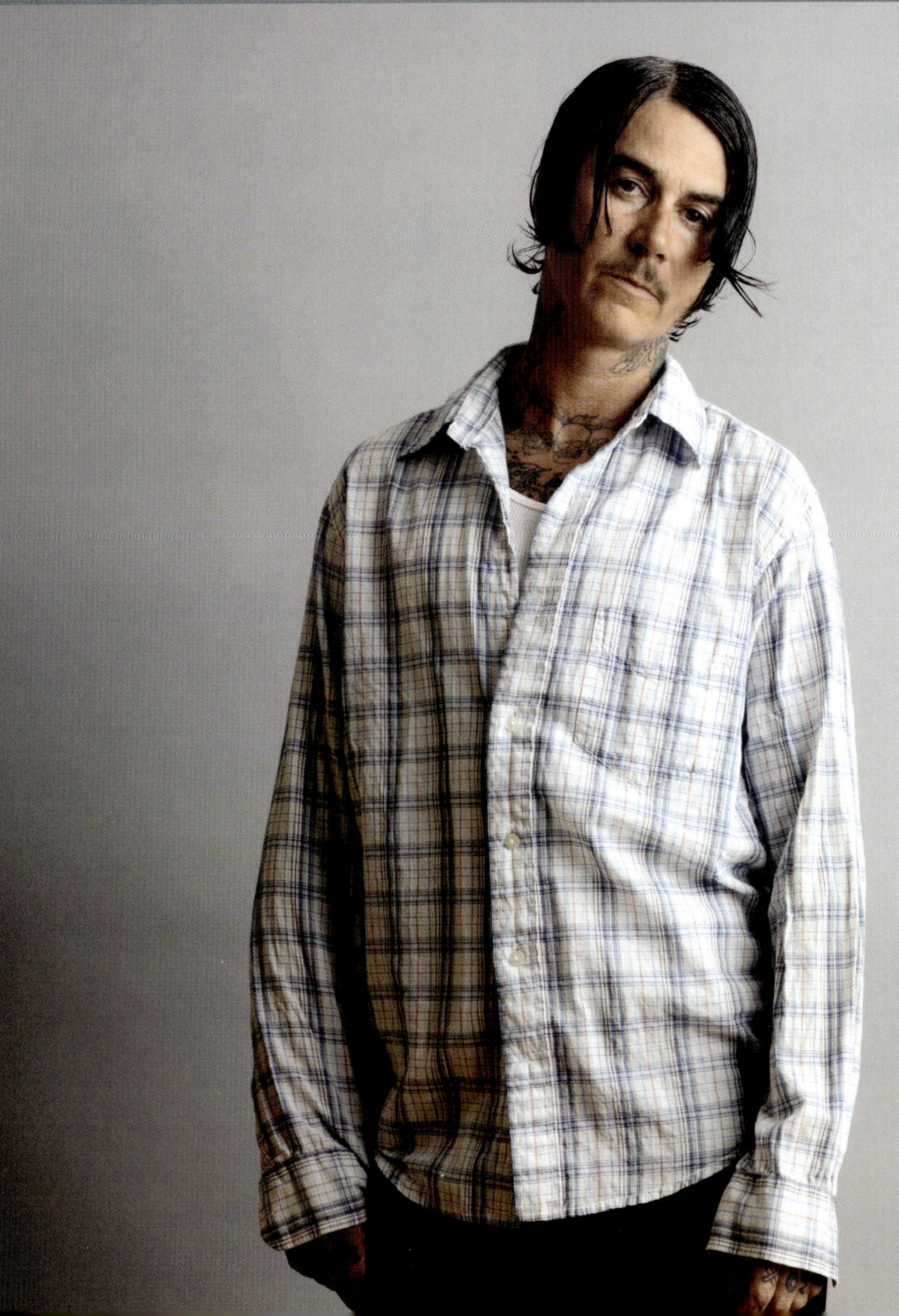

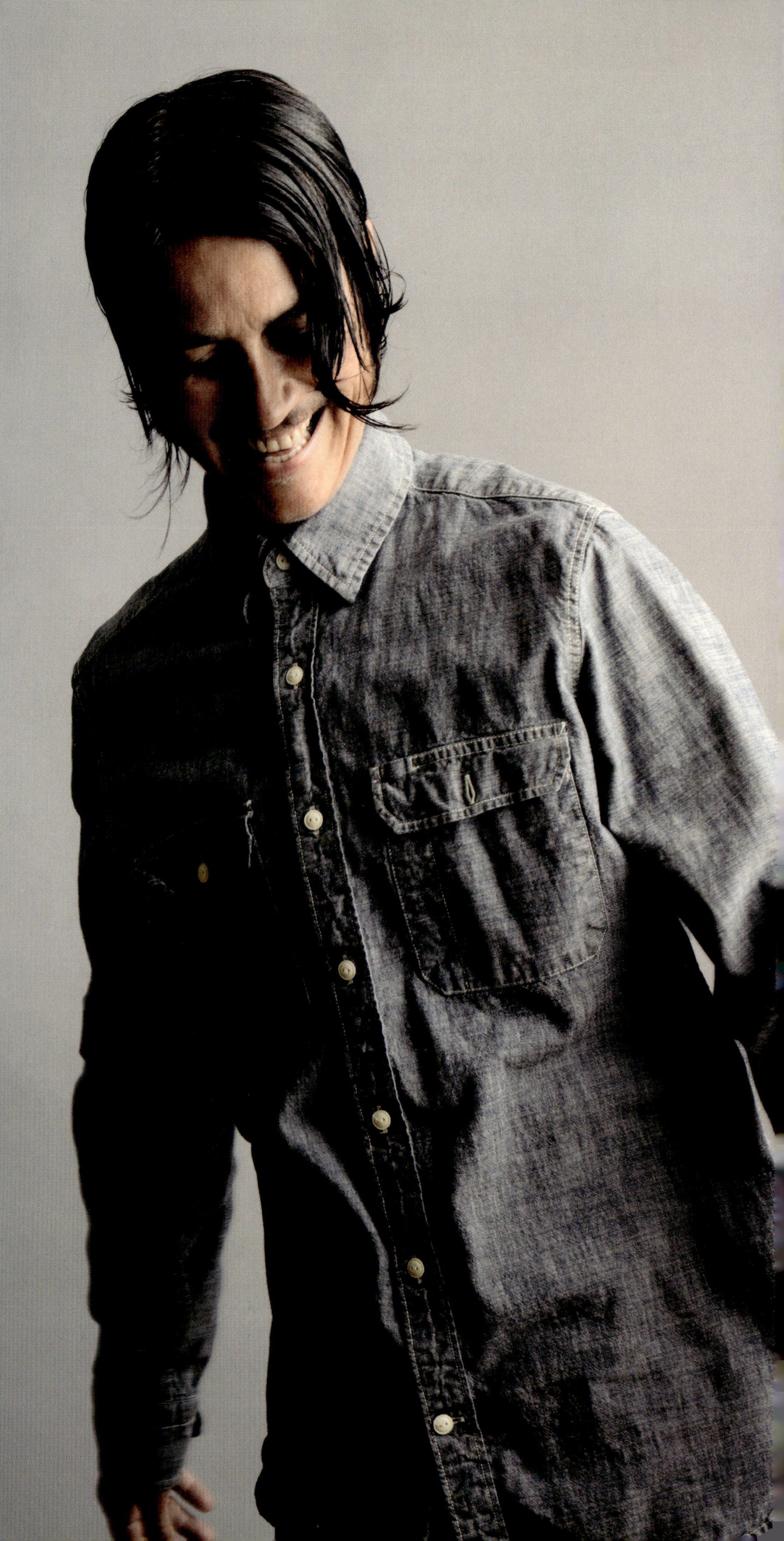

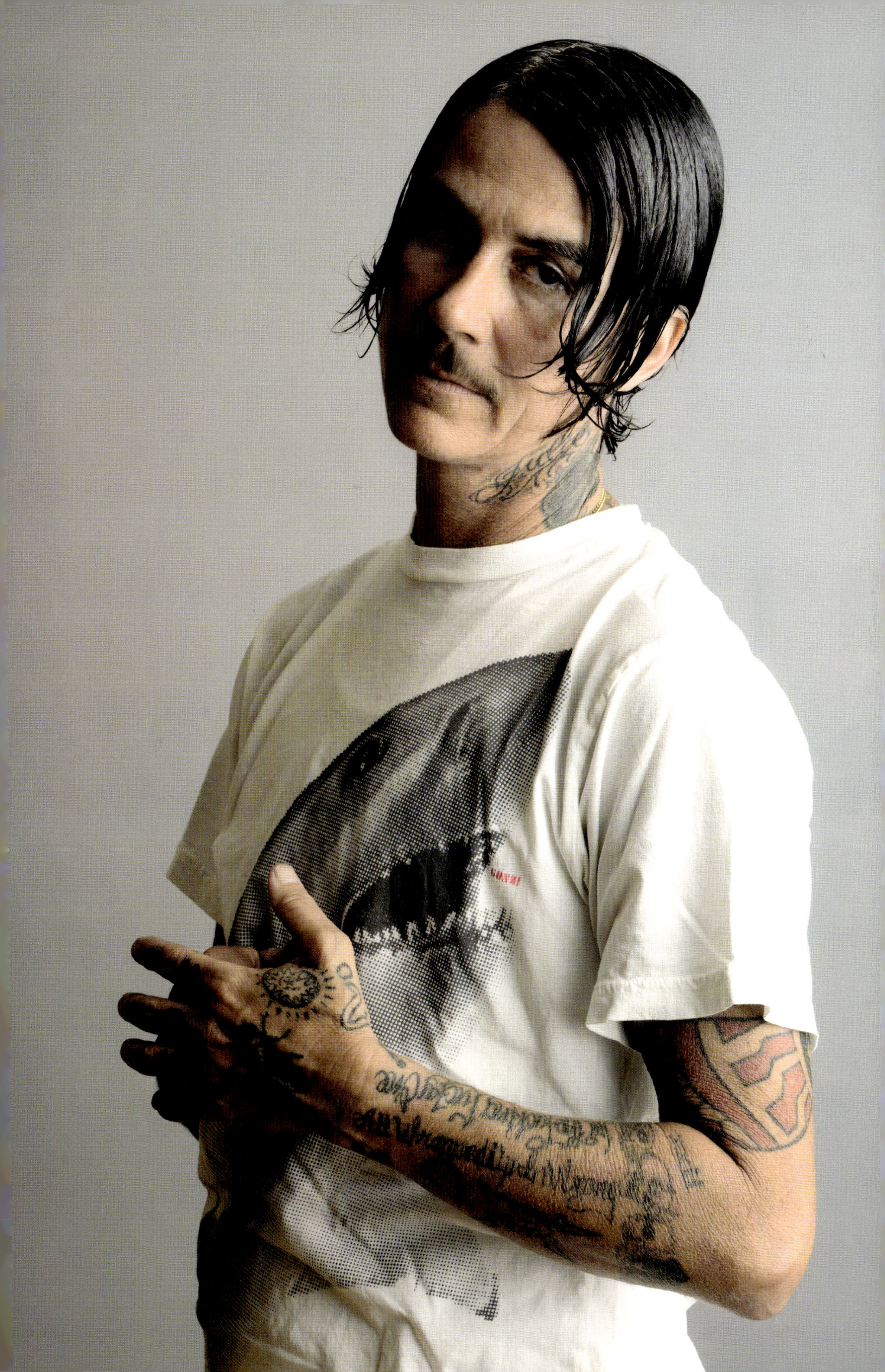
GONZ!

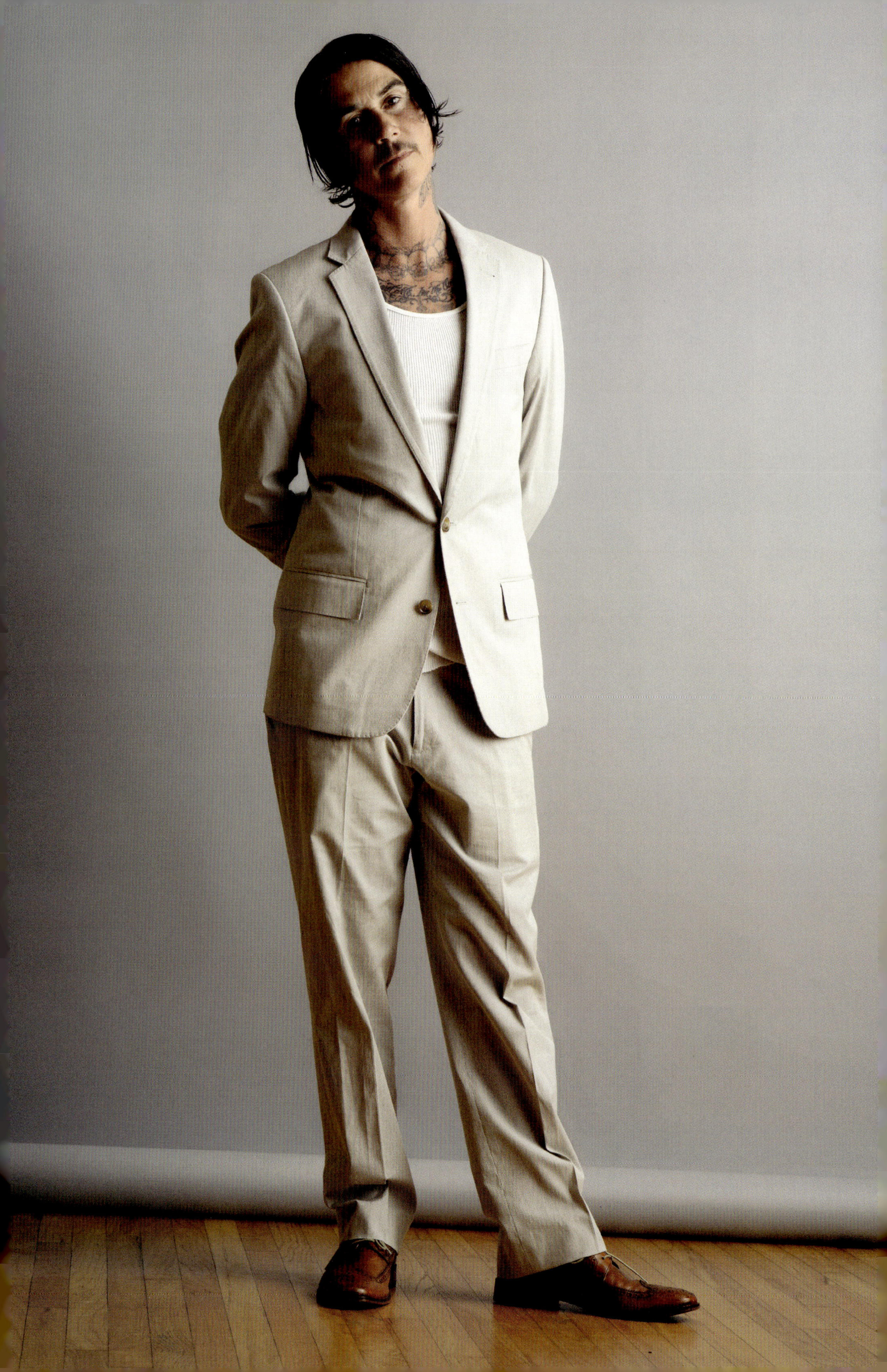

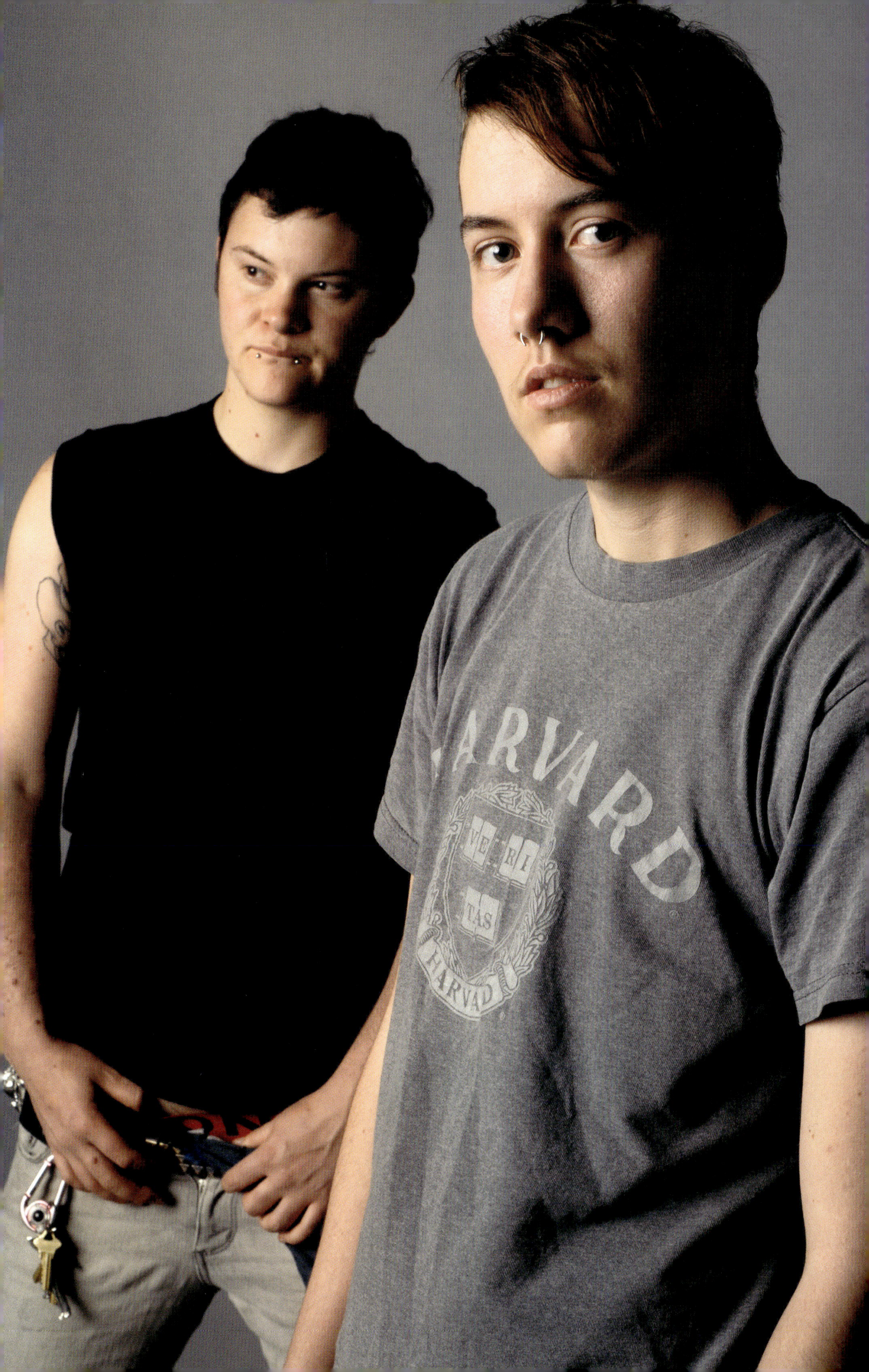
ARVARD
VE RI
TAS
HARVAD

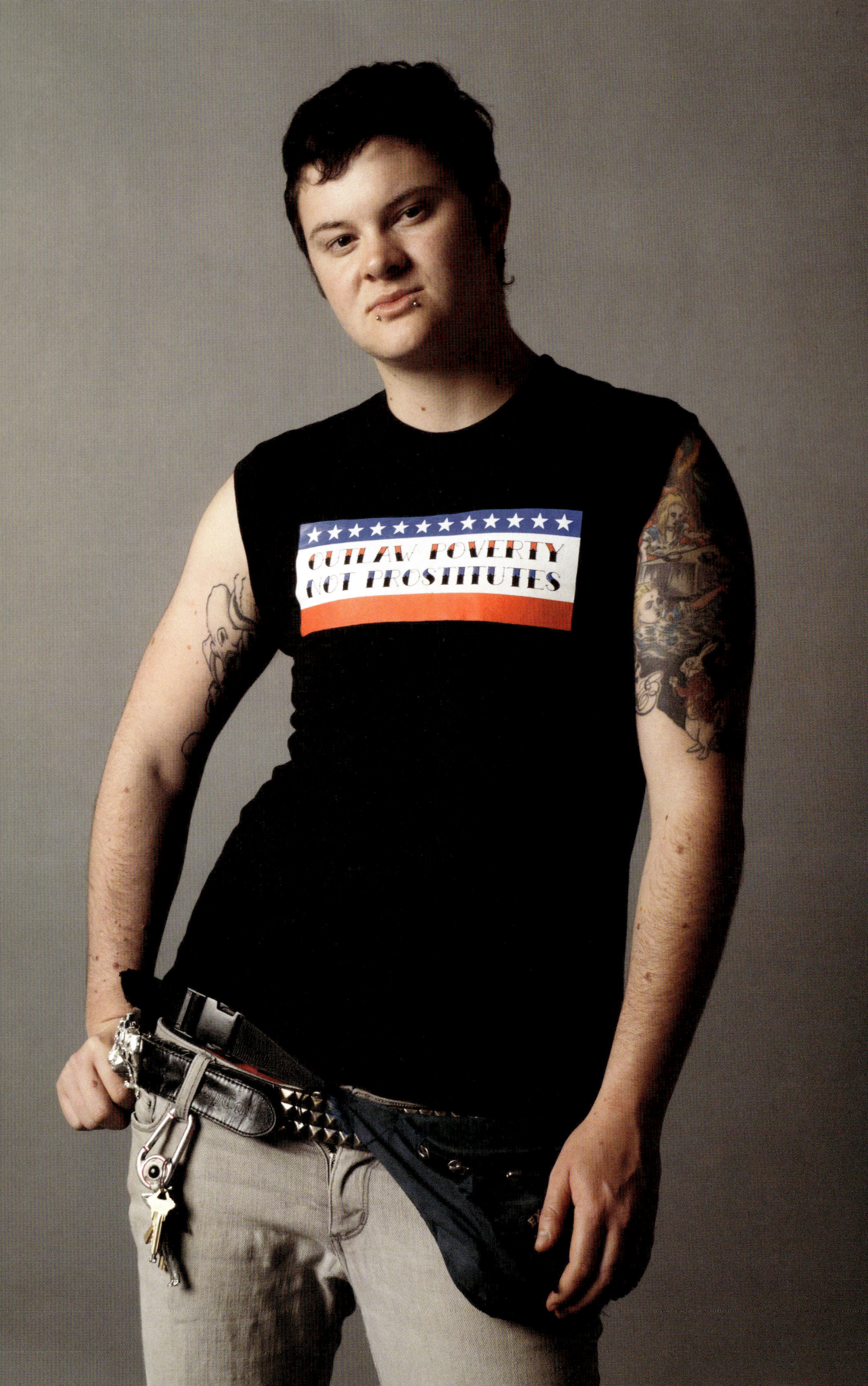
OUTLAW POVERTY
NOT PROSTITUTES

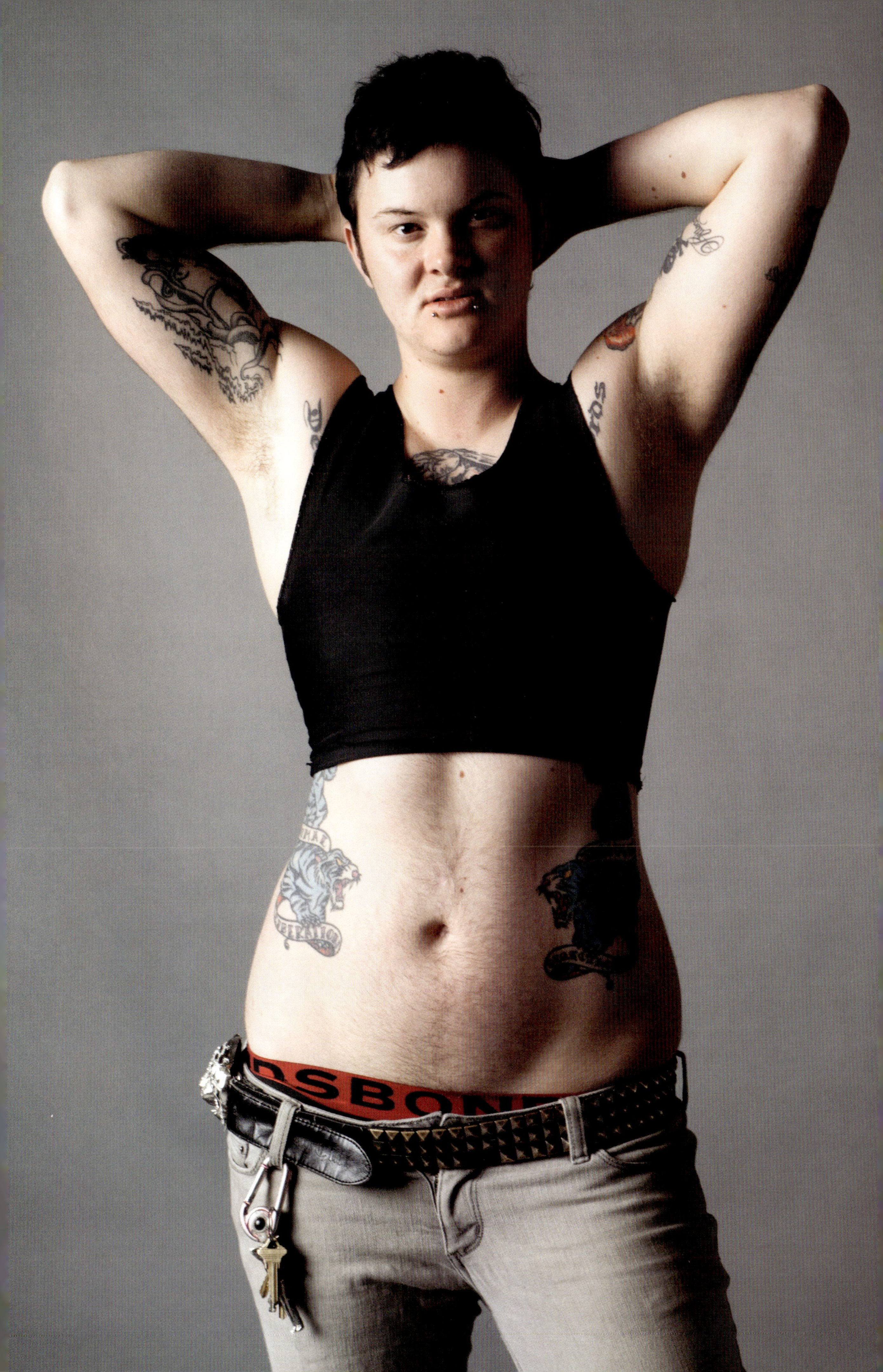

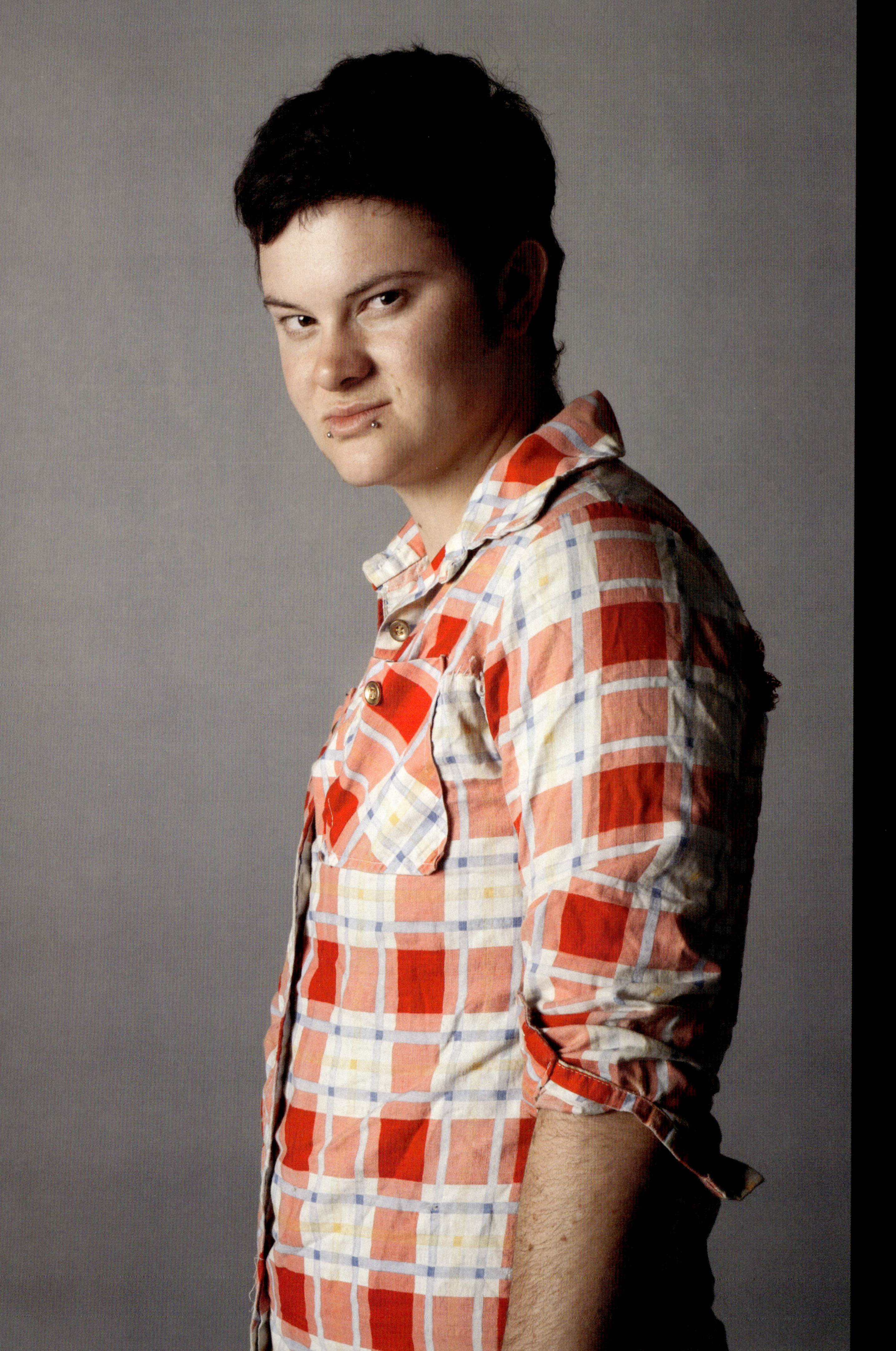

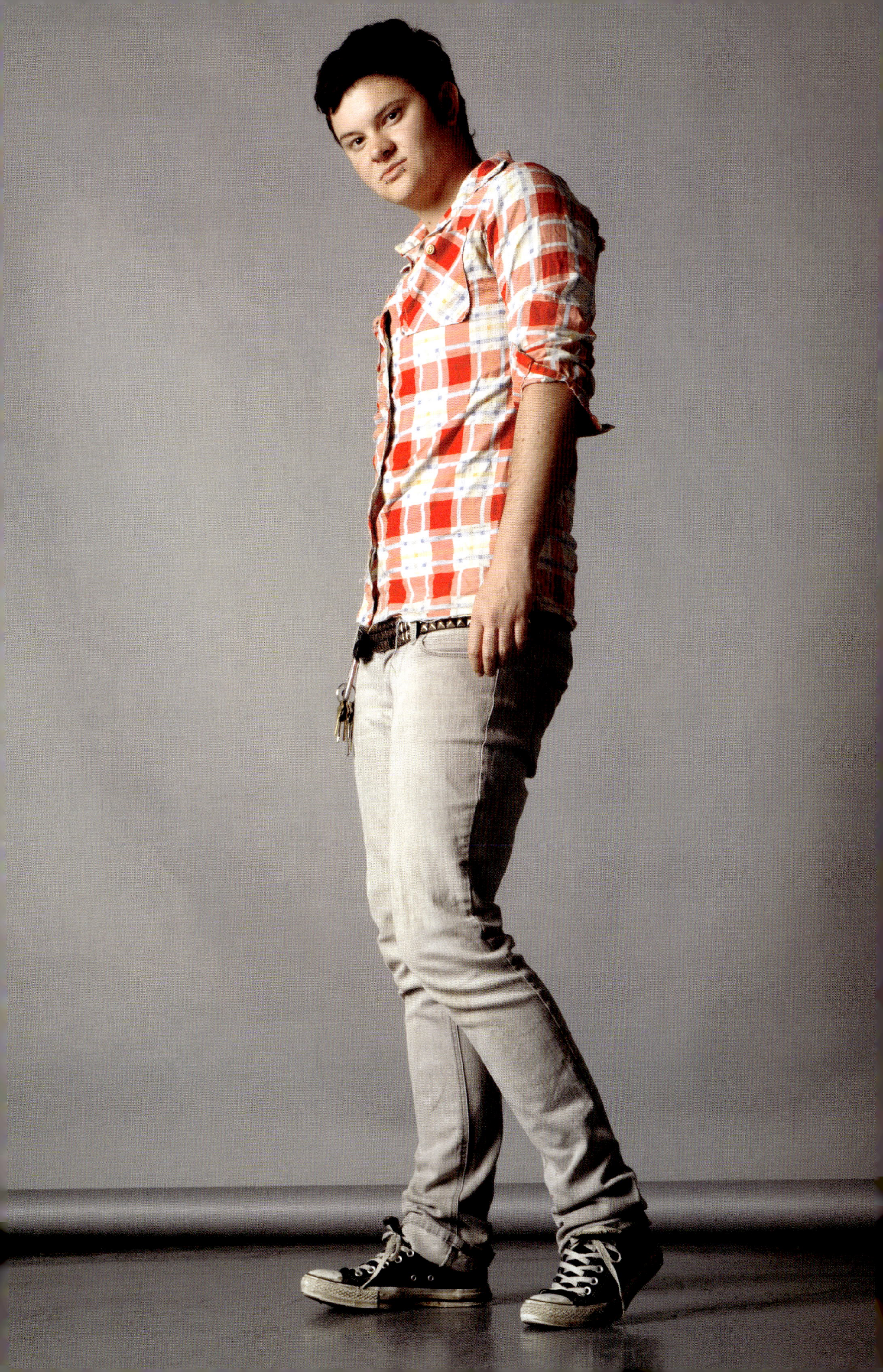

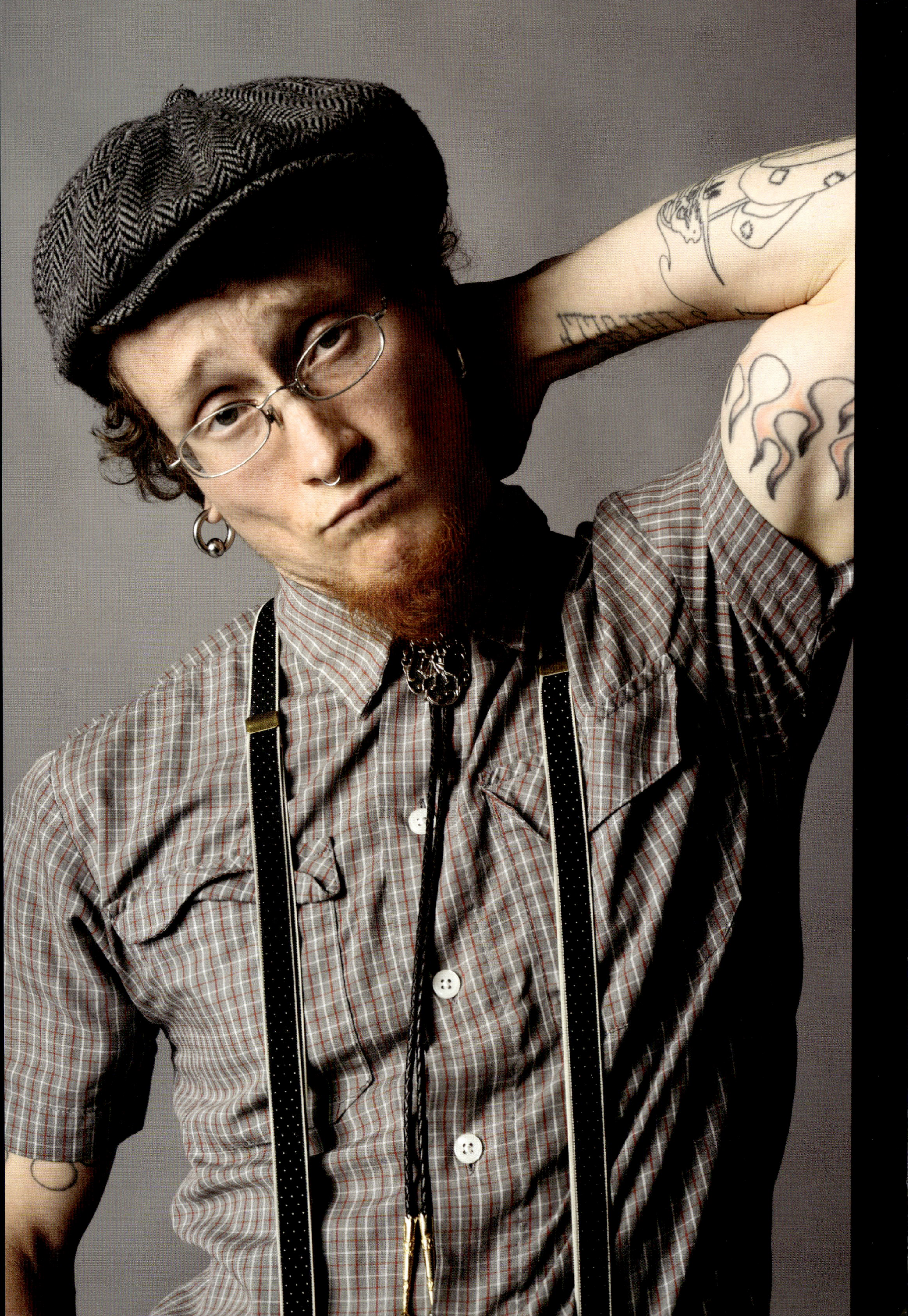

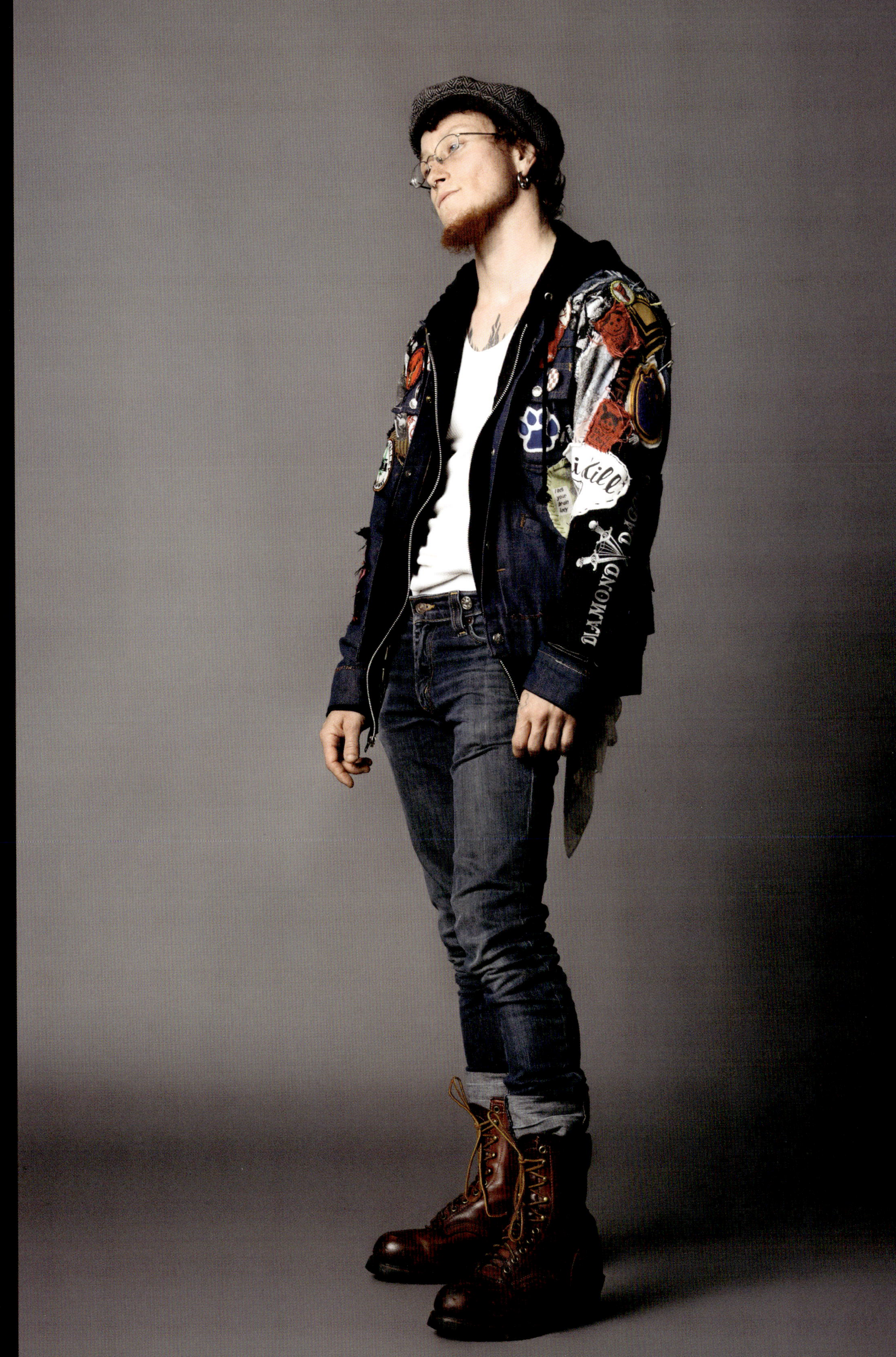
DIAMOND

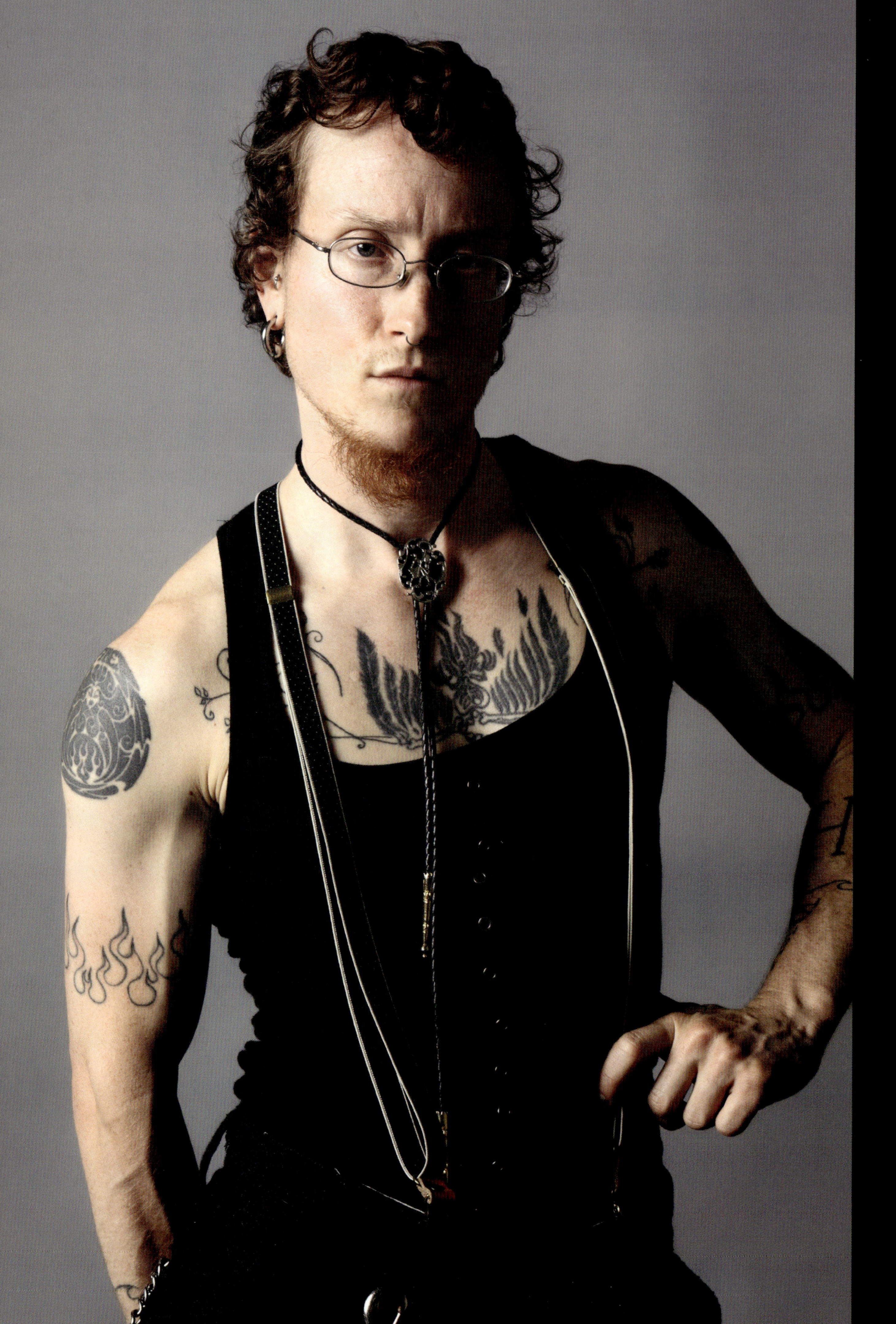

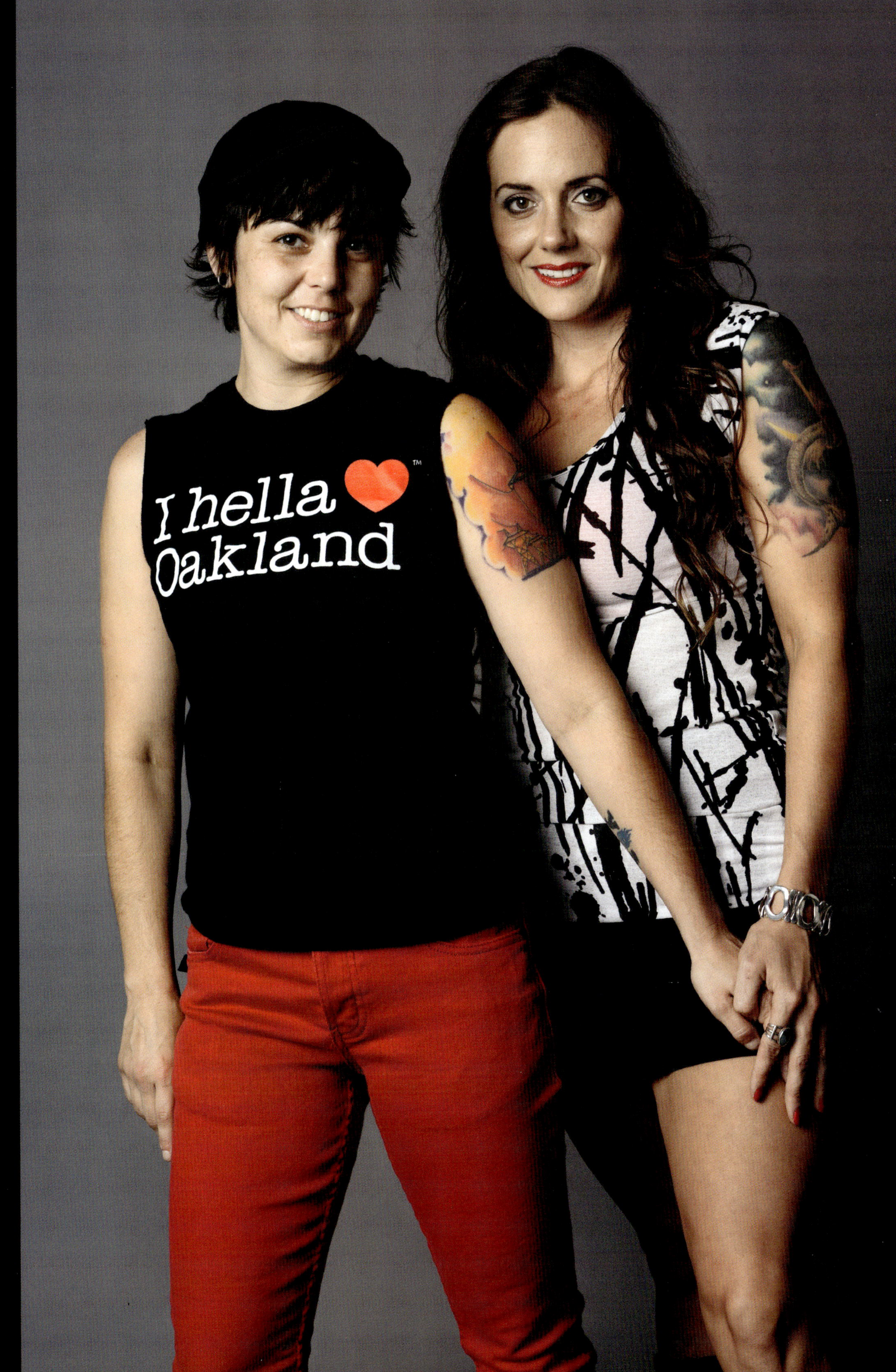

I hella
Oakland

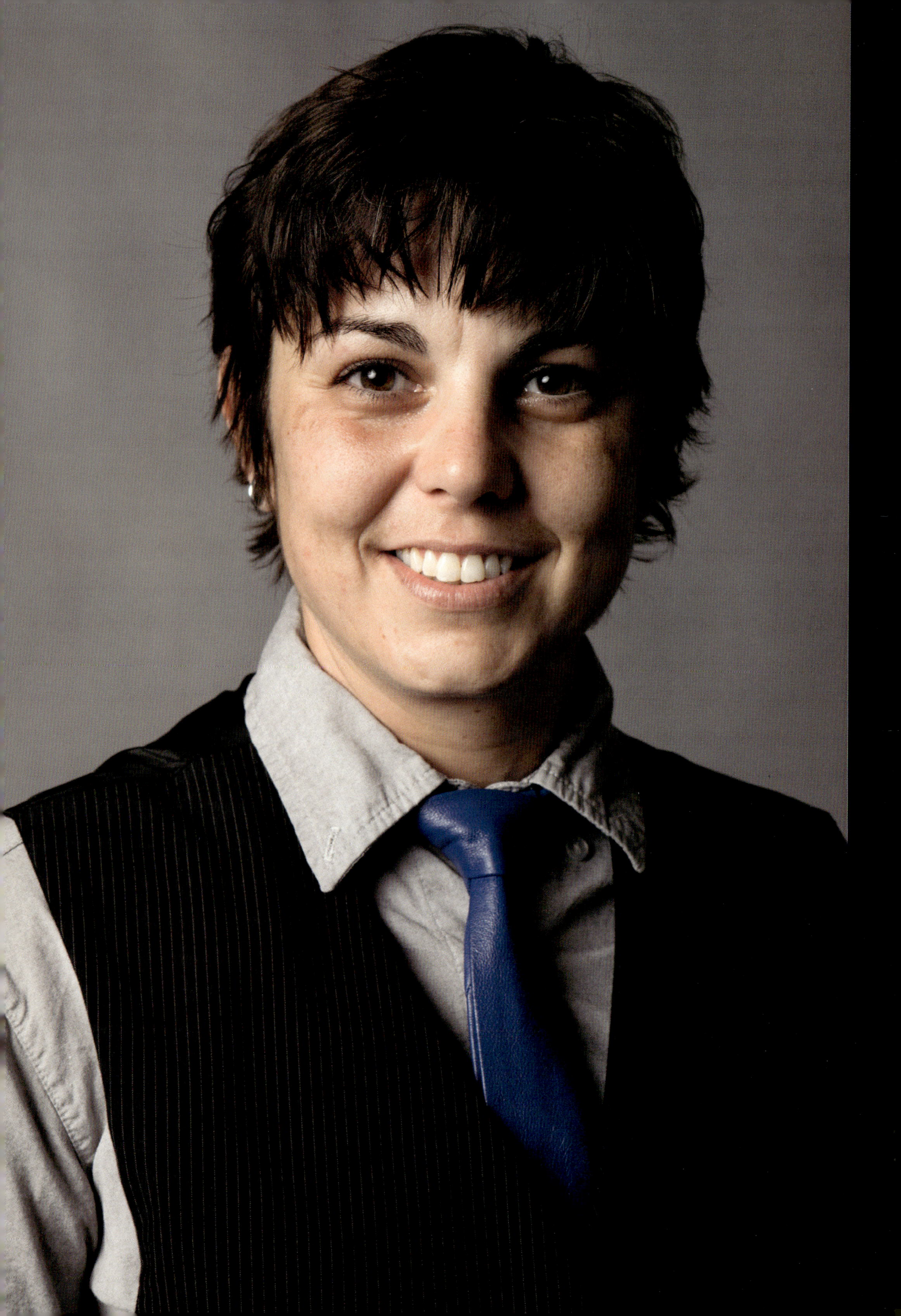

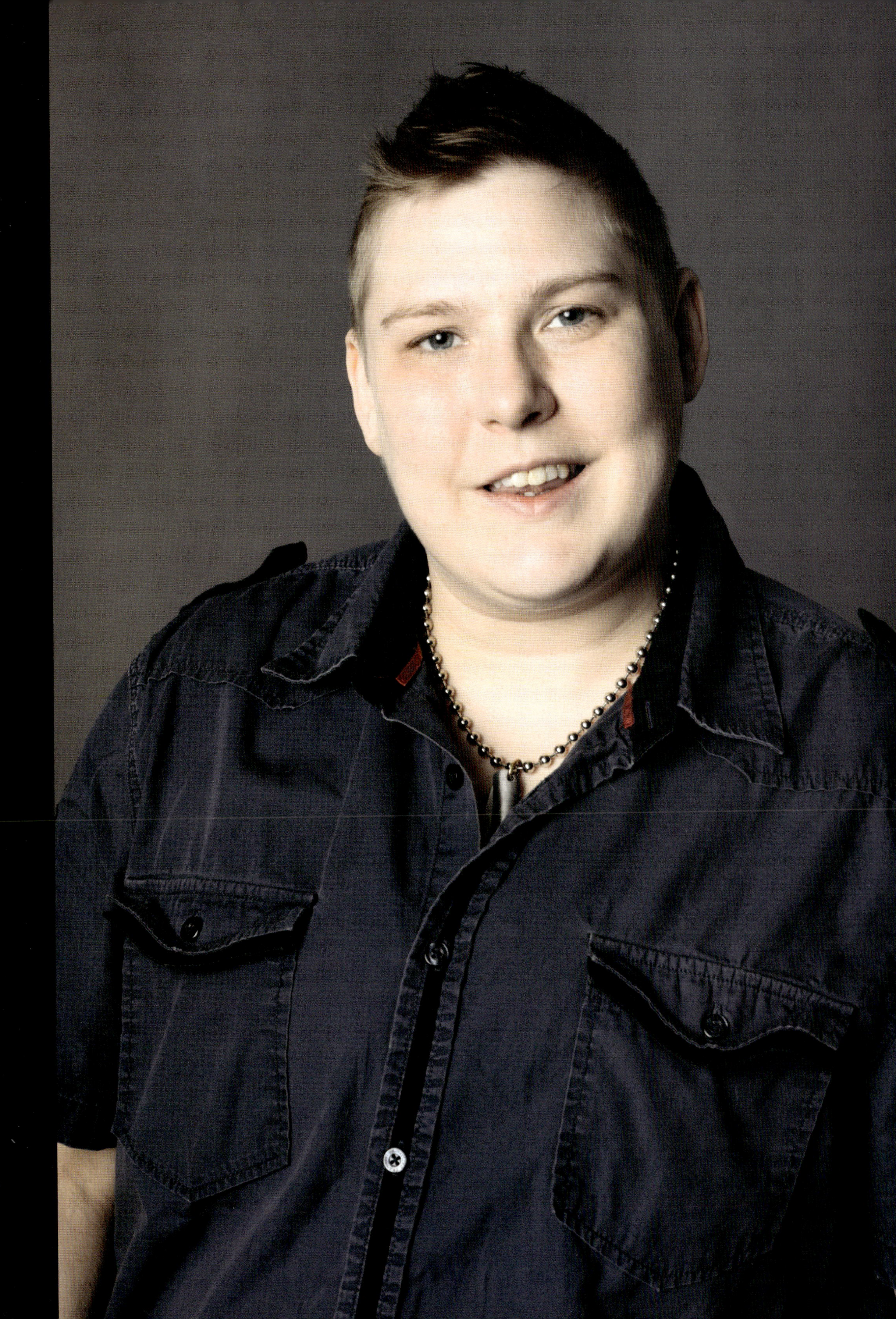

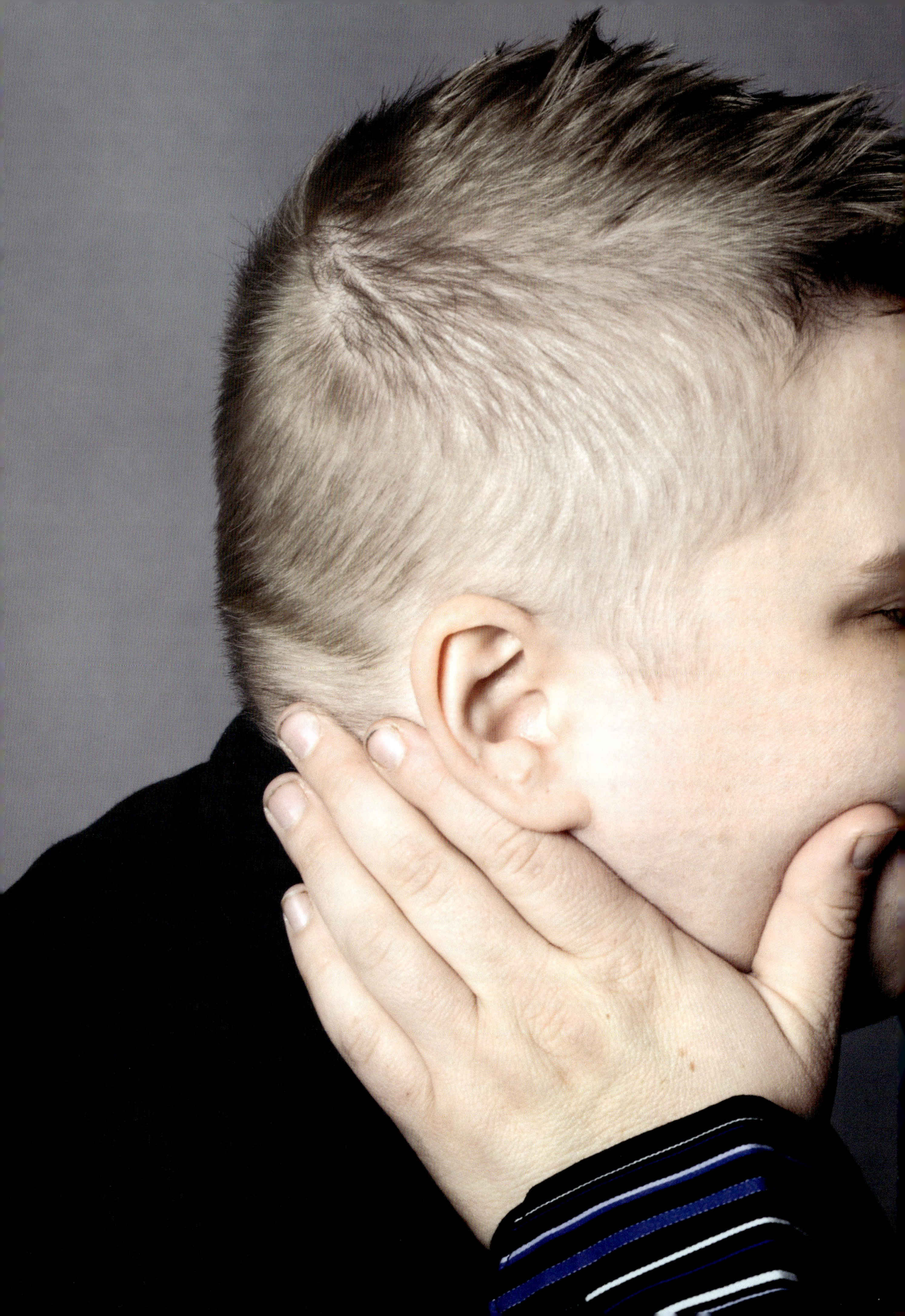

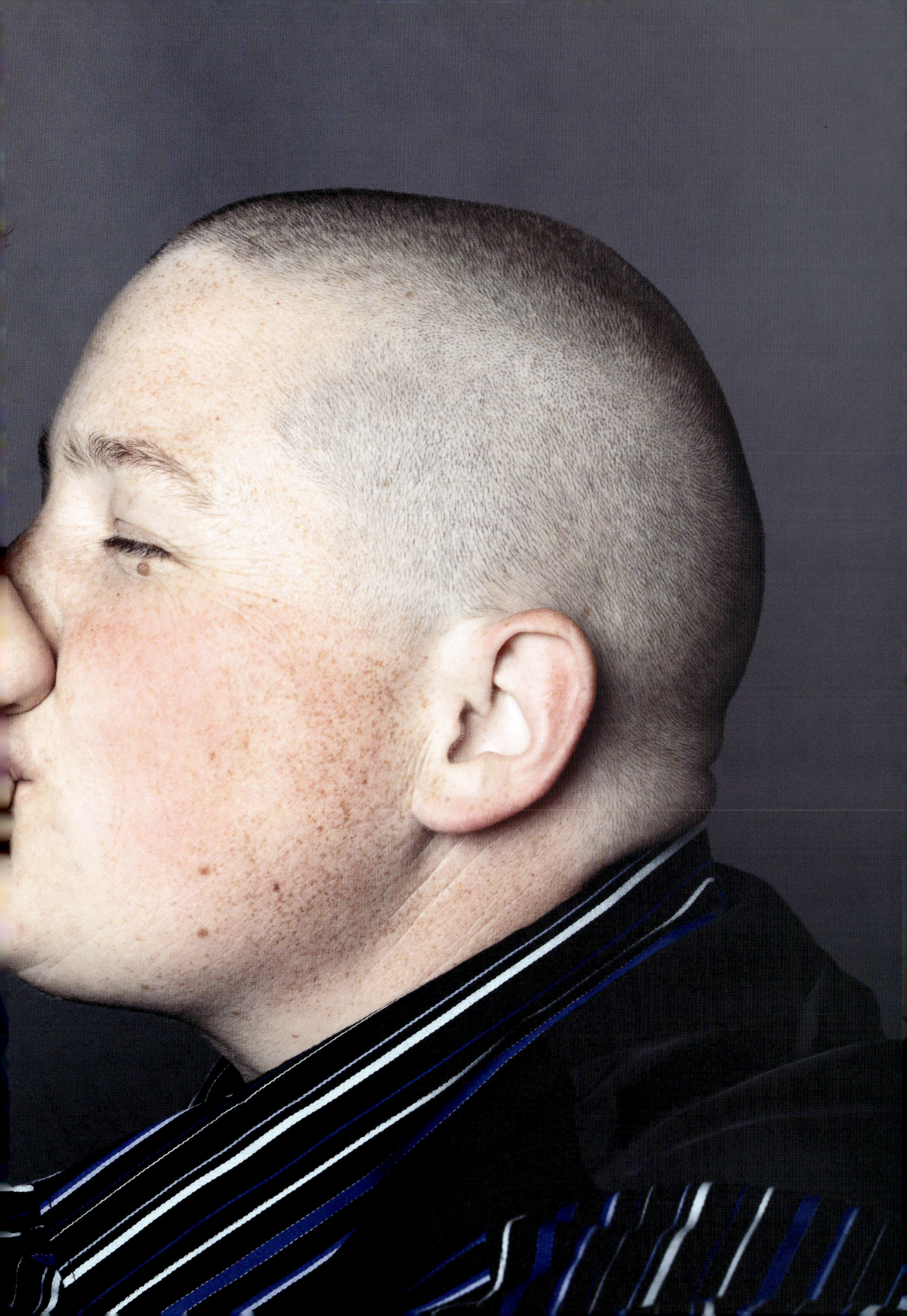

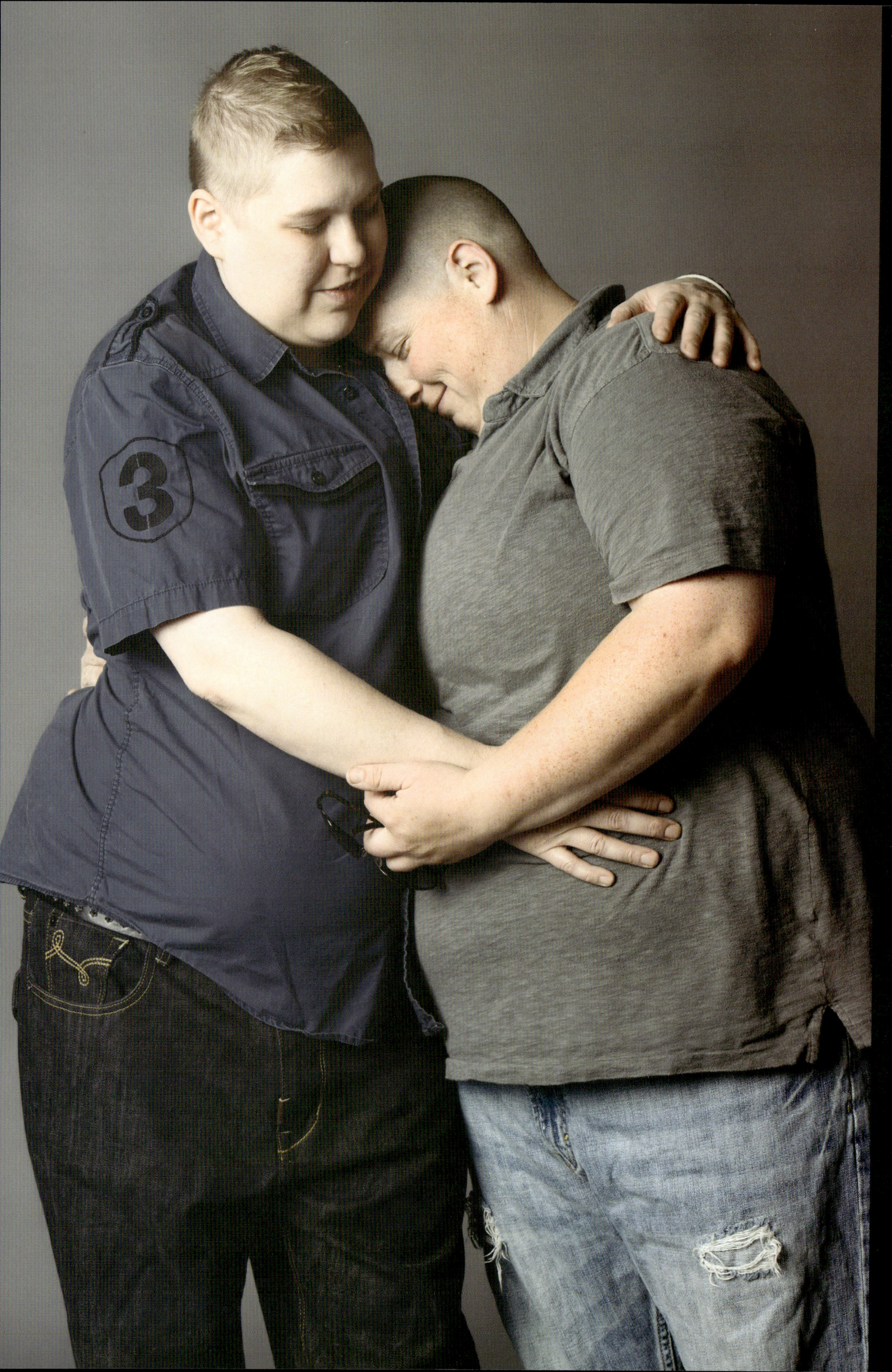

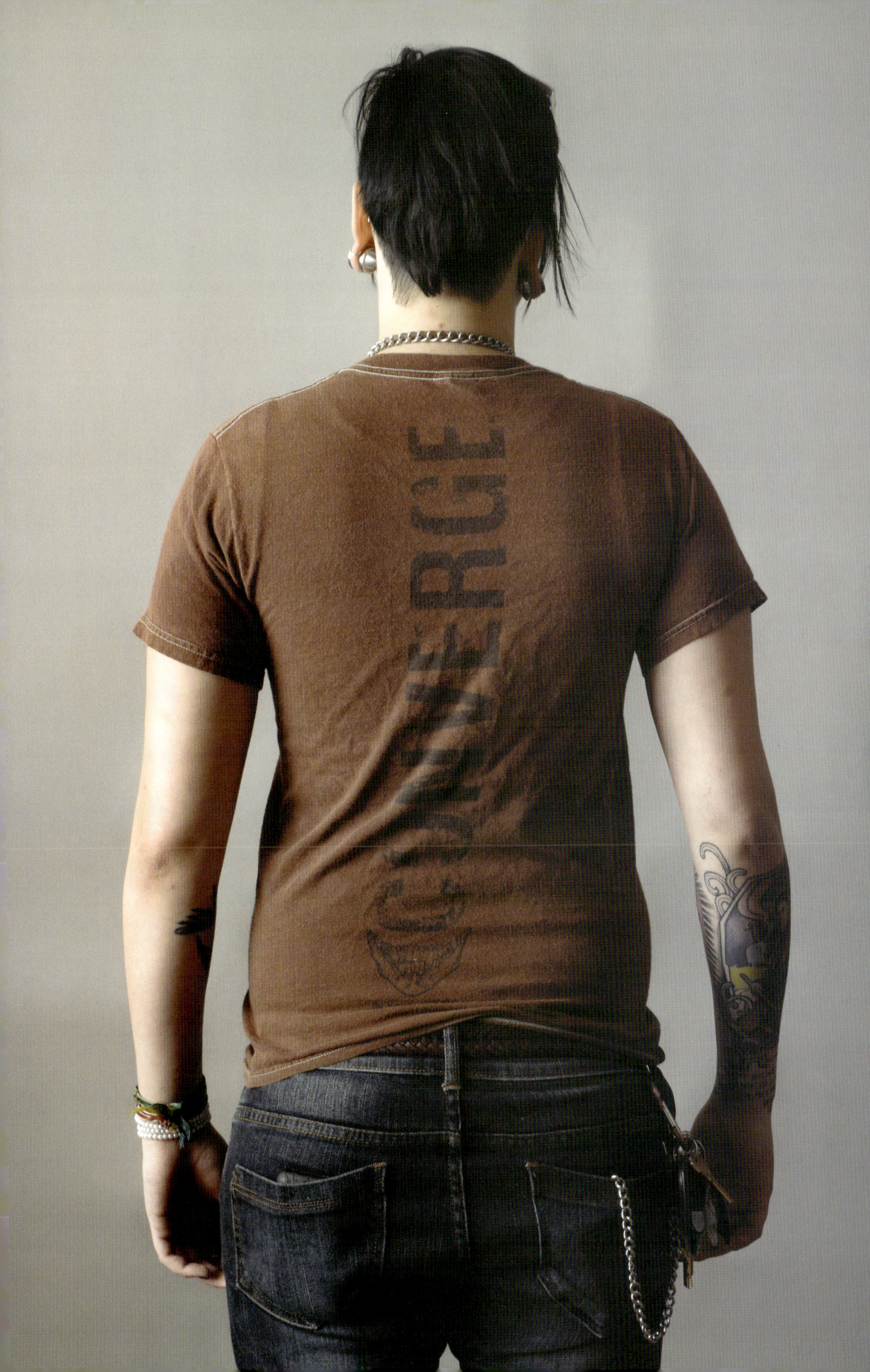
CONVERGE

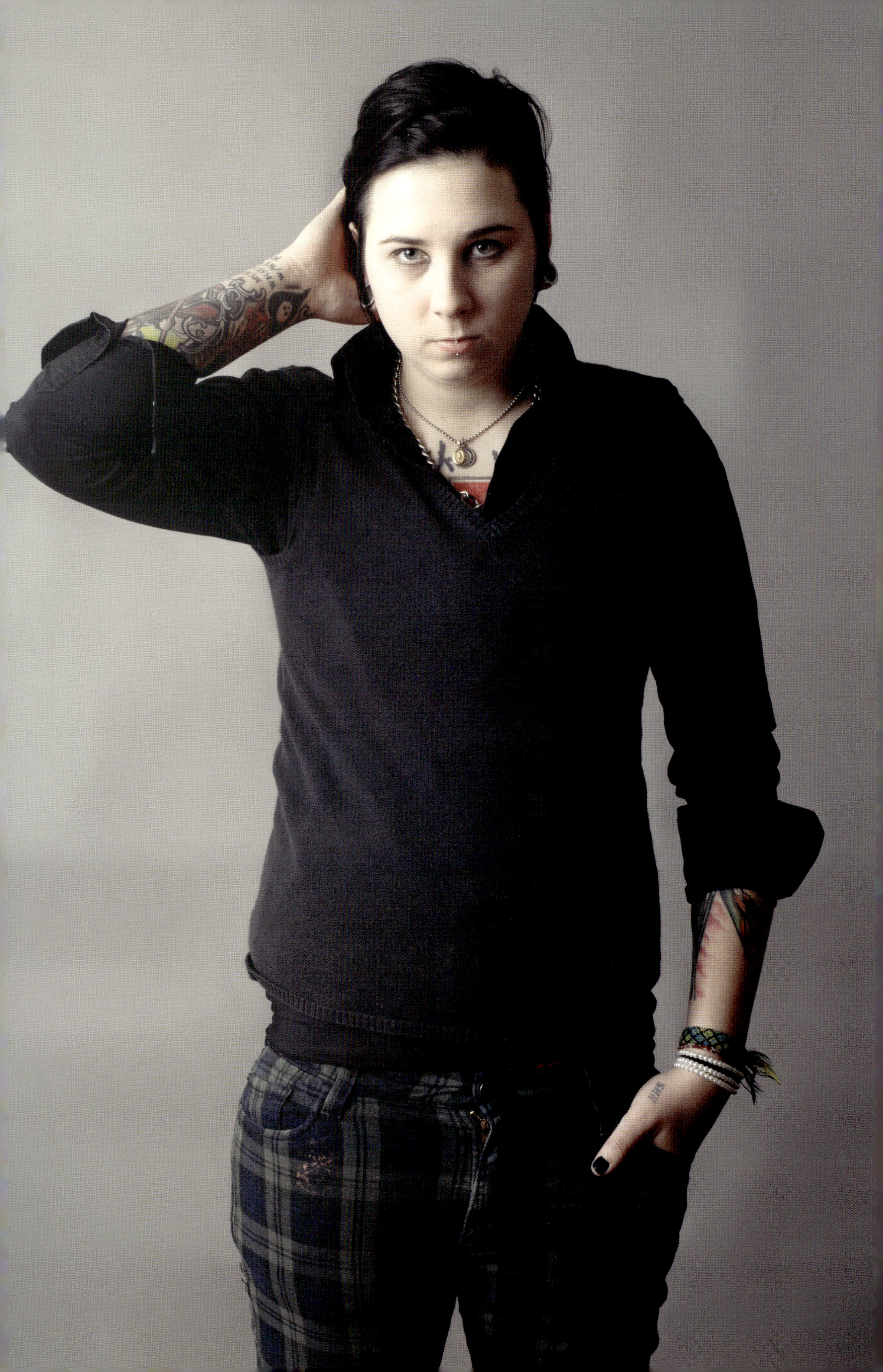

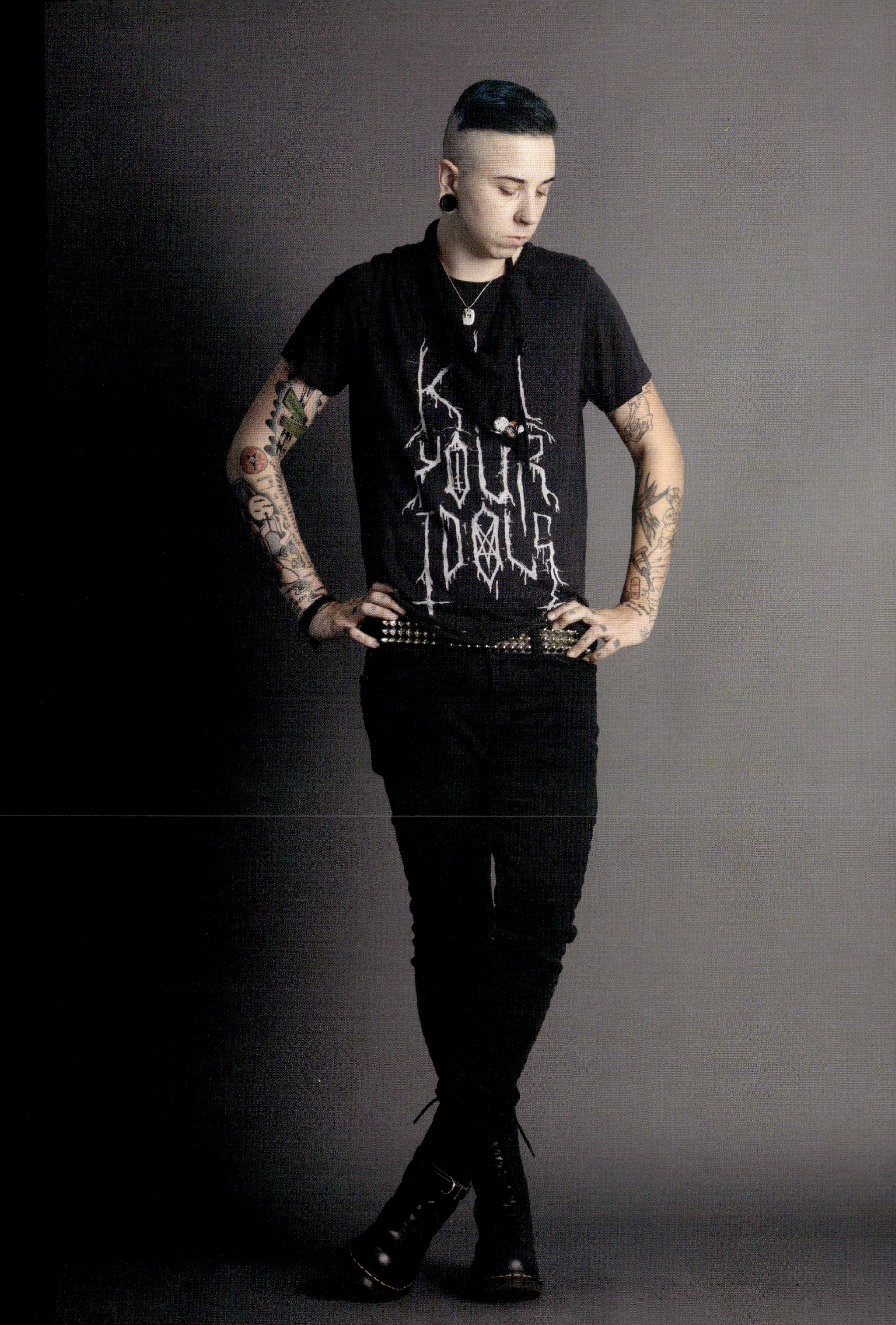
YOUR
IDOLS

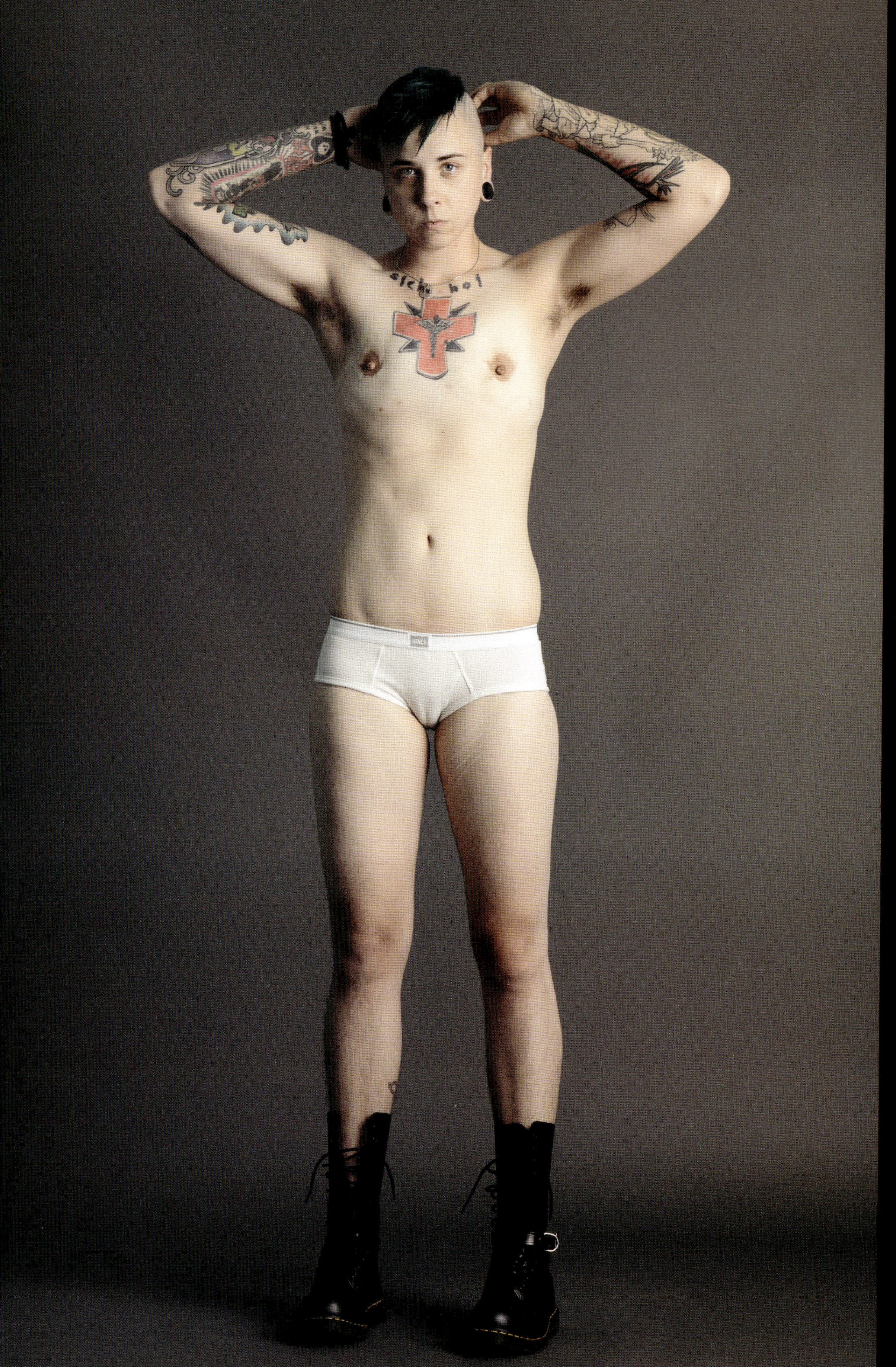
sick boi

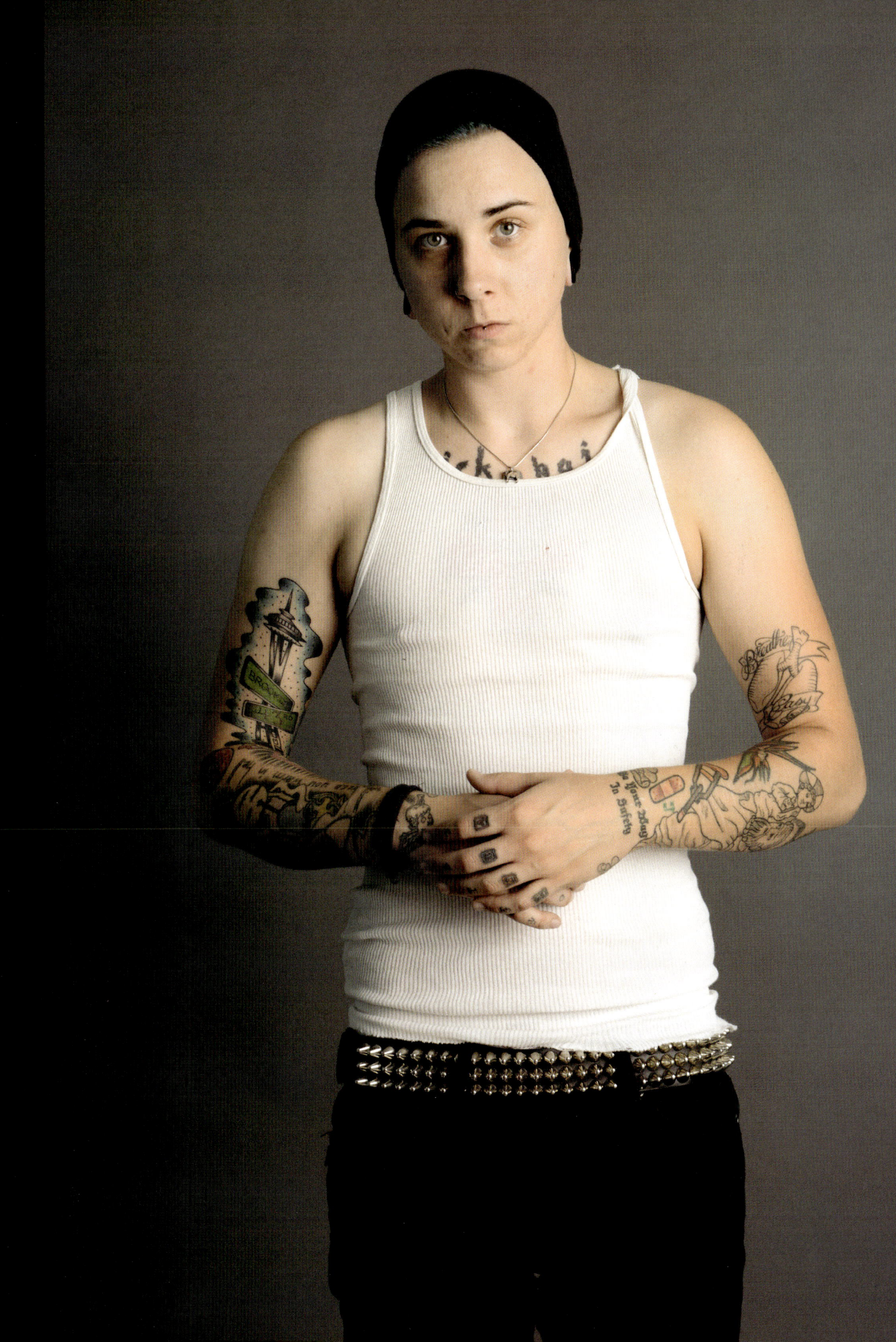

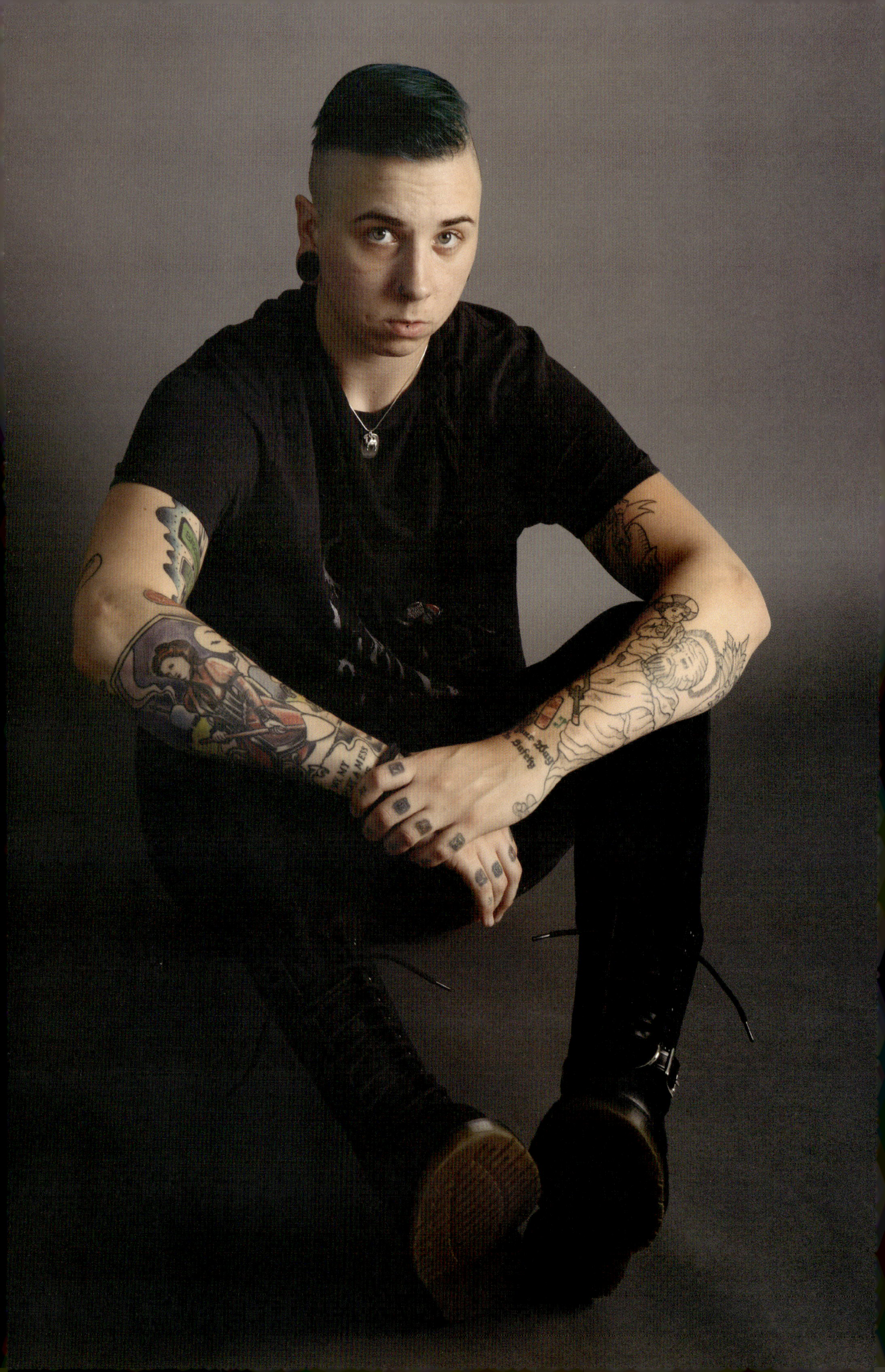

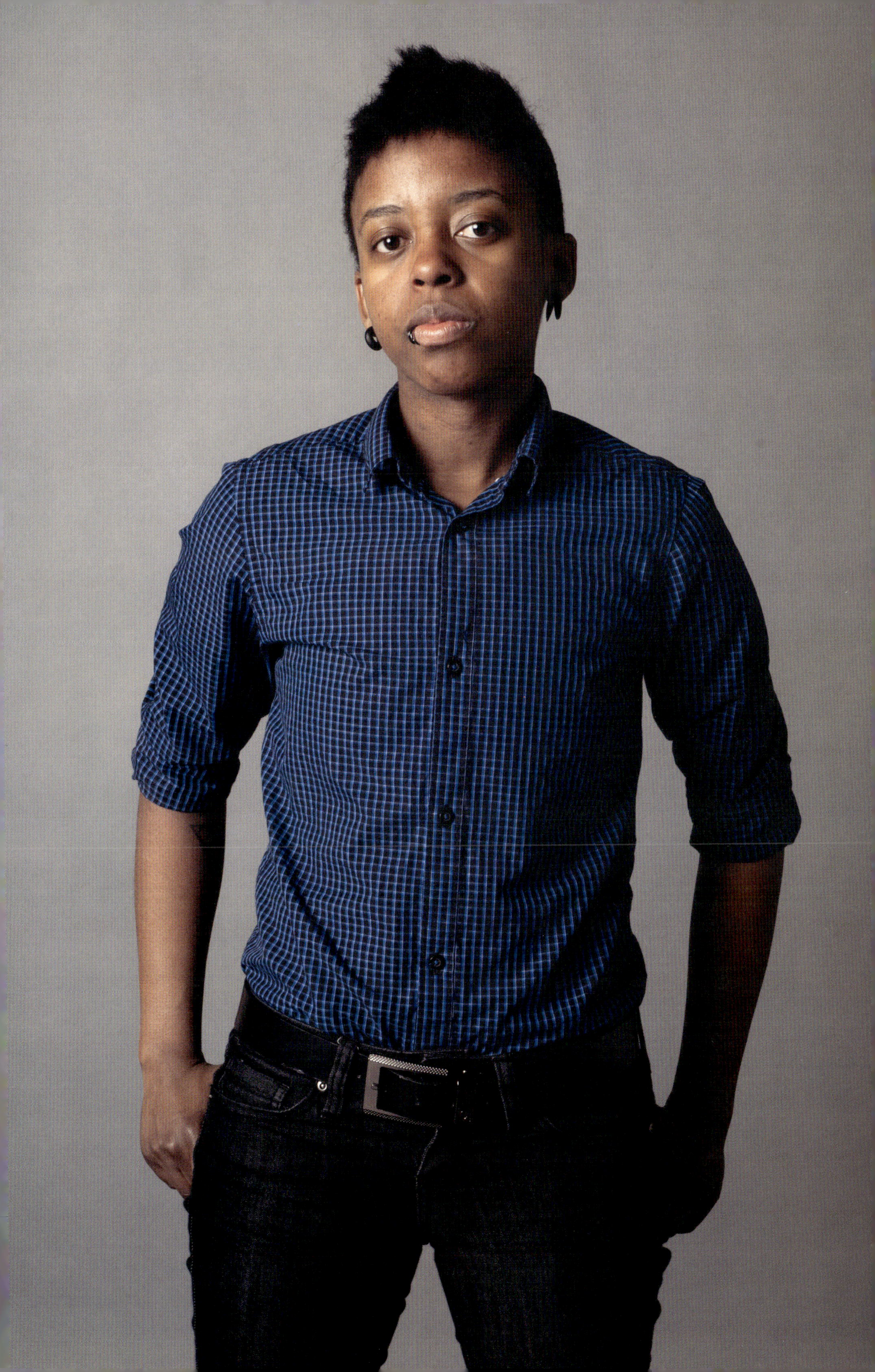

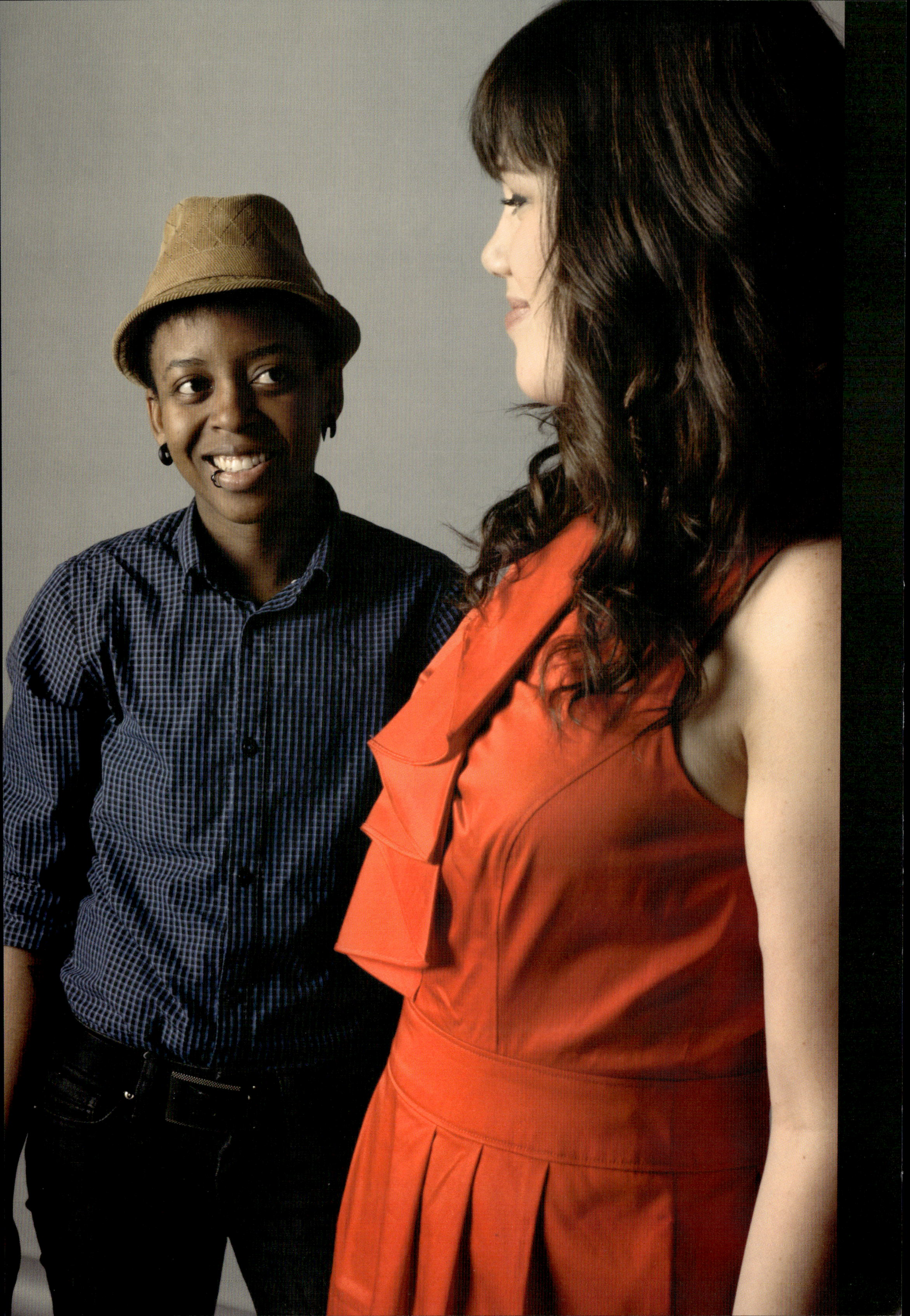

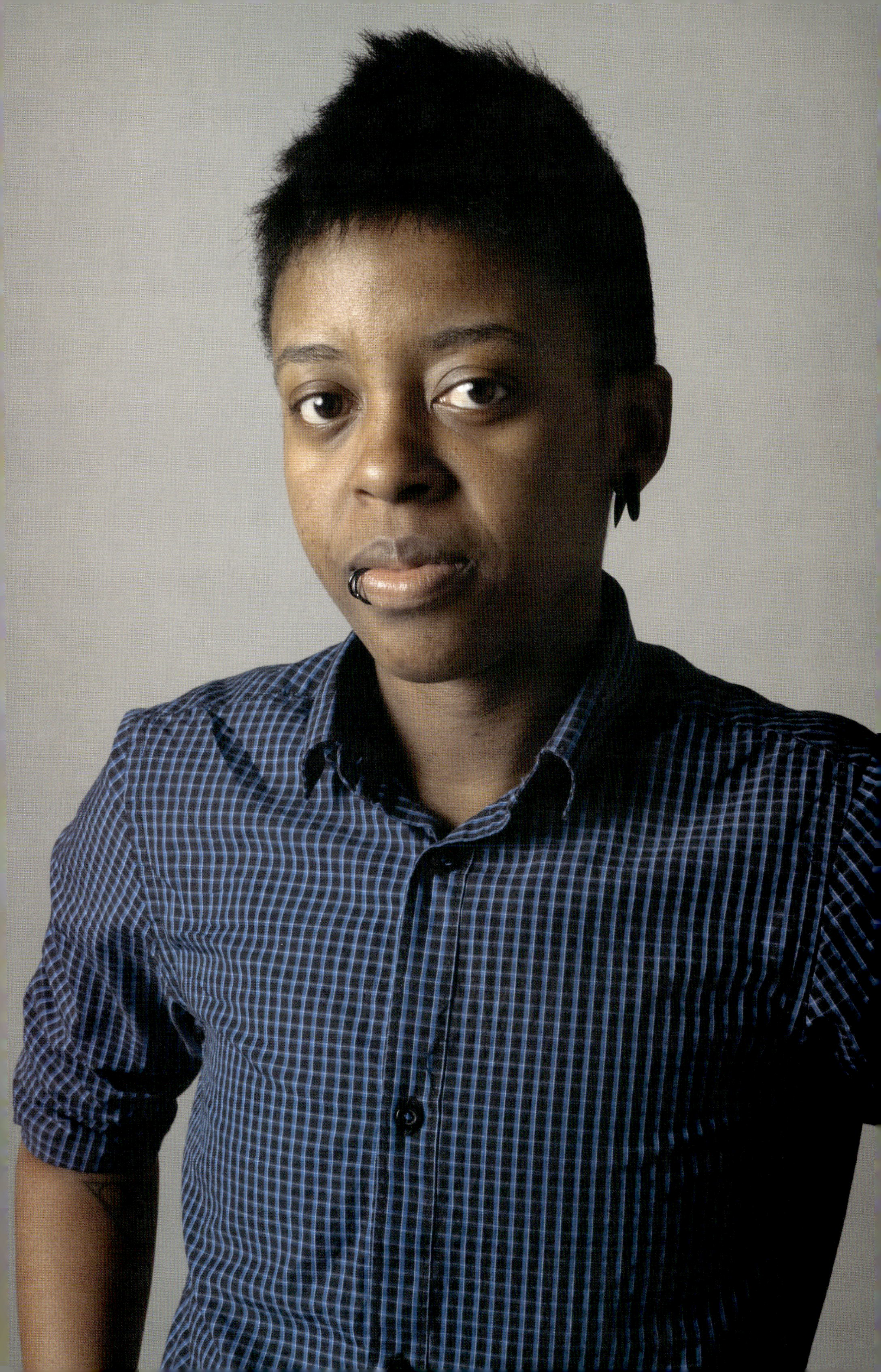

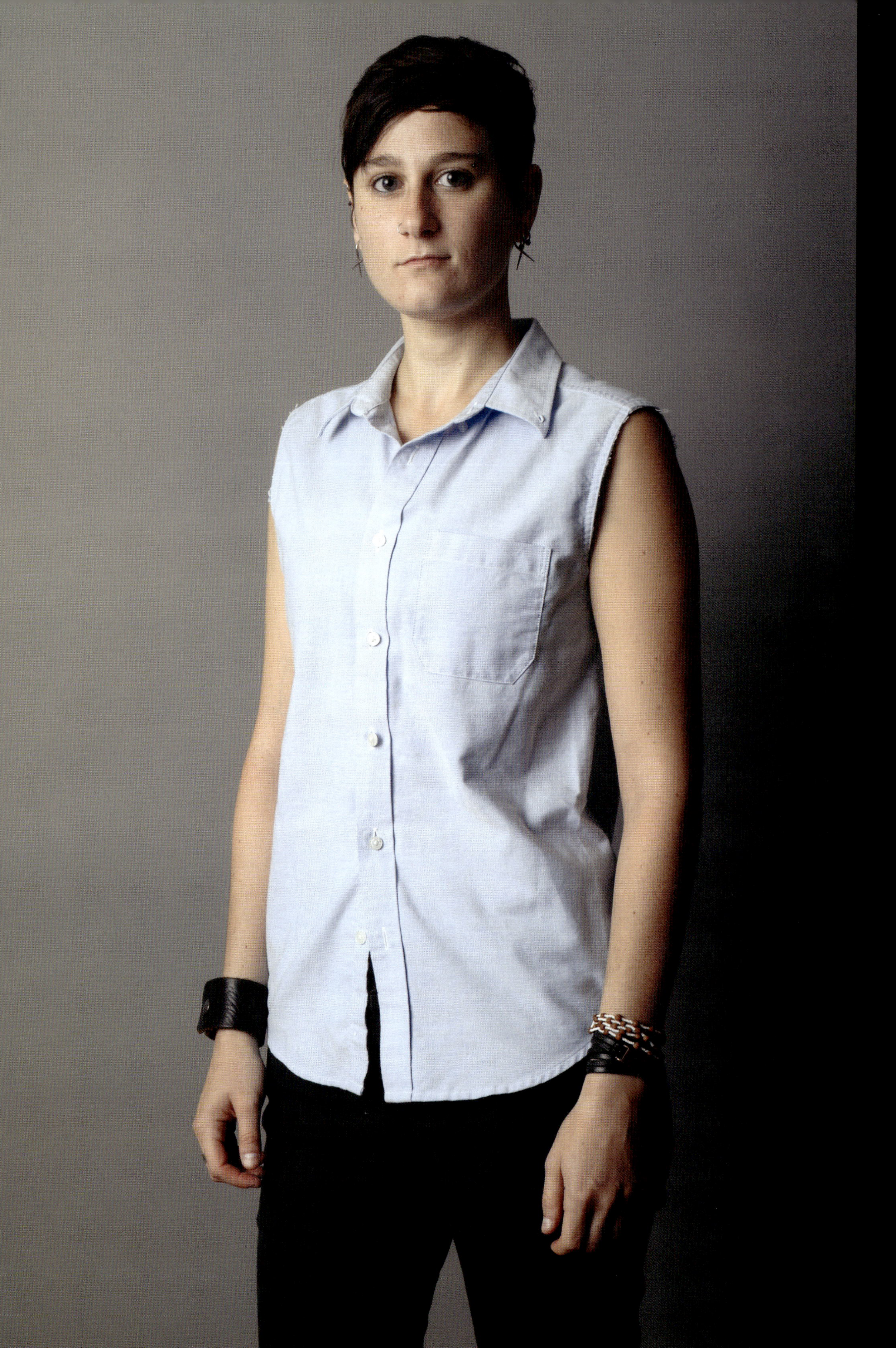

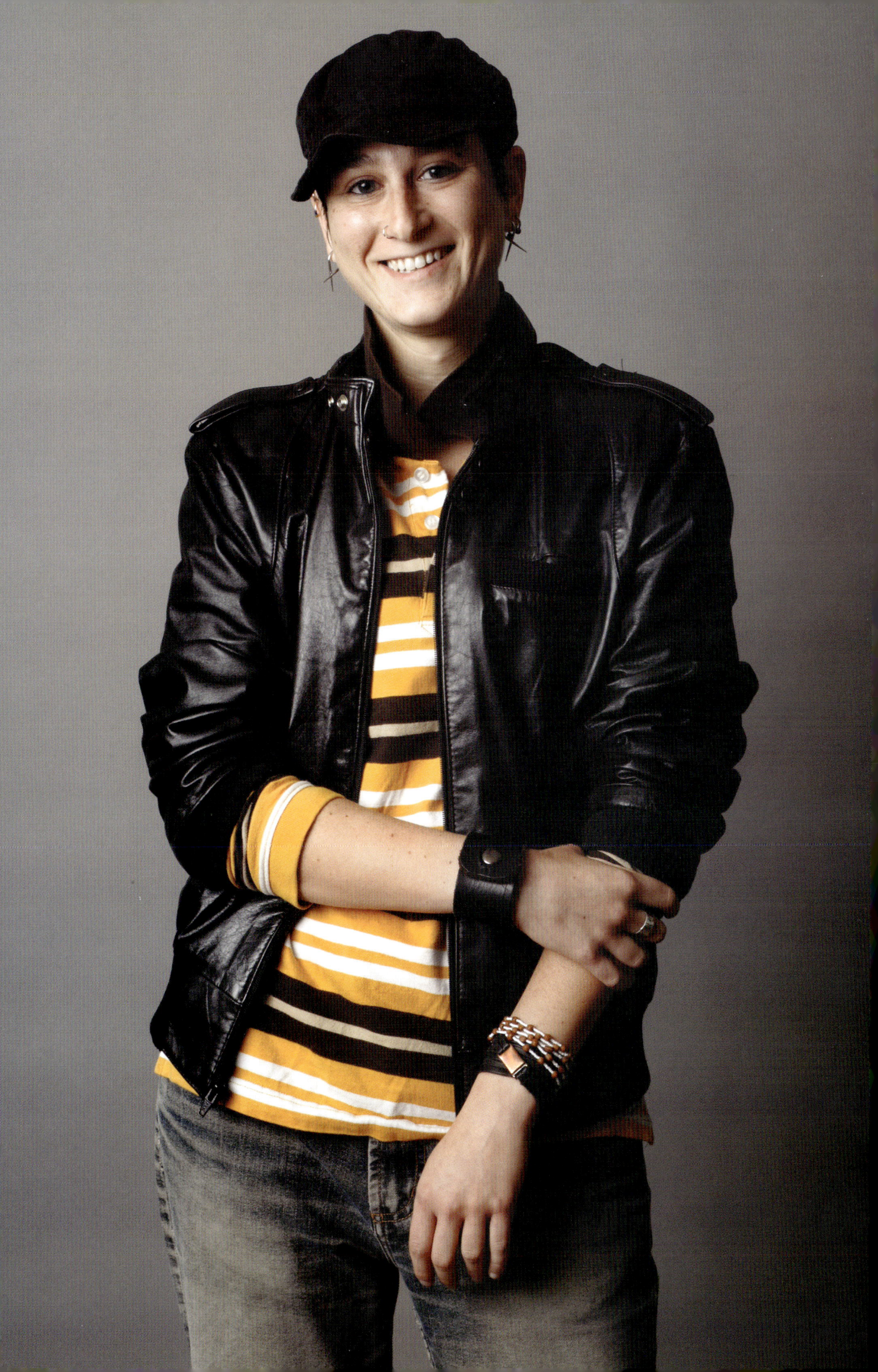

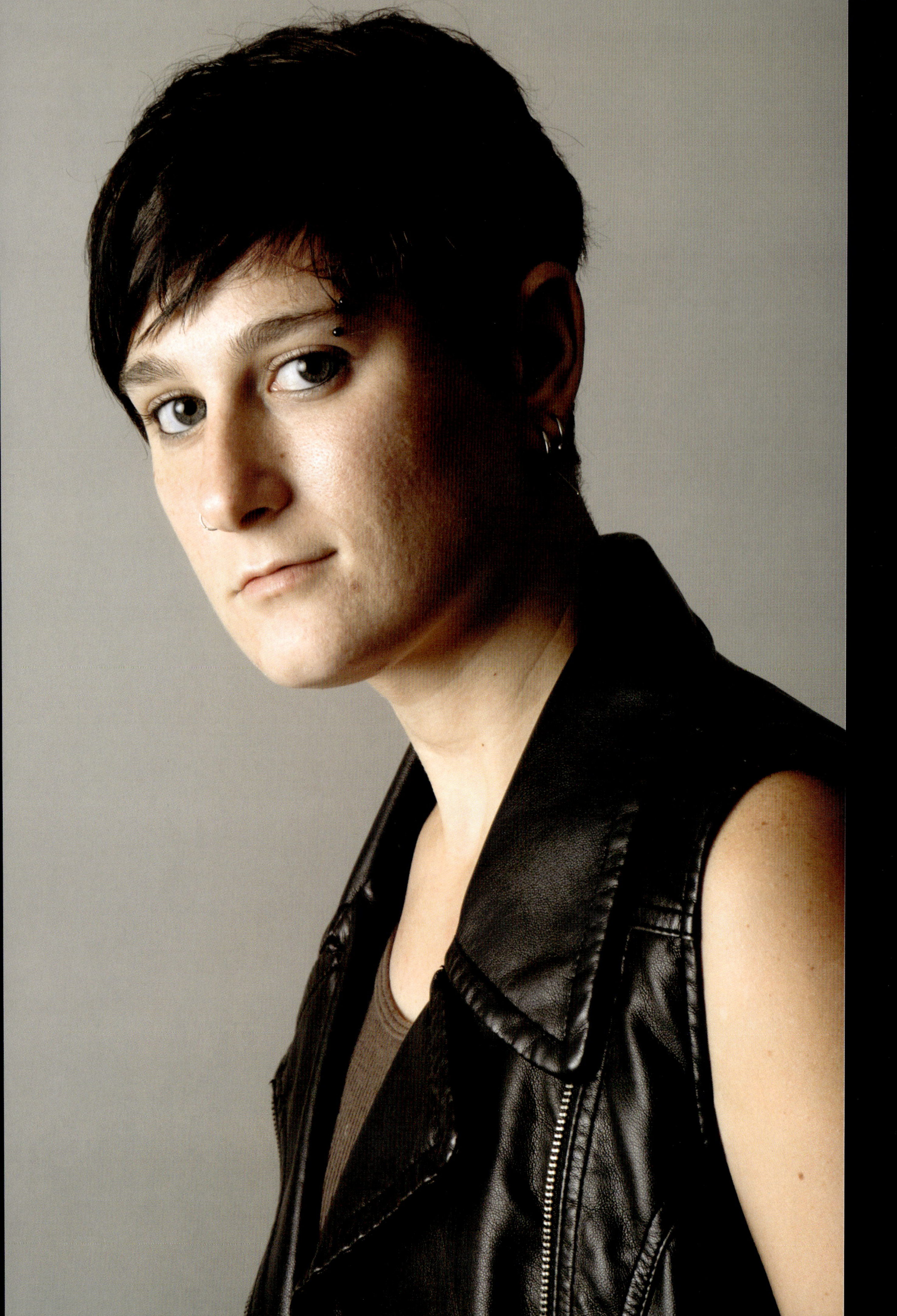

NOAH ENACTION

I was never a tomboy. I don't have any of the expected baby-dyke stories about being forced into dresses as a girl, or stealing my brothers' action figures and ignoring my dolls. No, I was a house-playing, cherry chapstick-wearing, stuffed animal lover. Patent leather slip-ons and long skirts were staples of the synagogue uniform I wore every week. A quiet, anxious girl from an Orthodox Jewish home, I was always tuned into my body's sensations. Part from fear, part from perverse curiosity (perverse in the Orthodox community, anyway), paying attention to how my skin or gut felt in a certain outfit, or noticing how physically close I was to the people around me, was constantly part of my mindscape.

As a survivor of sexual assault, as a queer, and as a woman, exploring new ways of engaging with my body and listening to its sometimes subtle, sometimes cacophonous utterances is not only a matter of survival, but also a distinct place of joy. From a stern religious context where gender codes were absolute to experiencing my woman's body as a site of danger, I hadn't realized I wanted something new from my body till I looked at myself in the mirror with my new crew cut, tucking a too big button-down into my baggiest pair of jeans. Trying to ignore my bunching boxers, I ran a palm full of gel through my hair till it clumped into a crop of glazed half-waves. Who was this person staring back at me? They looked vaguely familiar, the shape of the face, the faintly dimpled chin, the unclouded eyes—but I couldn't quite place them. I was riveted. Could this be me, too?

This was in college. Every day I stepped out of my room and felt the air on my scalp, every time I found myself swaggering along campus paths like I could have anything I wanted, was an experiment, an adventure. I realized I could create a new relationship with my body. That I could unrecognize myself.

But this is not about self-loathing, festering anger at my Orthodox community, or about attempting to reverse the effects of trauma. For me, playing with gender is about defamiliarization. Through this exercise, it is possible see new parts of myself all the time. That moment in front of the mirror, I saw someone inside me I hadn't known was there. I gave him a name: Noah.

The differences between Sarah and Noah are not so great. It takes an eye trained to nuance to perceive the distinction. But for me, however subtly, the shift is felt.

Sarah and Noah share the same assertive nose and half smirk. But Sarah sits cross-legged, her eyes dashing between her surroundings and her own body, always assessing. She is conscious of her clavicle and hips. She intertwines her fingers and favors her right foot when she walks. Her breasts are valuable.

Noah feels other parts of my same body more deeply. For him, shoulders come into focus, overpowering the chest. He tosses his head back slightly to showcase the gentle swell of a pronounced Adam's apple, too big to be stuck in a woman's throat. Noah feels his feet on the floor. He rolls up his sleeves and leads from the presence between his hips. It's a benevolent weight, untamed and pure. Maybe Noah's hips sway less. Maybe he ignores the sensitivity of nipples and focuses instead on the sternum. He slouches into a quiet, but irrefutable confidence.

Their personalities, too, are only finely distinctive. They are both fidgety and inquisitive, but Sarah is anxious—nervous as a fluttering leaf. Twitchy like a set of fingers on a keyboard. Sarah tries too hard. Noah is simpler, undefined. He is a place of possibility within me. Because I know so little about Noah, there are no wrong answers and nothing to fear. The freedom to become anyone is a comfort. I do not need or want for people to call me Noah all the time. If they did, Noah would not be special. Instead, Noah remains rough—my unpolished stone.

I've expressed Noah as a restless teenage boy—sloppy, mischievous, curious, adorable. He has also been coy and inexperienced—a consummate, untainted bottom. He calculates his eye contact to produce the shimmer of a wily, forged innocence. Coltish but deferent, Noah is an accomplished flirt, always countering that direct eye contact with feigned resistance, tugging and slacking his end of the rope at twisted intervals. I love the way he walks into a bar: His white T-shirt hangs around his shoulders and torso in a way that makes him feel strong, like there's hidden muscle underneath. He shoves his hands into his pockets, keeps his stomach taut, hips stiff in their place, and his gaze coquettish from behind a short mess of hair. "How does this feel?" I ask myself. "What can I do with this posture? This temperament?"

Gender play helps me navigate some of the most ineffable parts of myself. Noah is not a binder or a jacket. Not a thick belt, a button-down, or a tie. Noah is a feeling. Noah is an attitude. I could be wearing baggy pants or drainpipes. I could be binding or wearing underwire. It could be boots or flip-flops. As much as gender is about style, it is not the whole story. Gender is an experience deeply felt in the body.

There are at least as many stories about gender play as there are genderqueer people. They can tell you about their experiences. This is mine. What brings me from Sarah to Noah, from cunt to cock, from woman to boy, is a suspension of disbelief. Becoming Noah, for me, is about making space for a new experience of my body. My imagination, if I surrender to the wild leaps it can make in just a hair of a second, is the magic that calms the ego, and releases insecurities and fears. Noah is for pleasure and we are on a wonderfully peculiar passage through this single body, looking for all of me.

SARAH BURGHAUSER

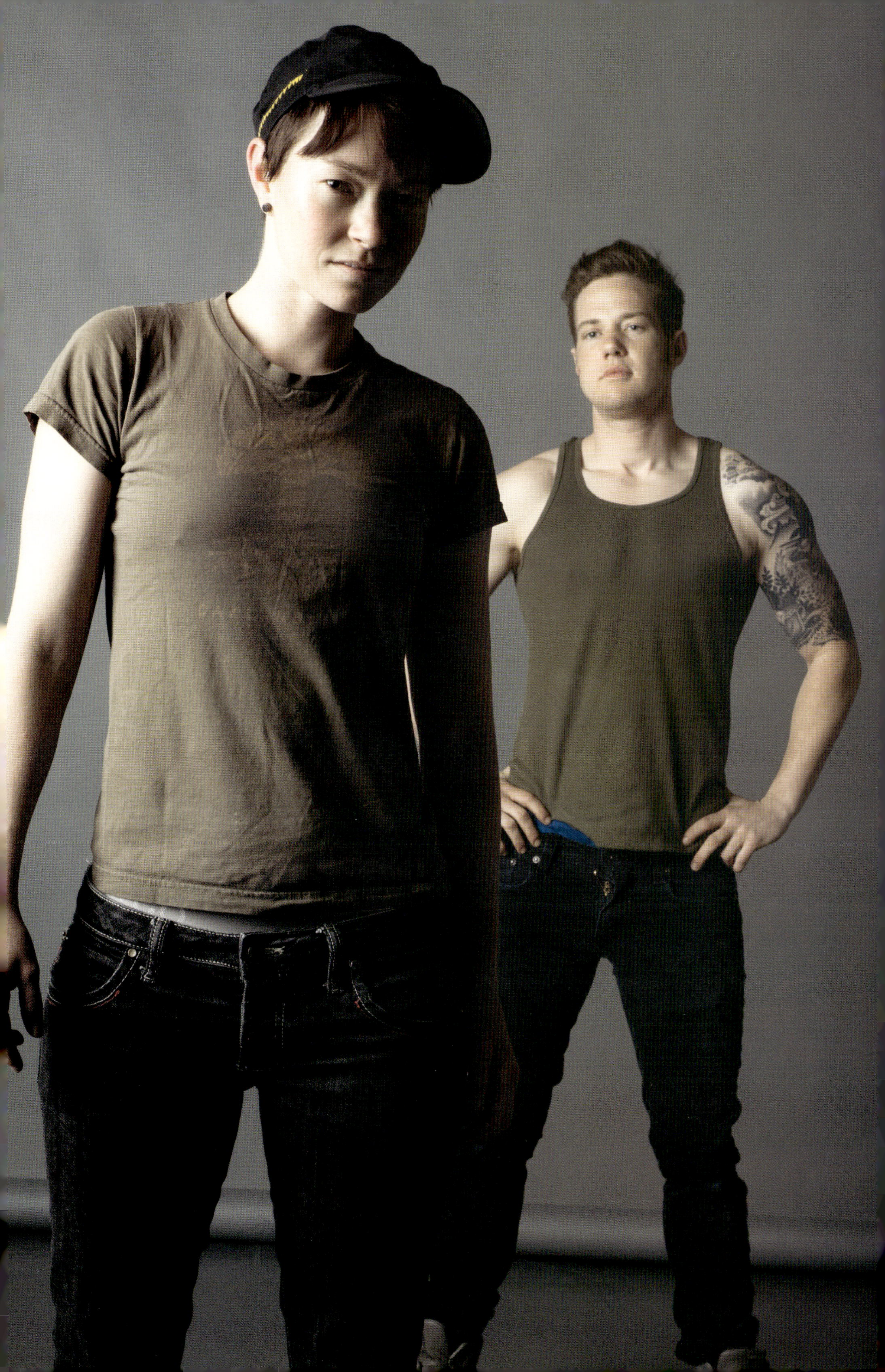

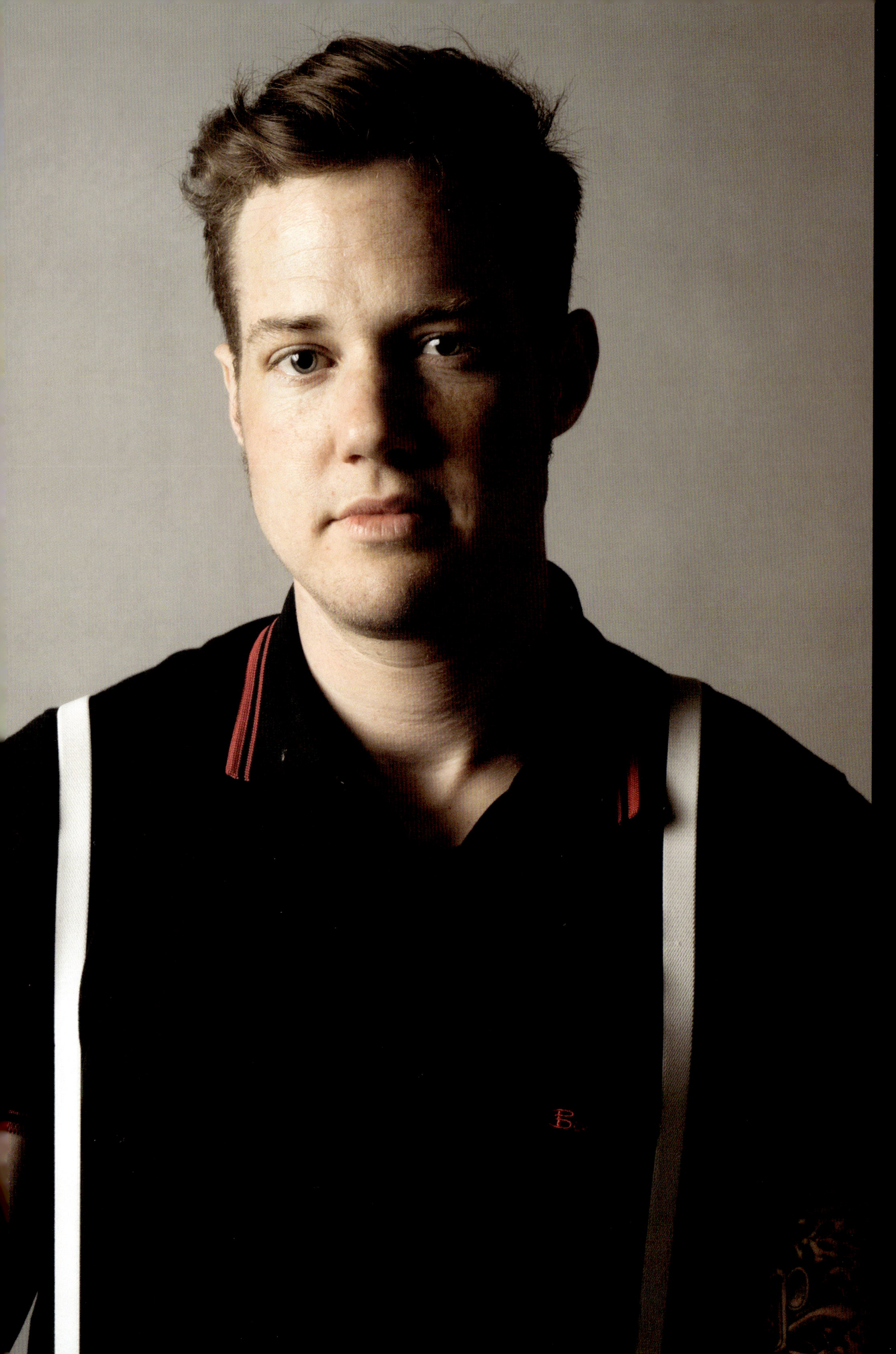

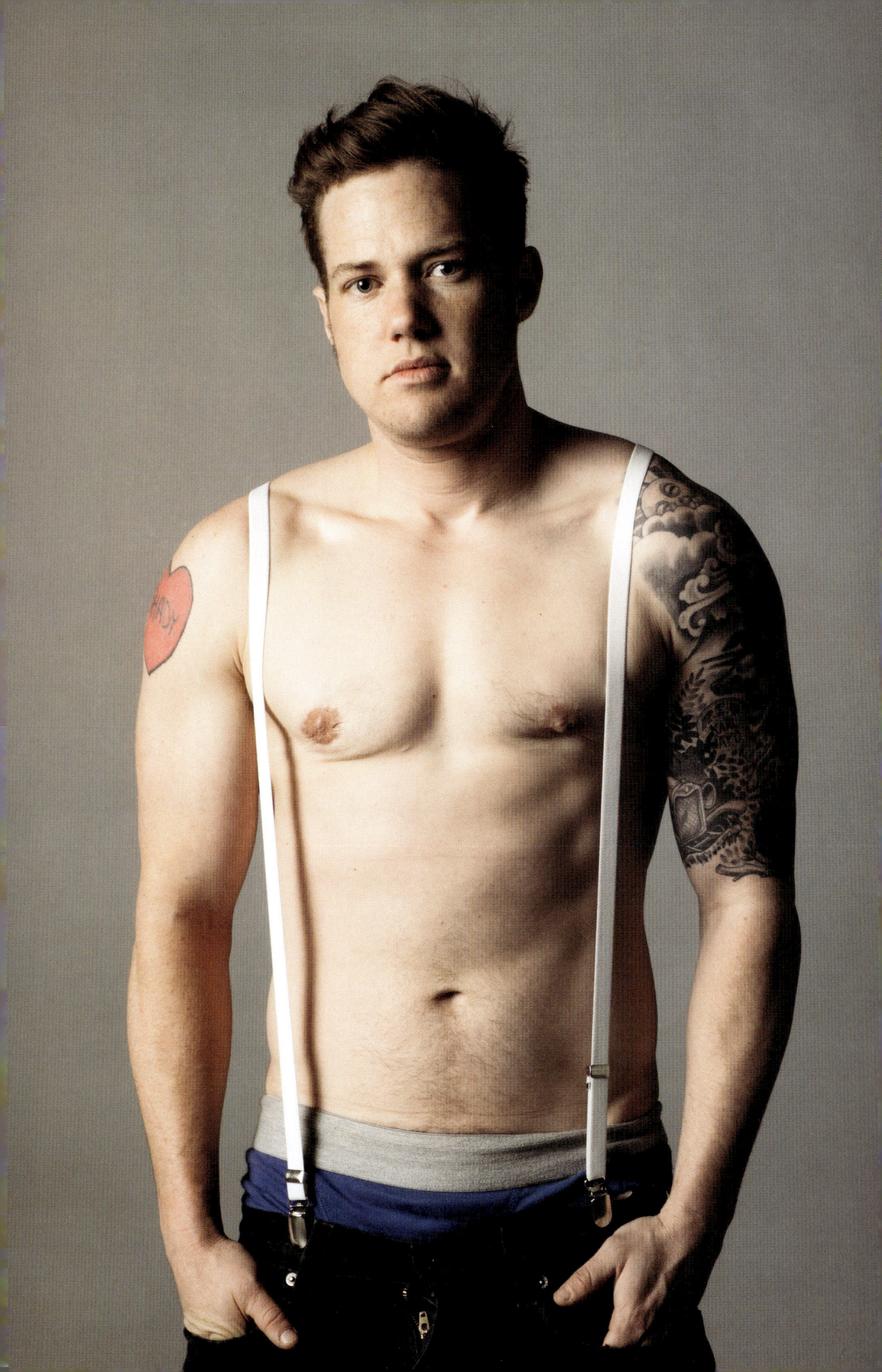

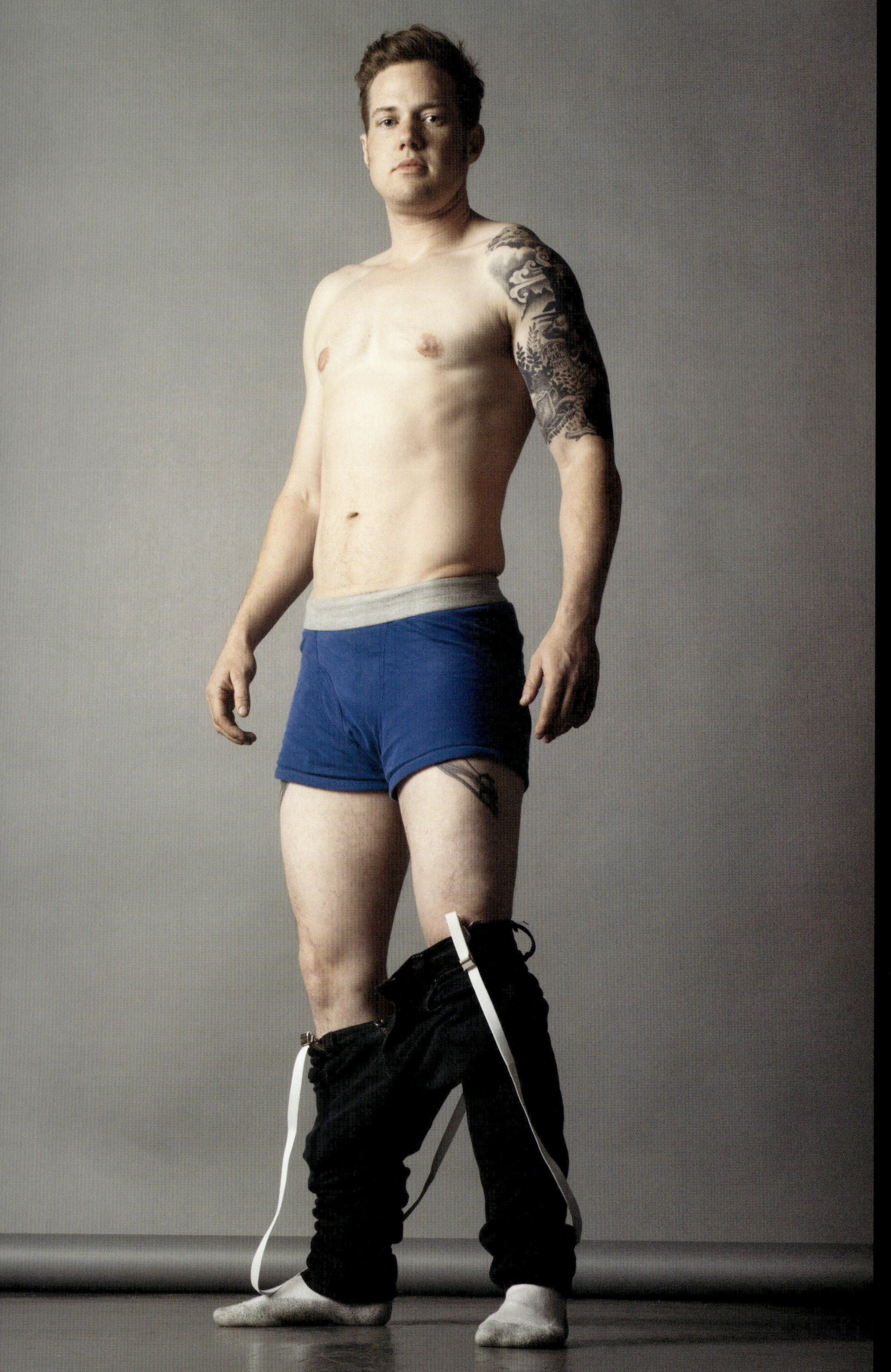

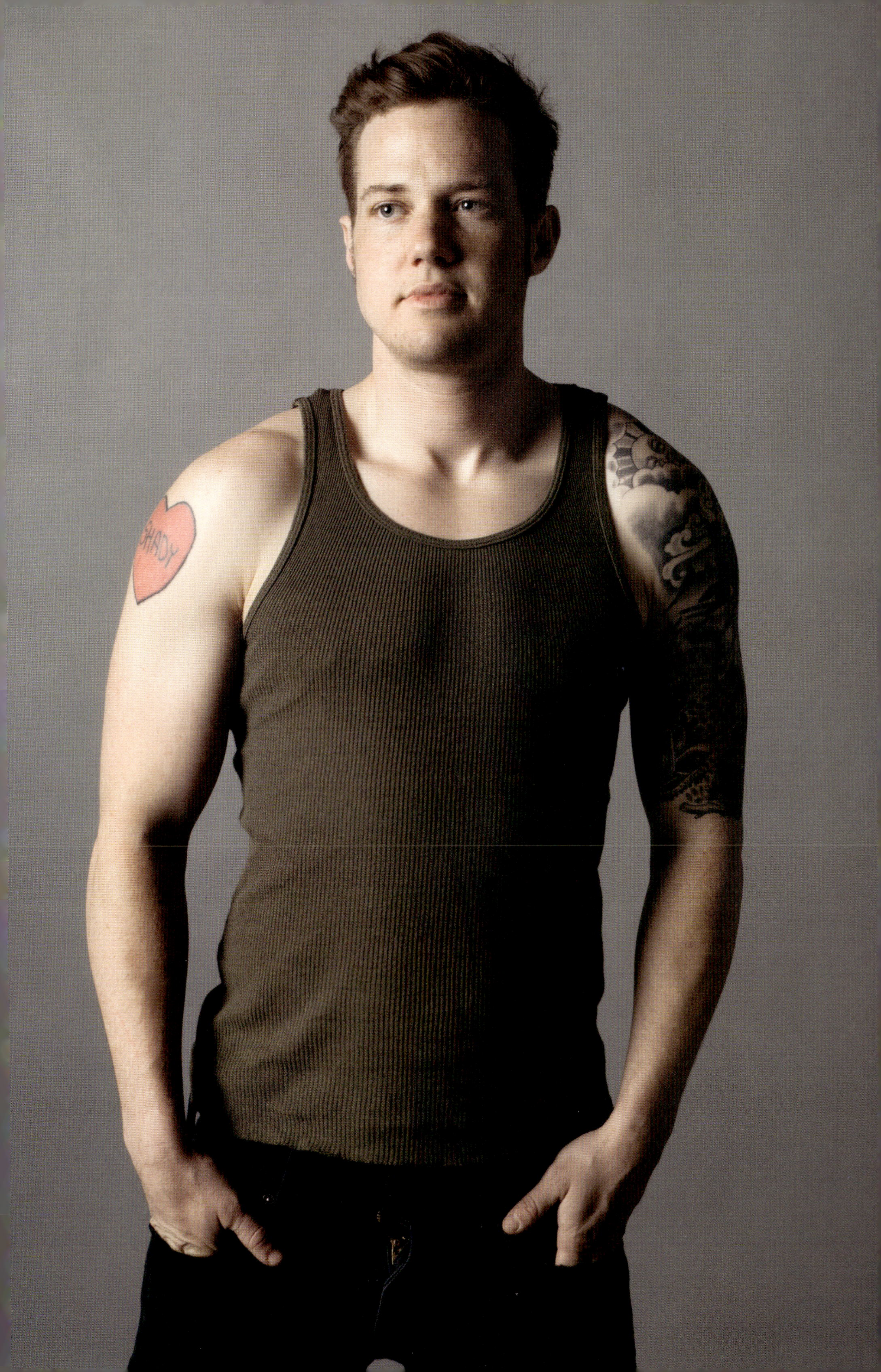
SHADY

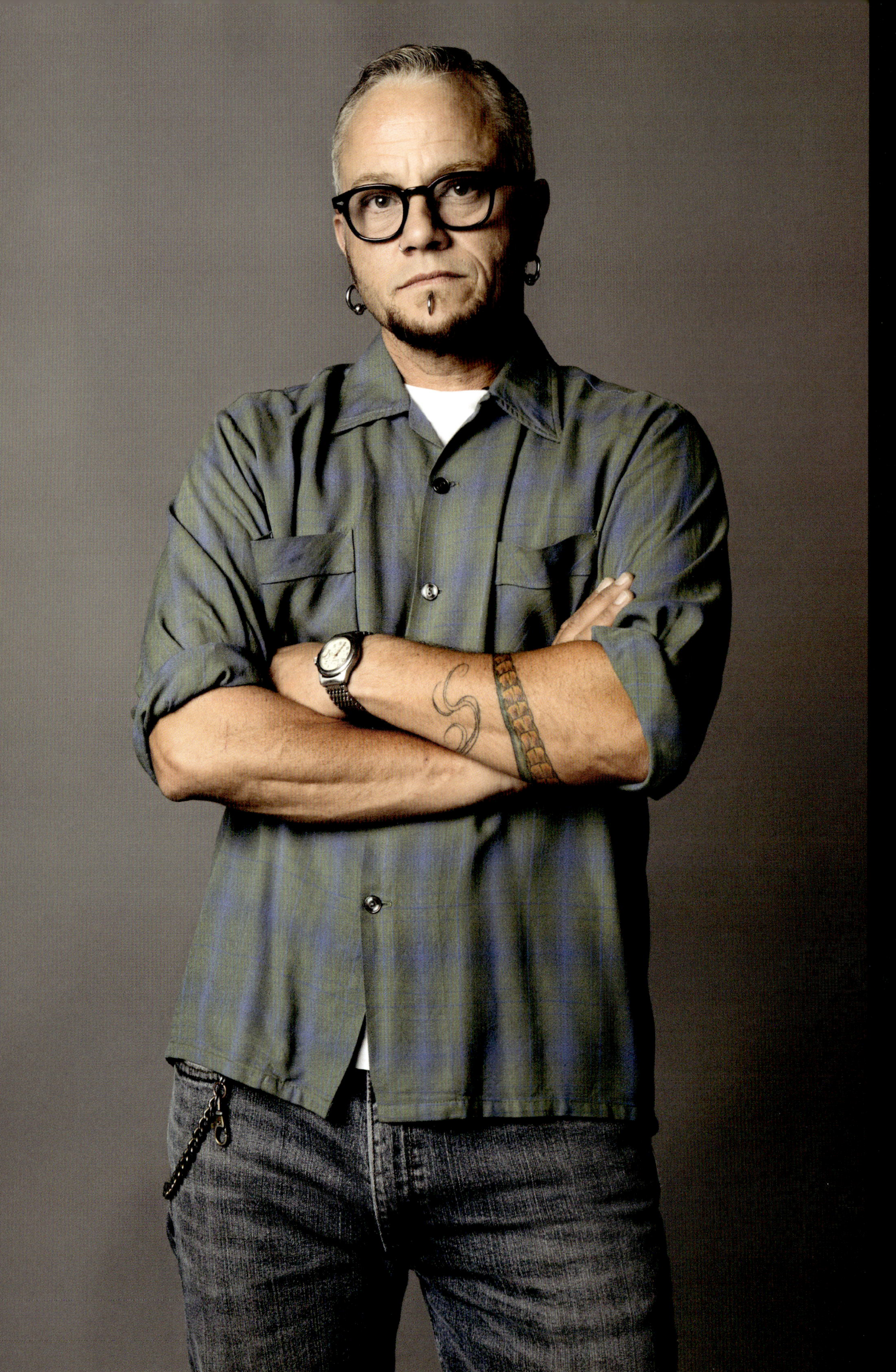

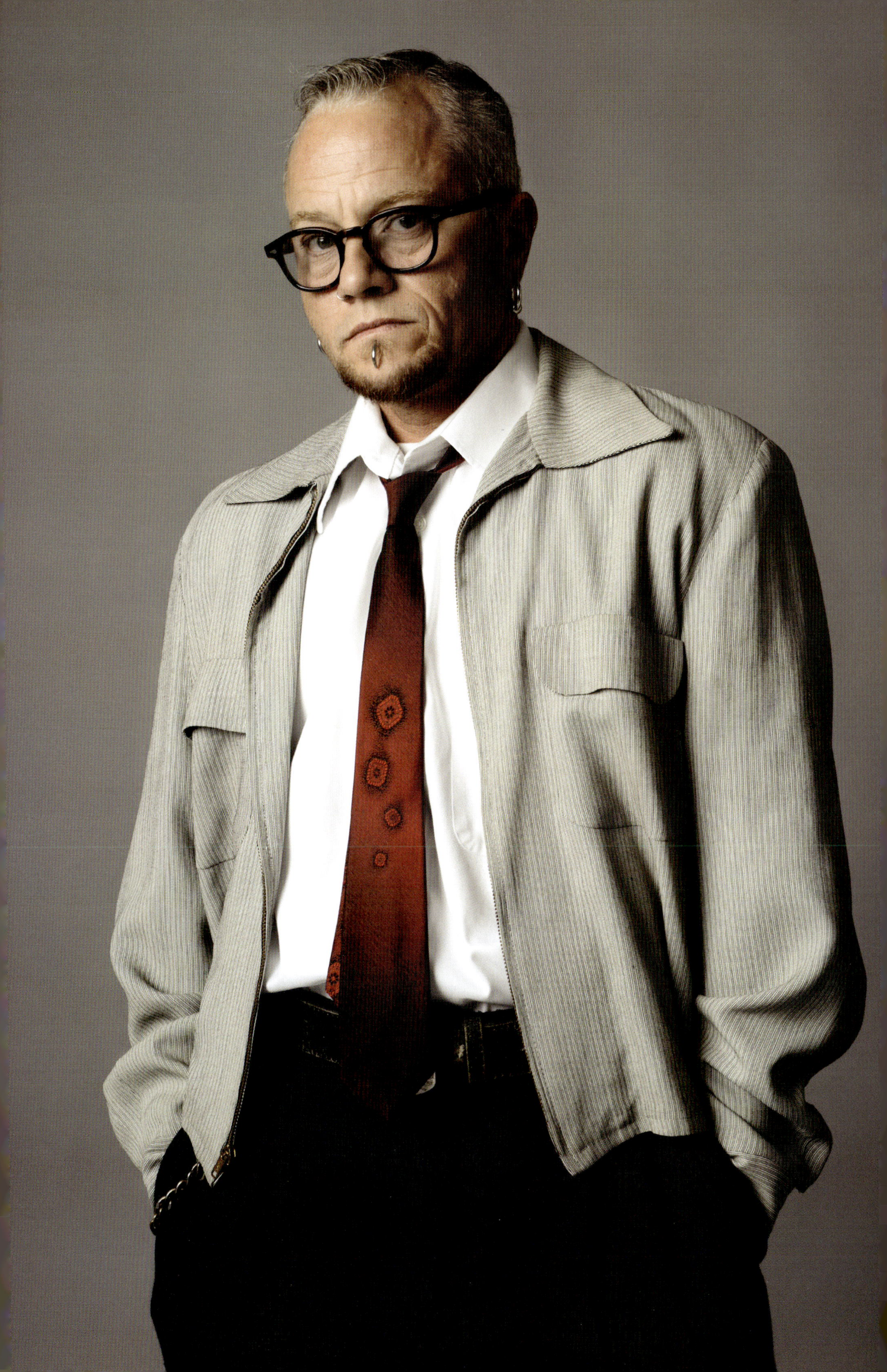

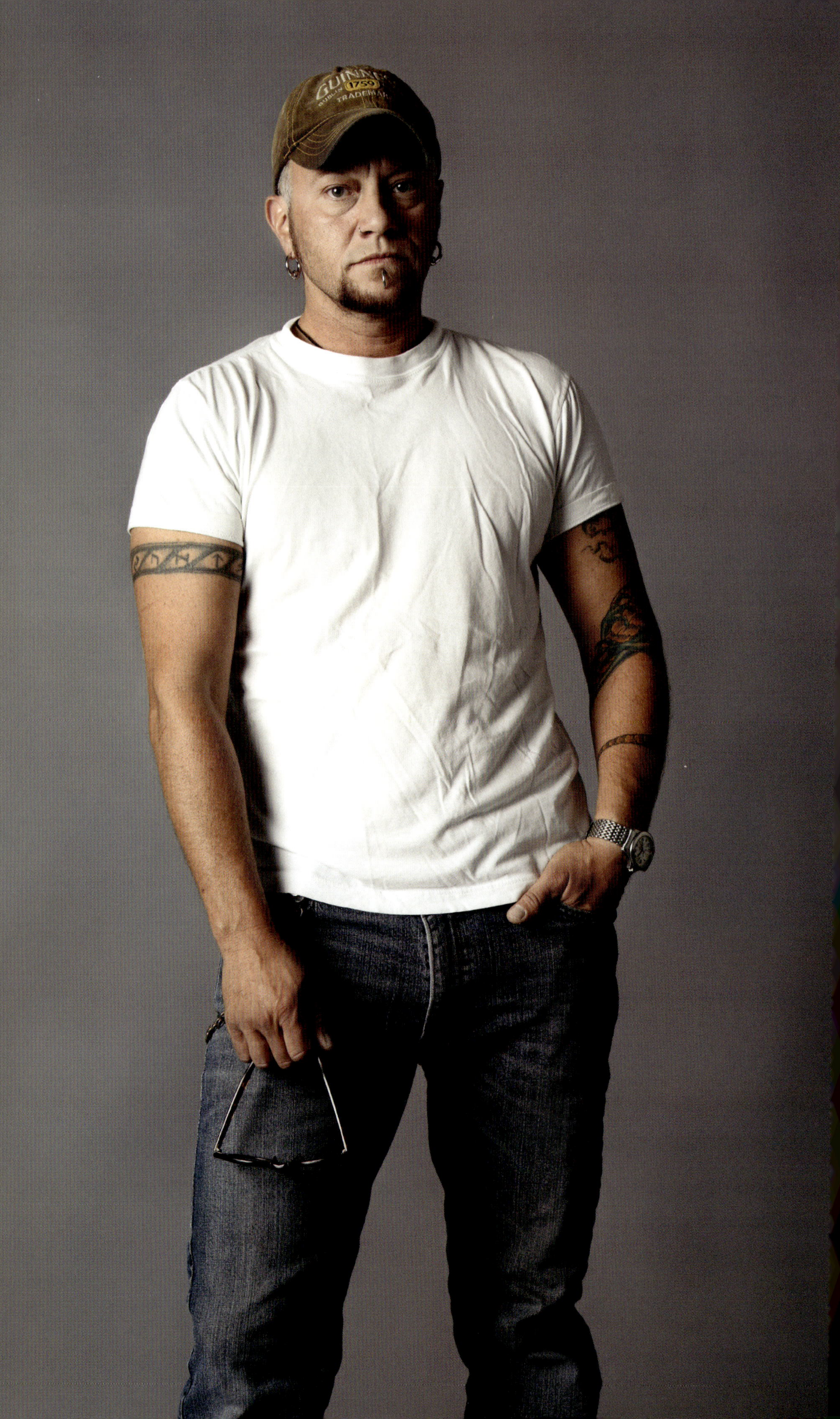
1759

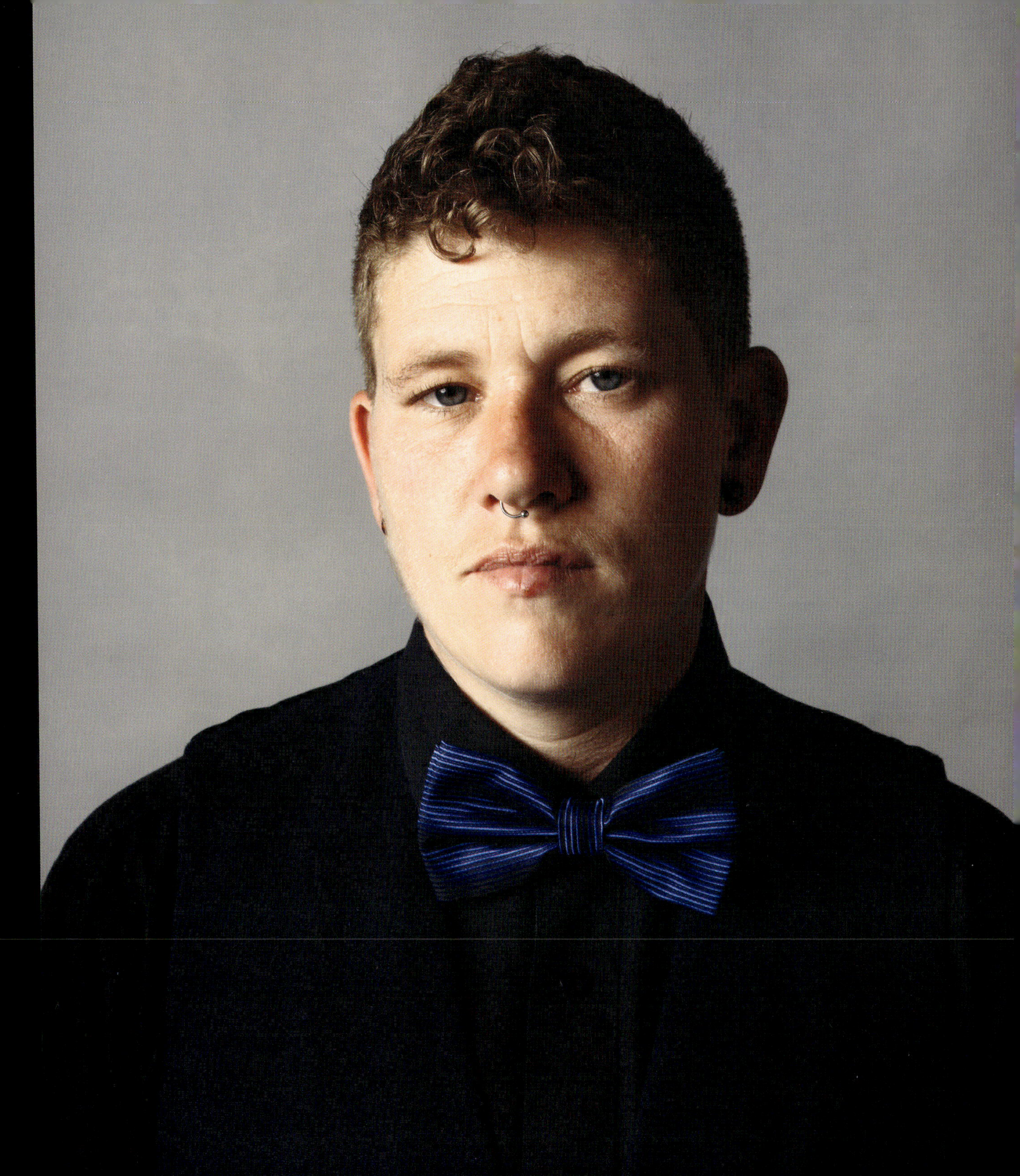

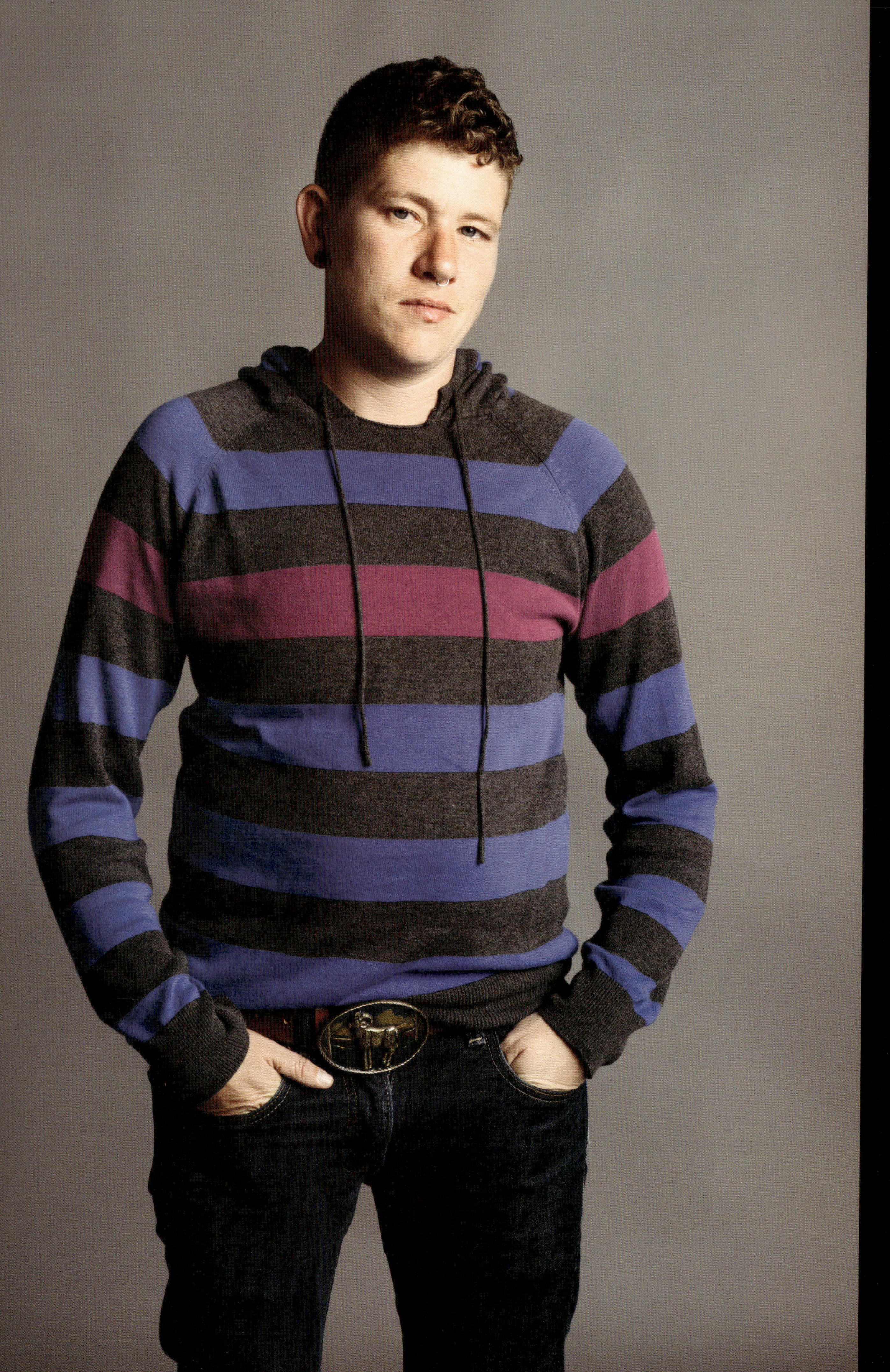

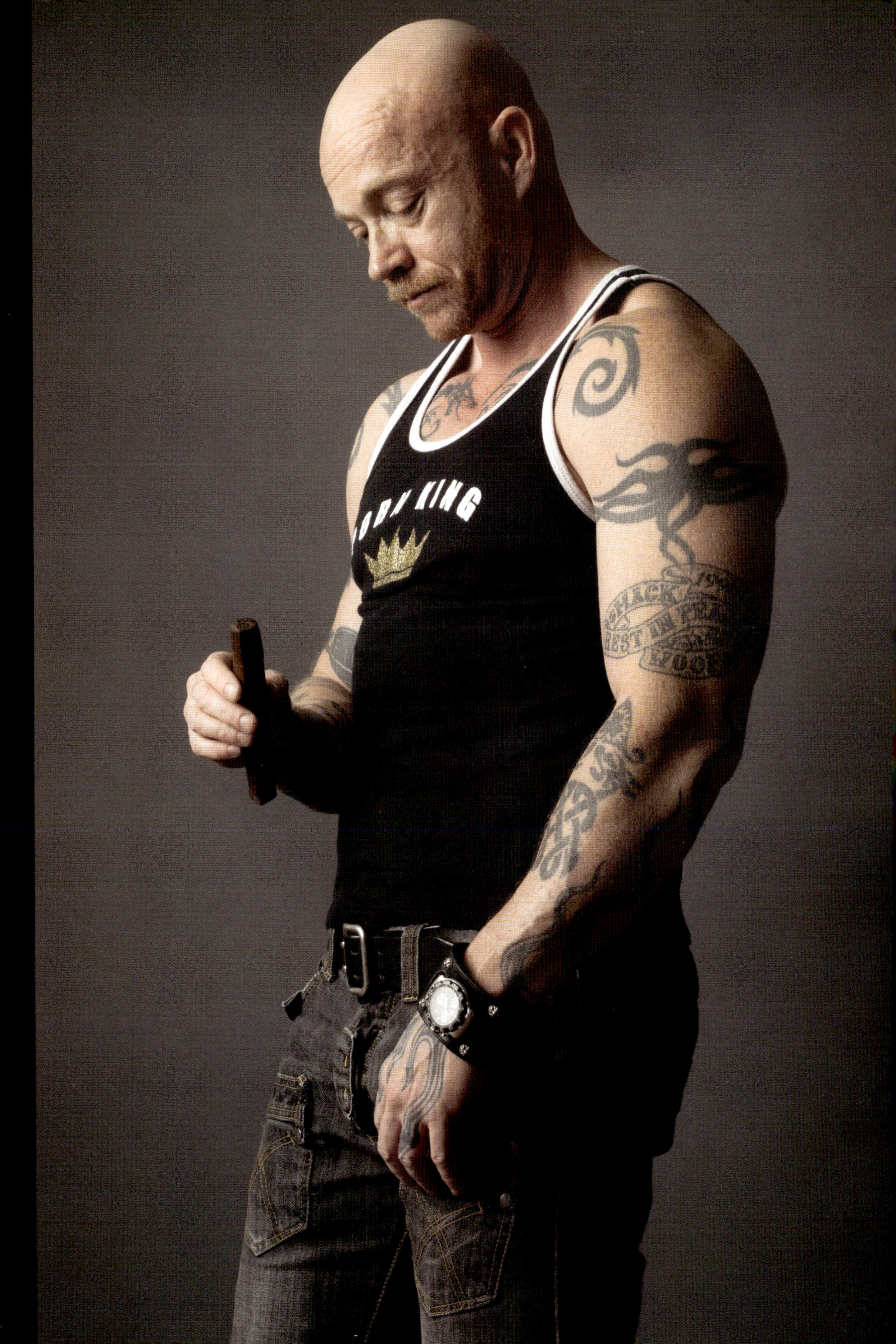
KING
SMACK
REST IN

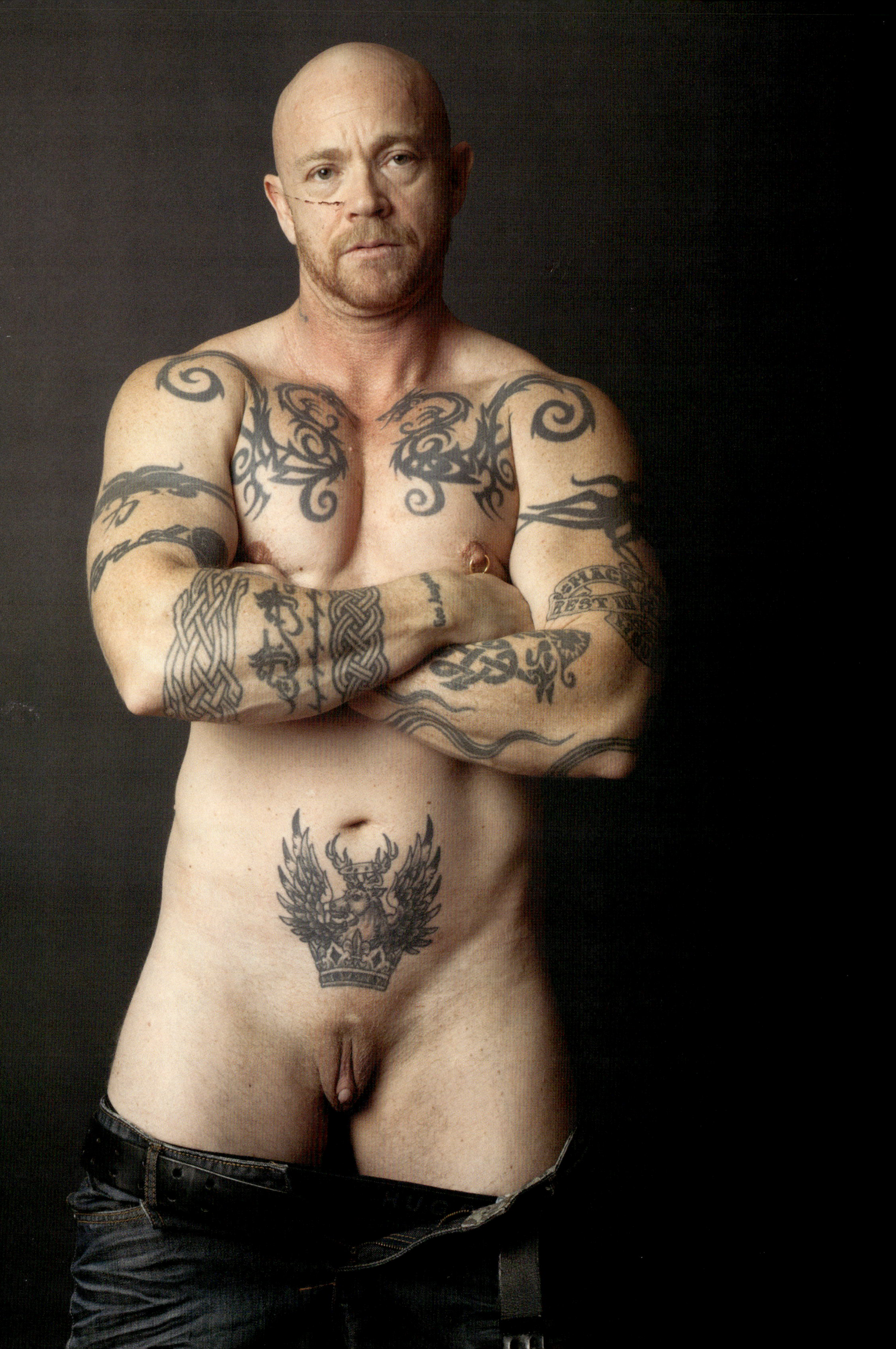

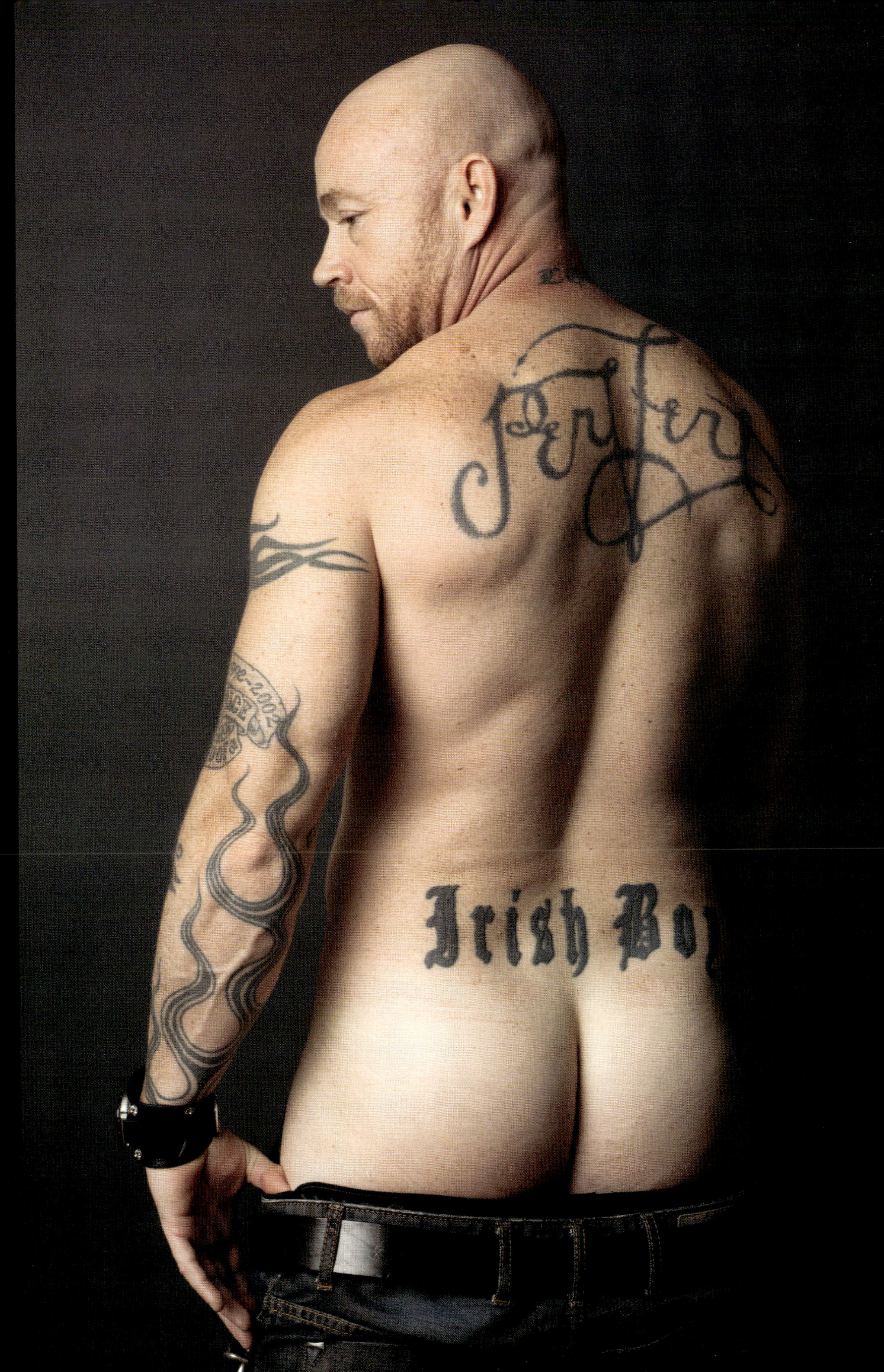
Irish Bo

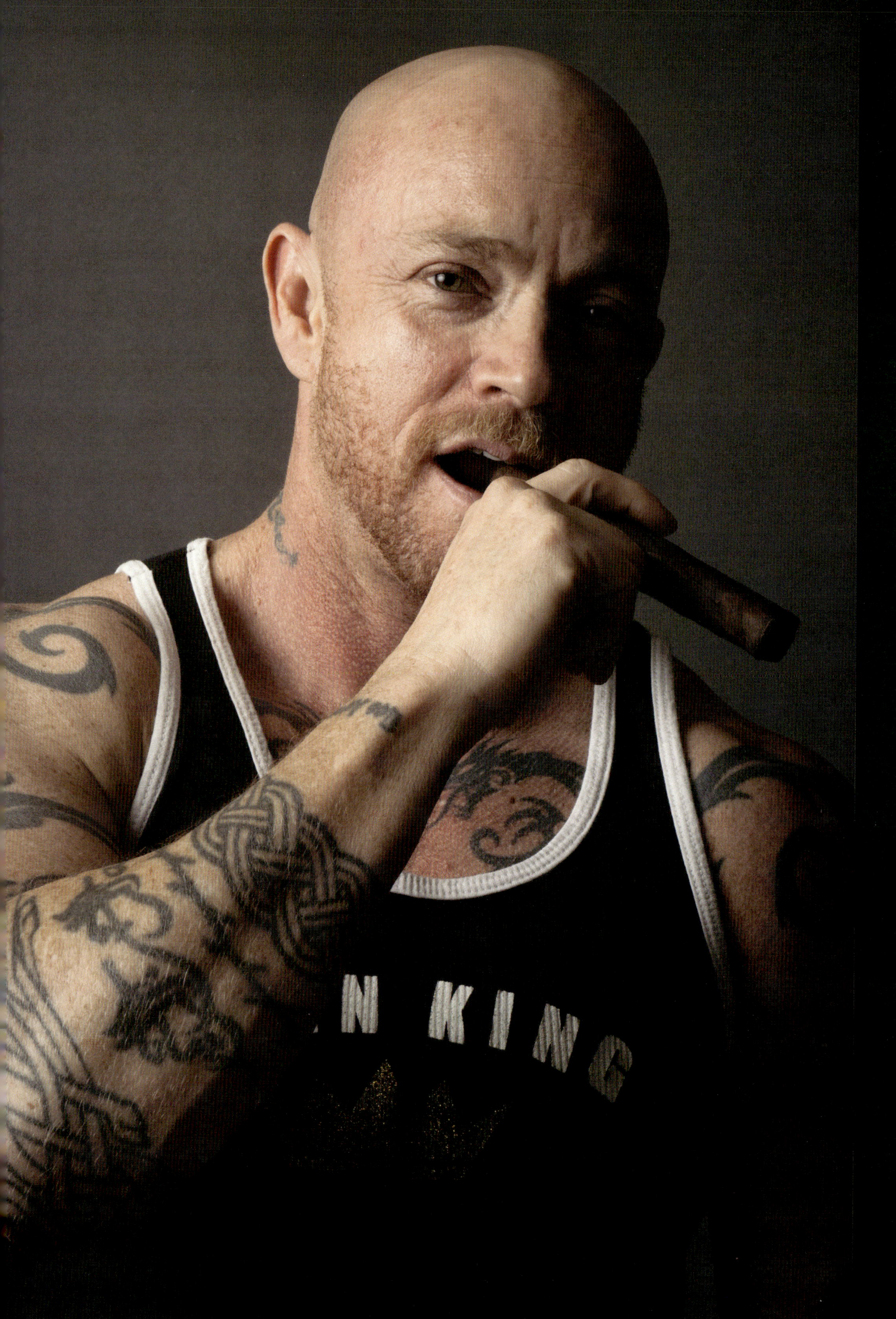
N KING

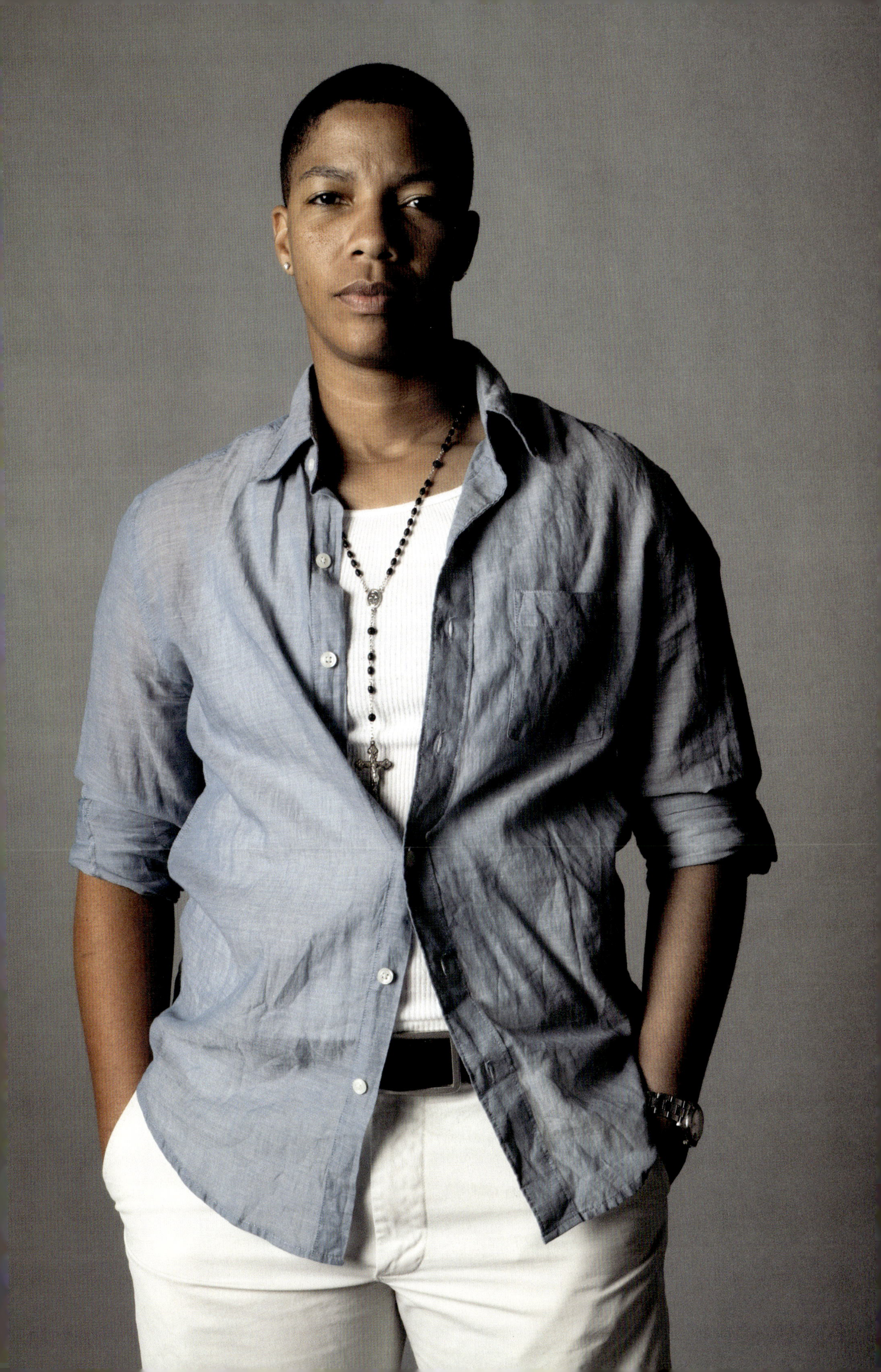

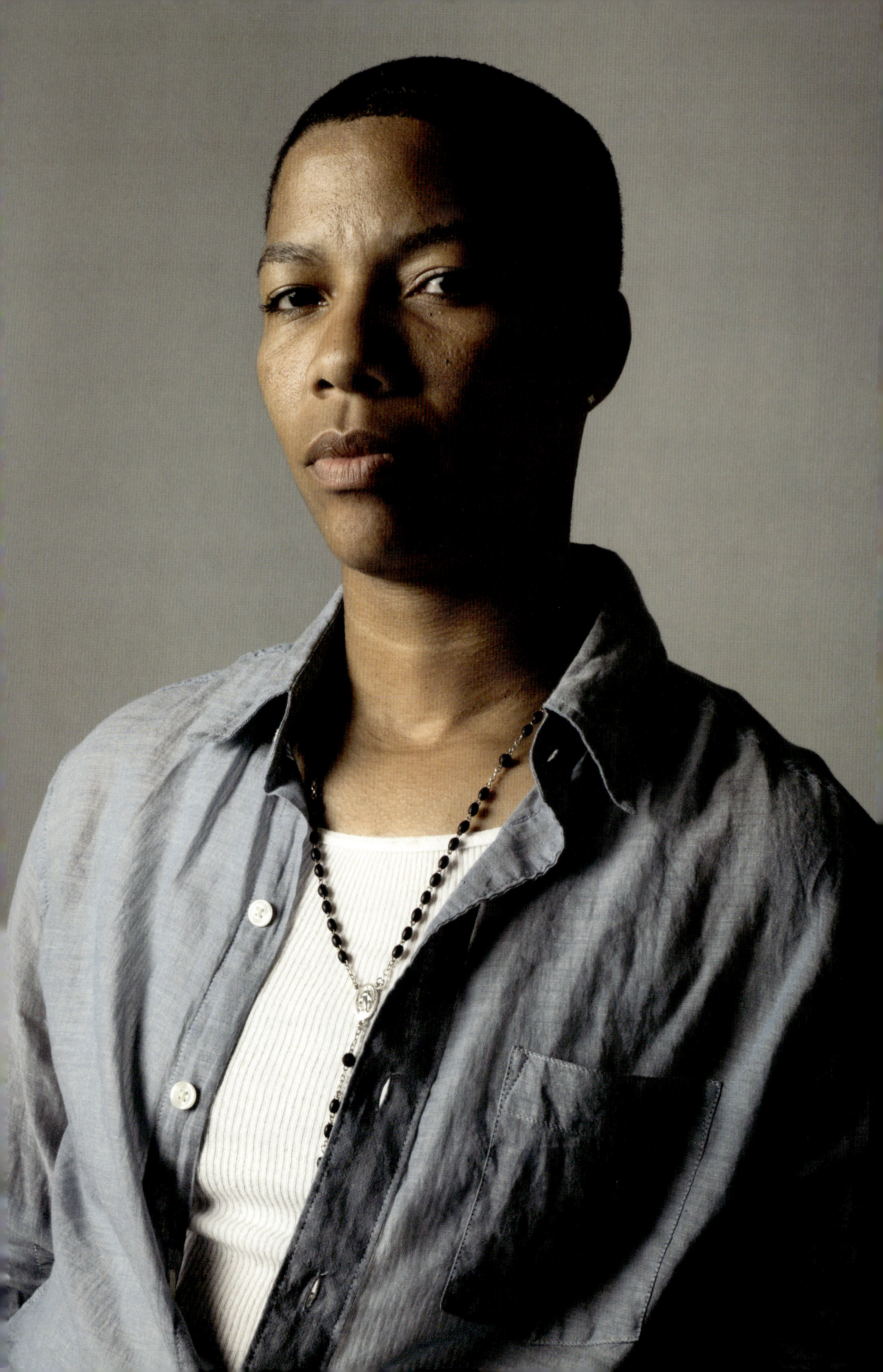

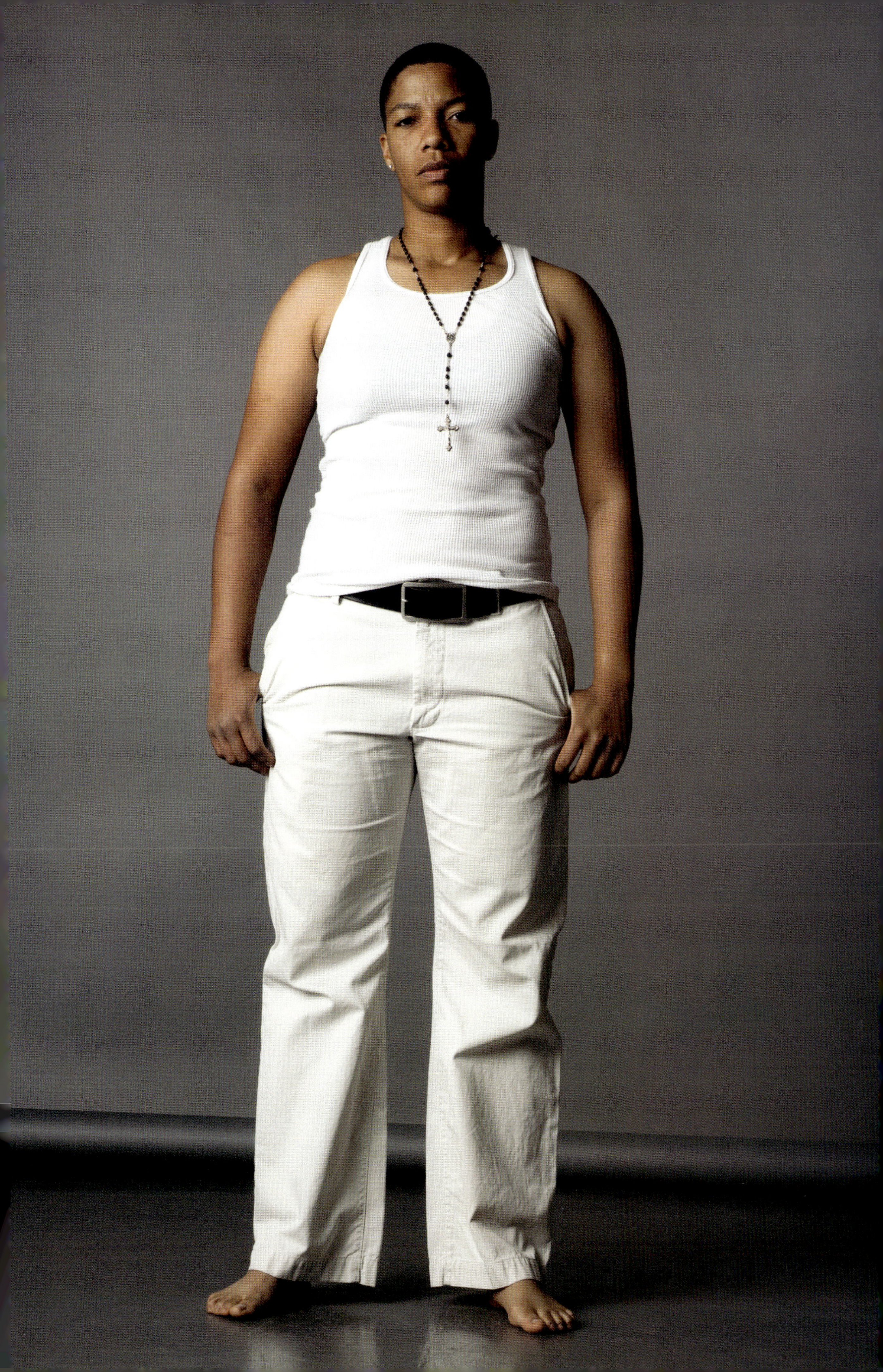

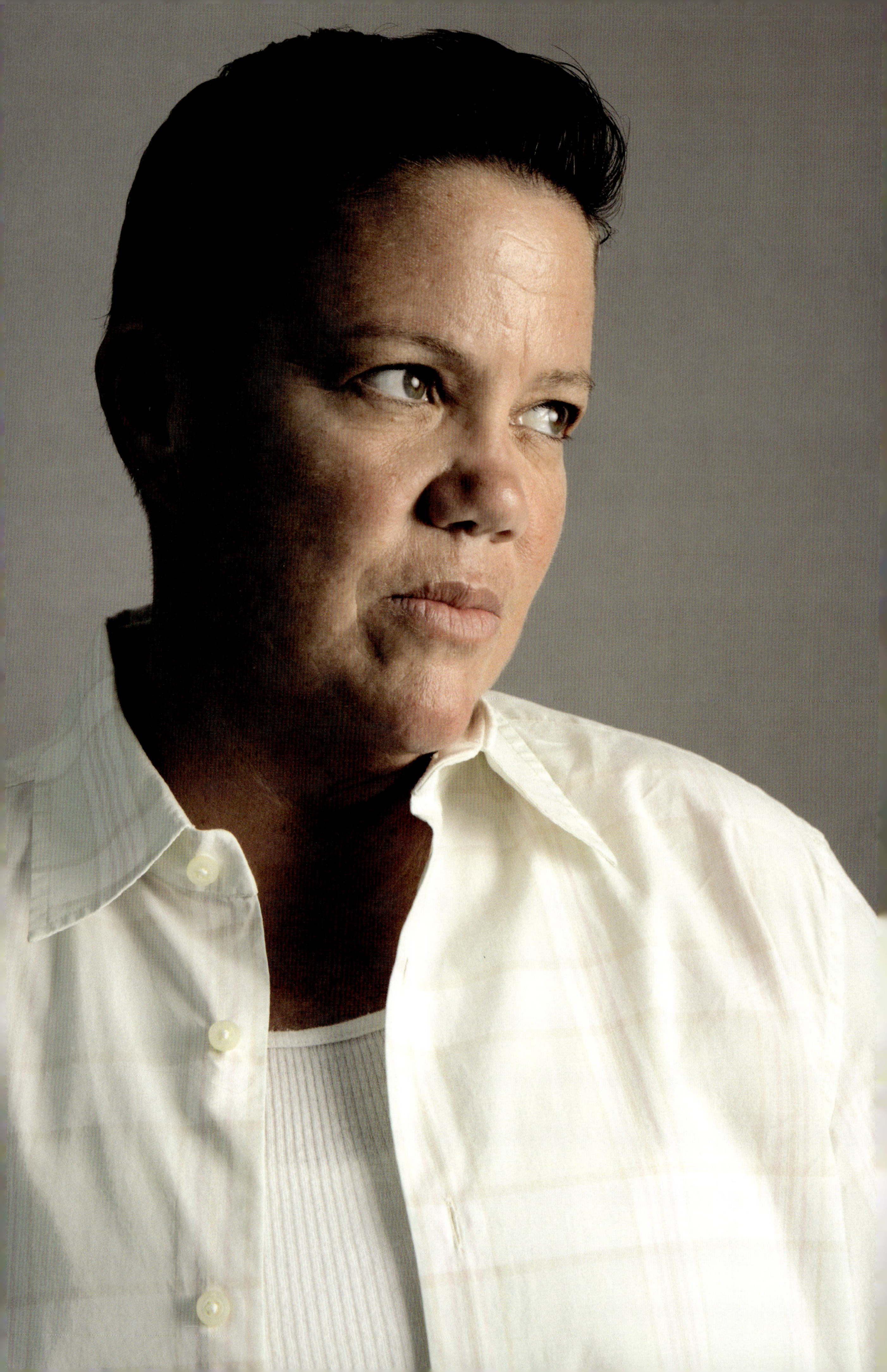

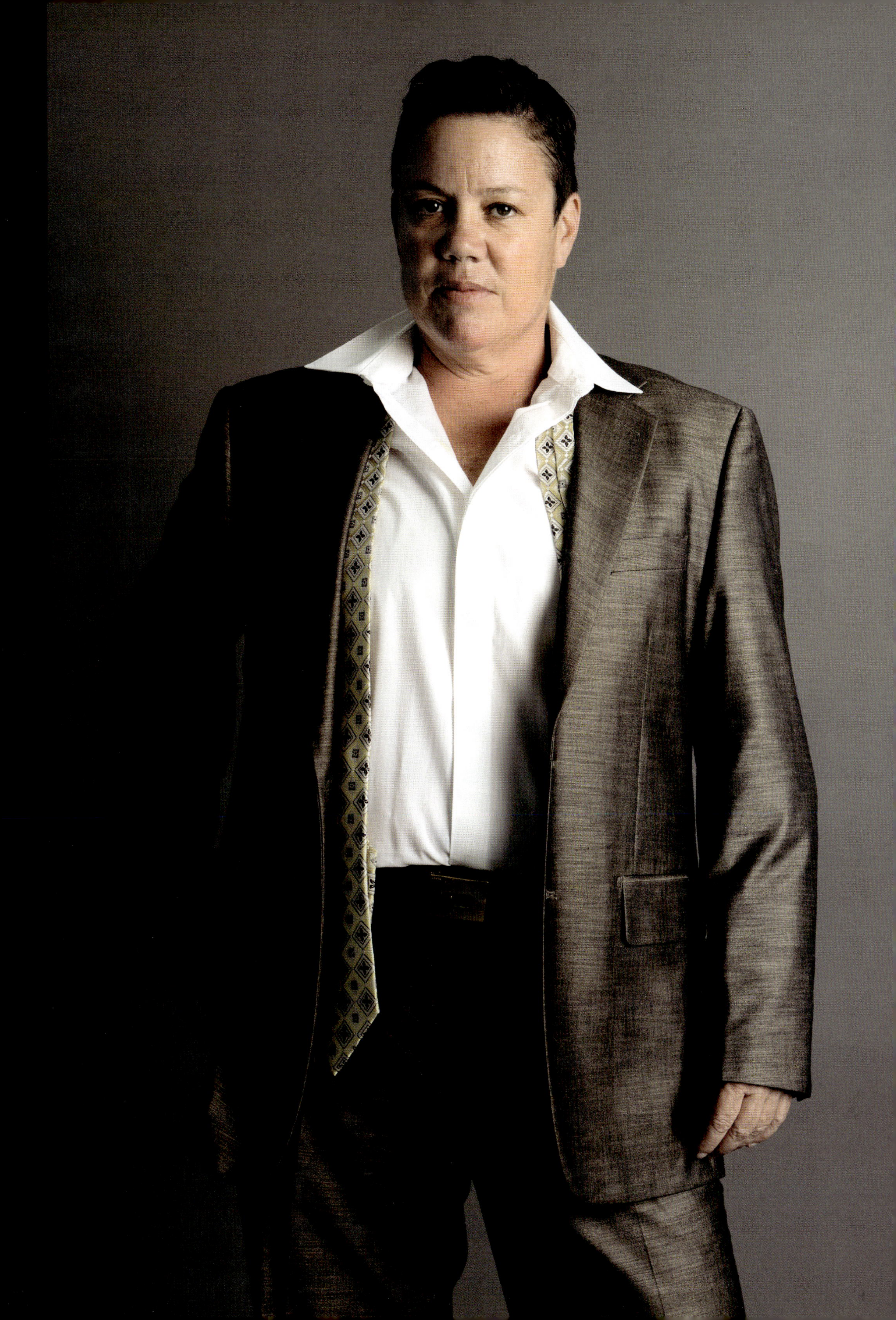

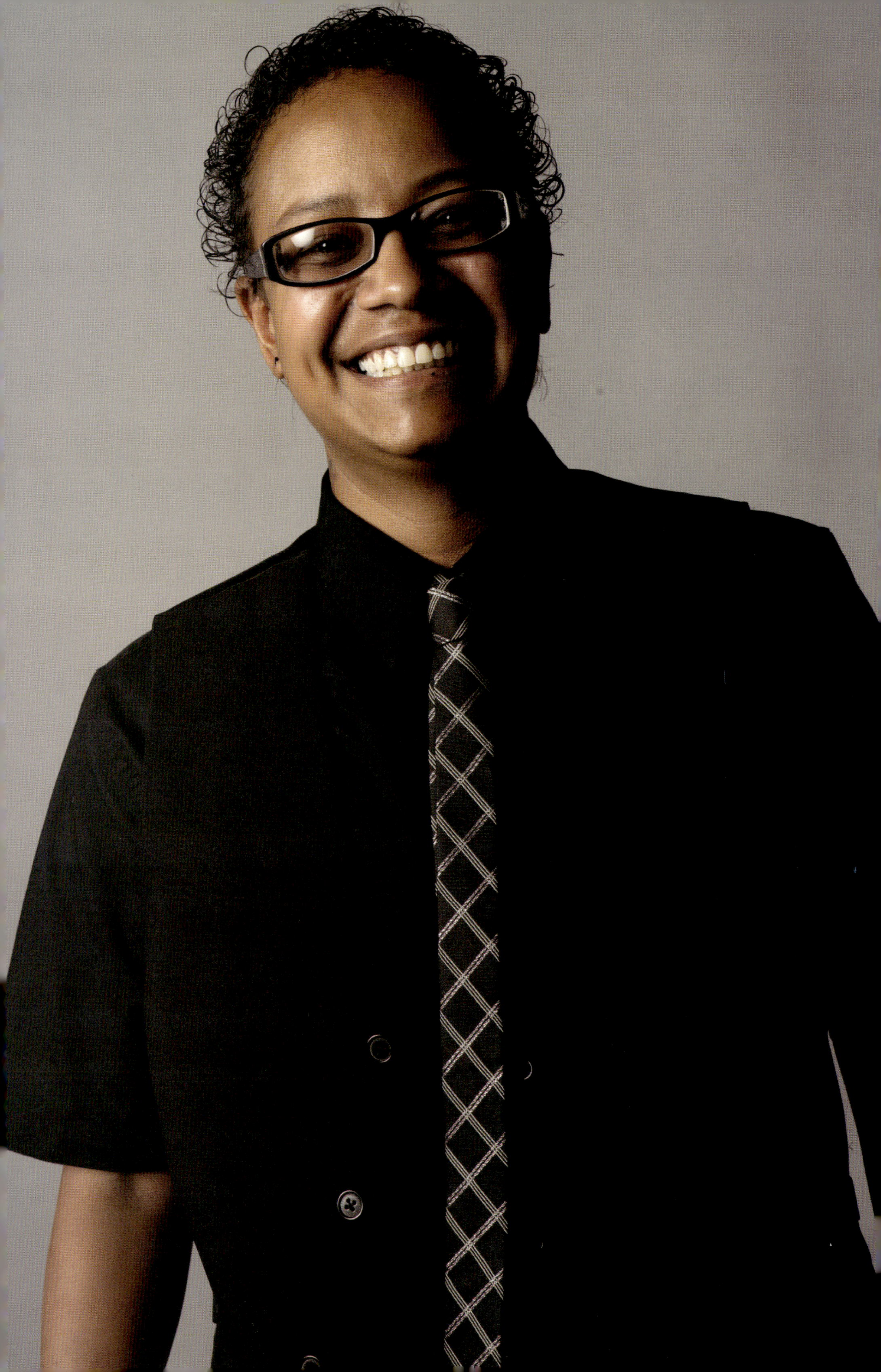

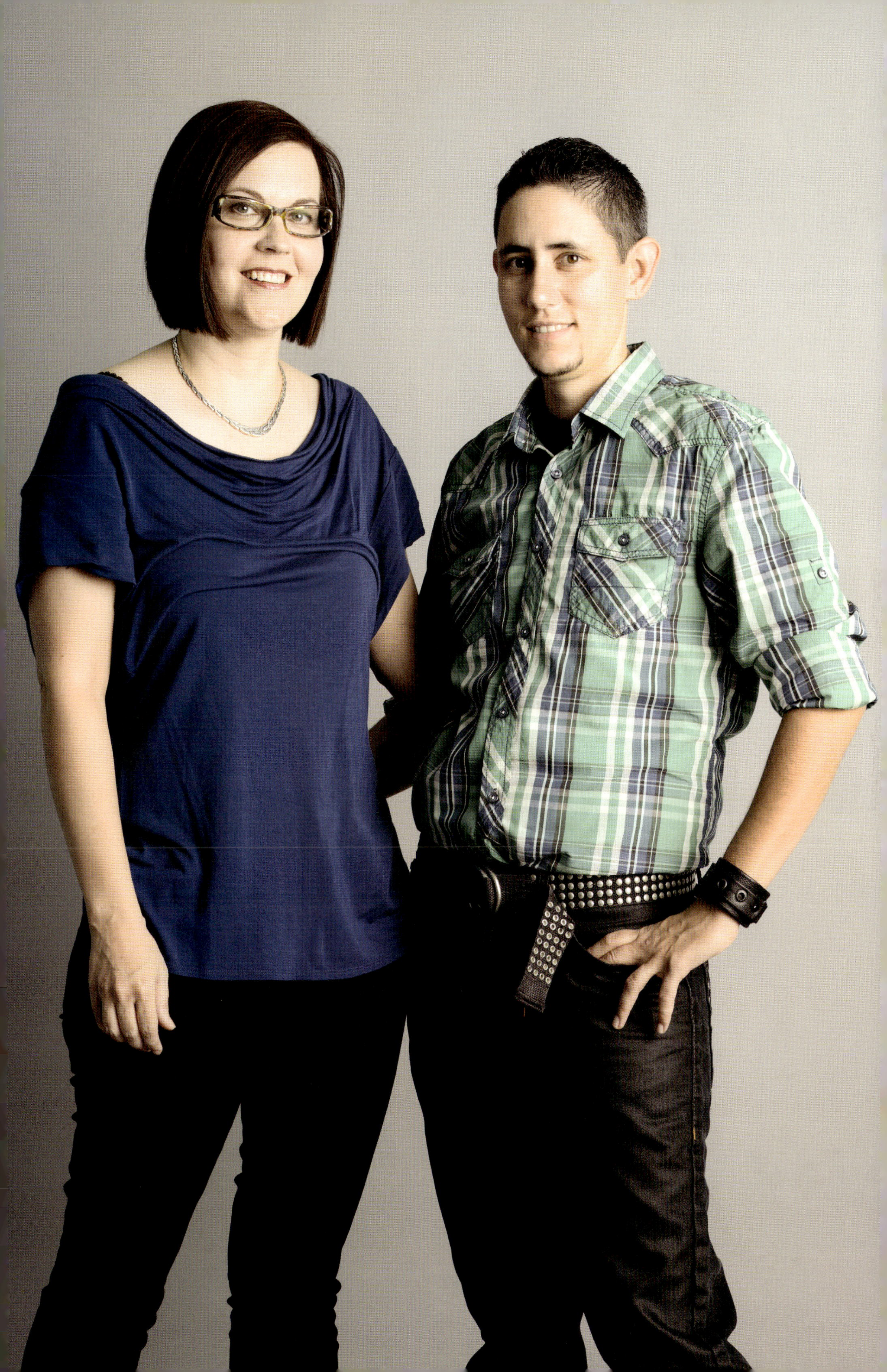

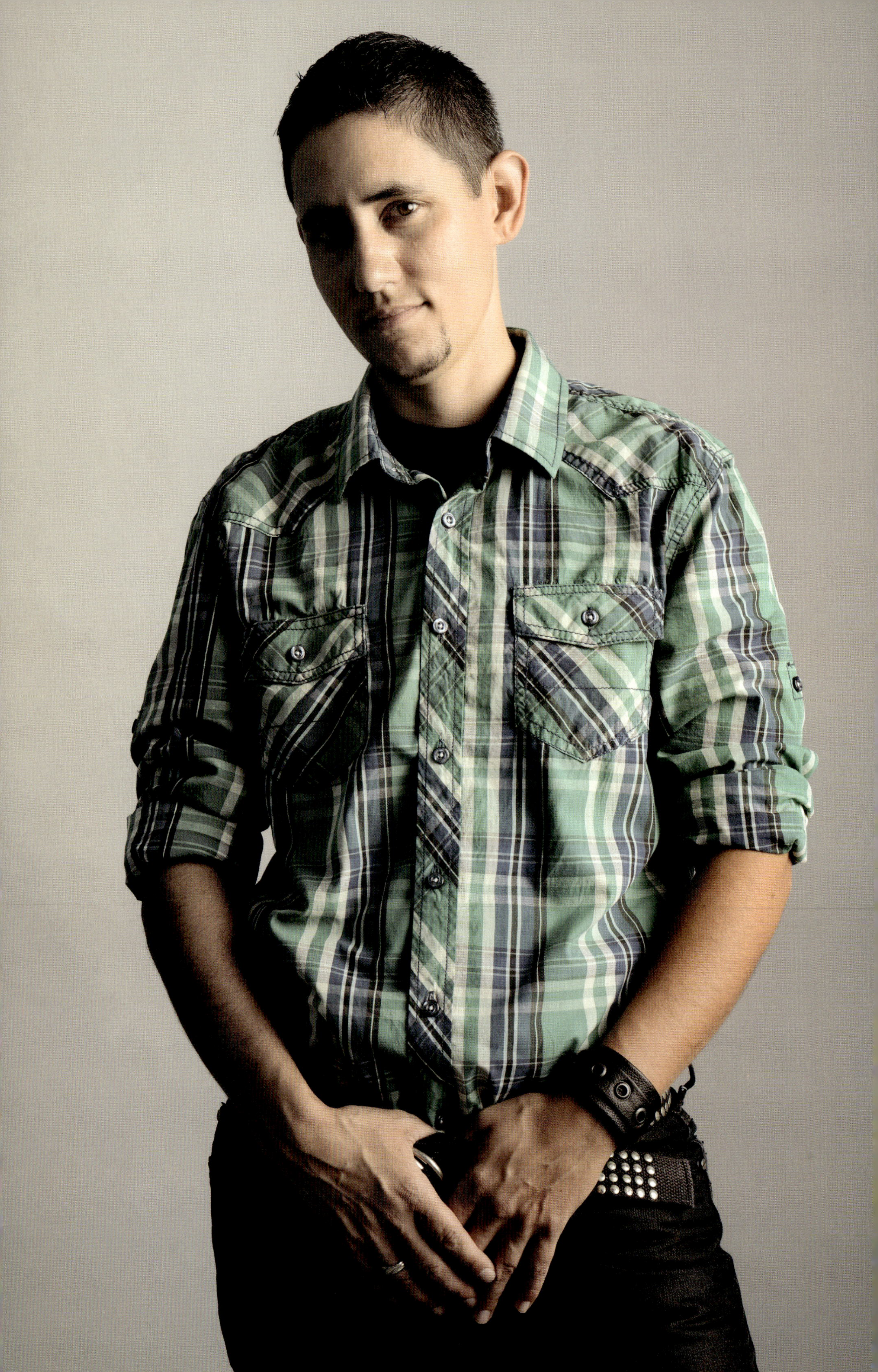

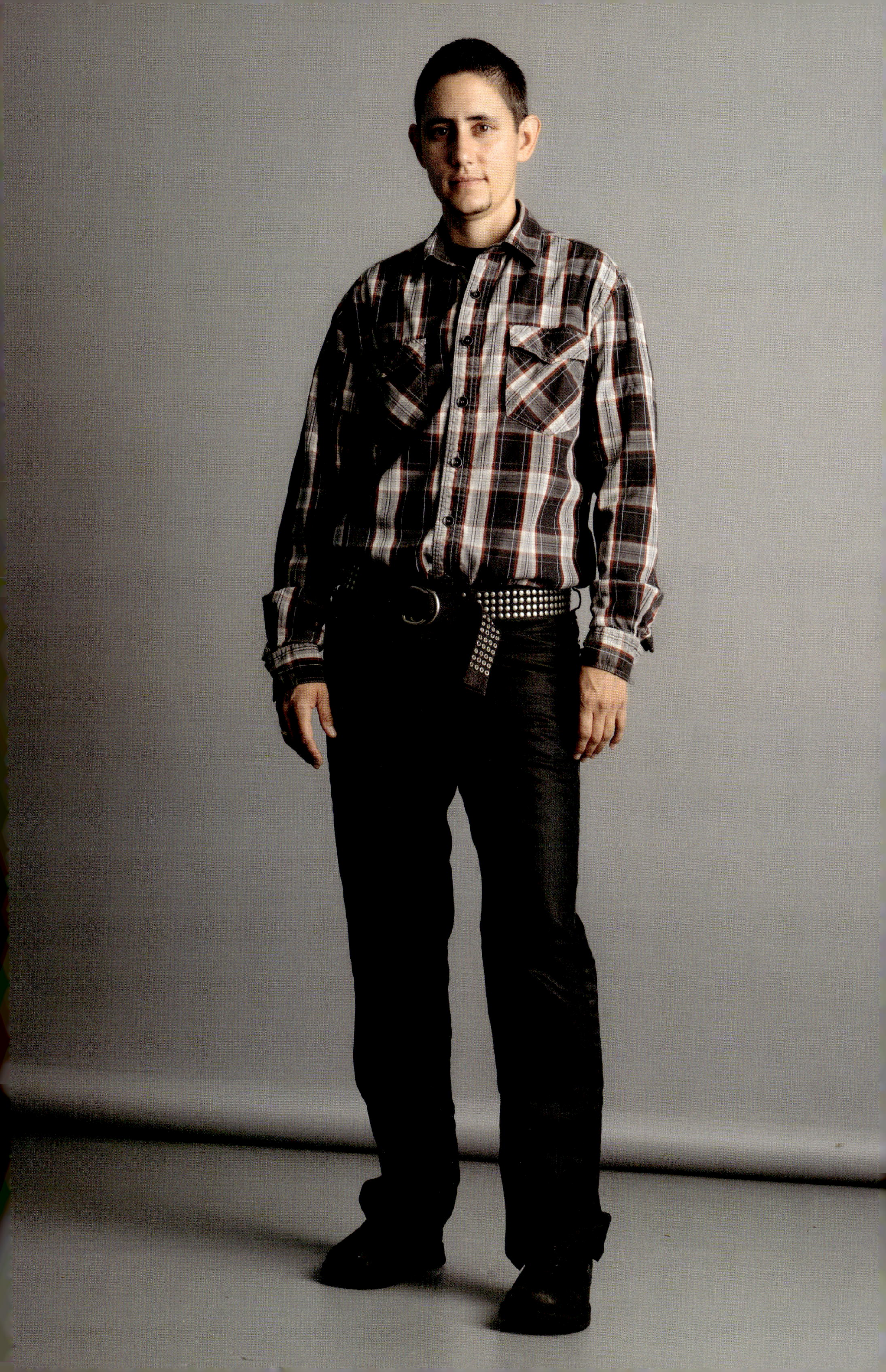

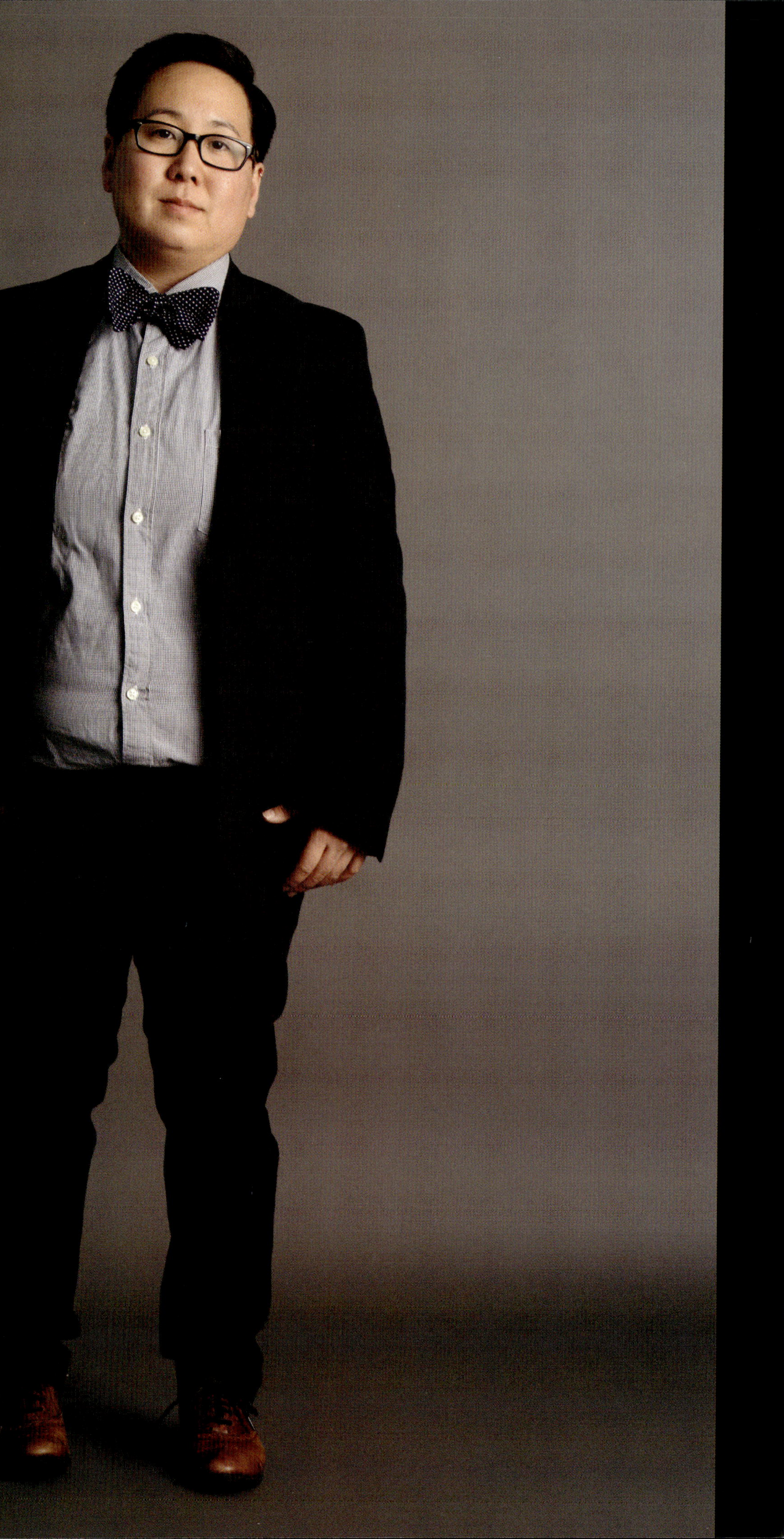

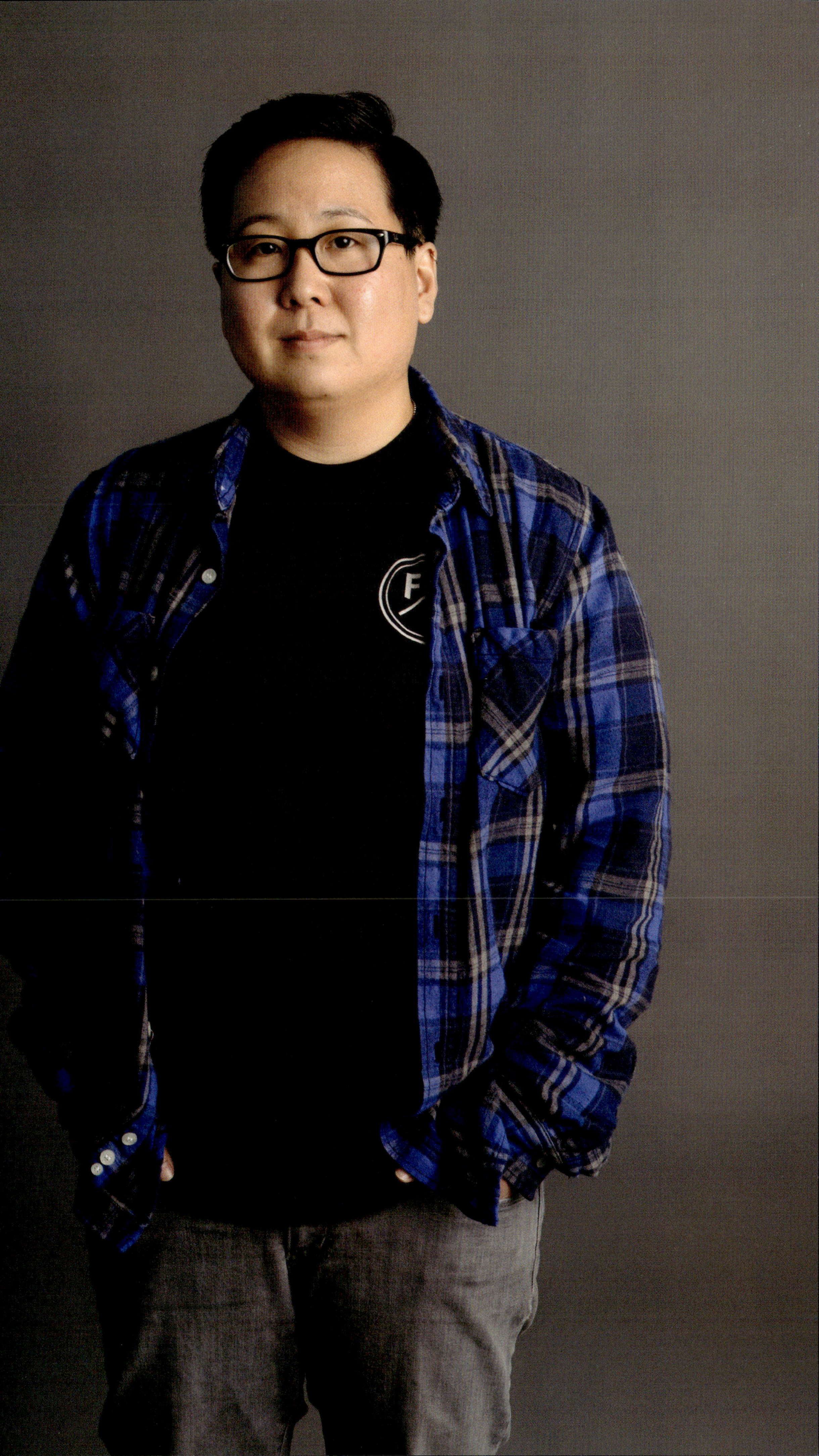

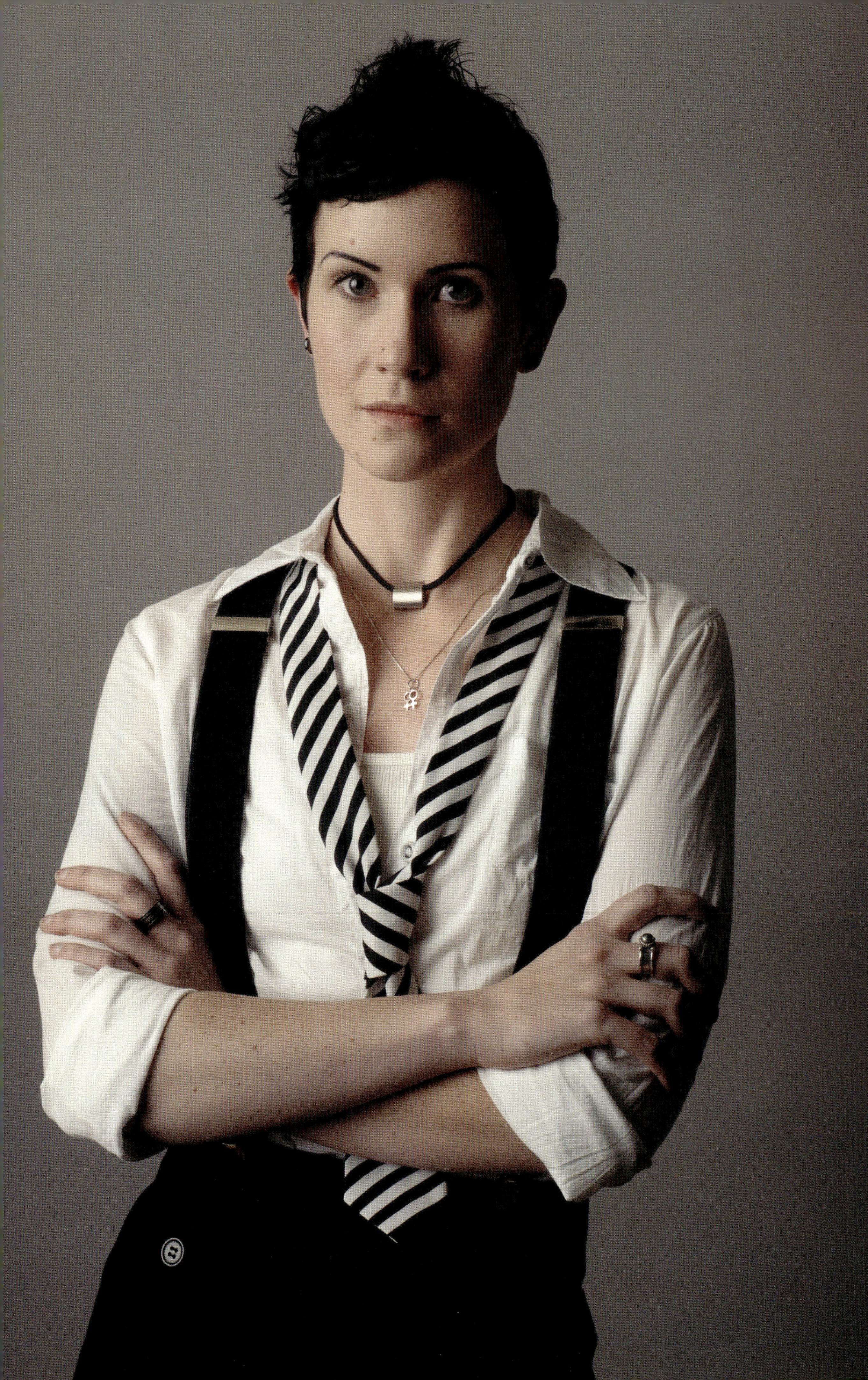

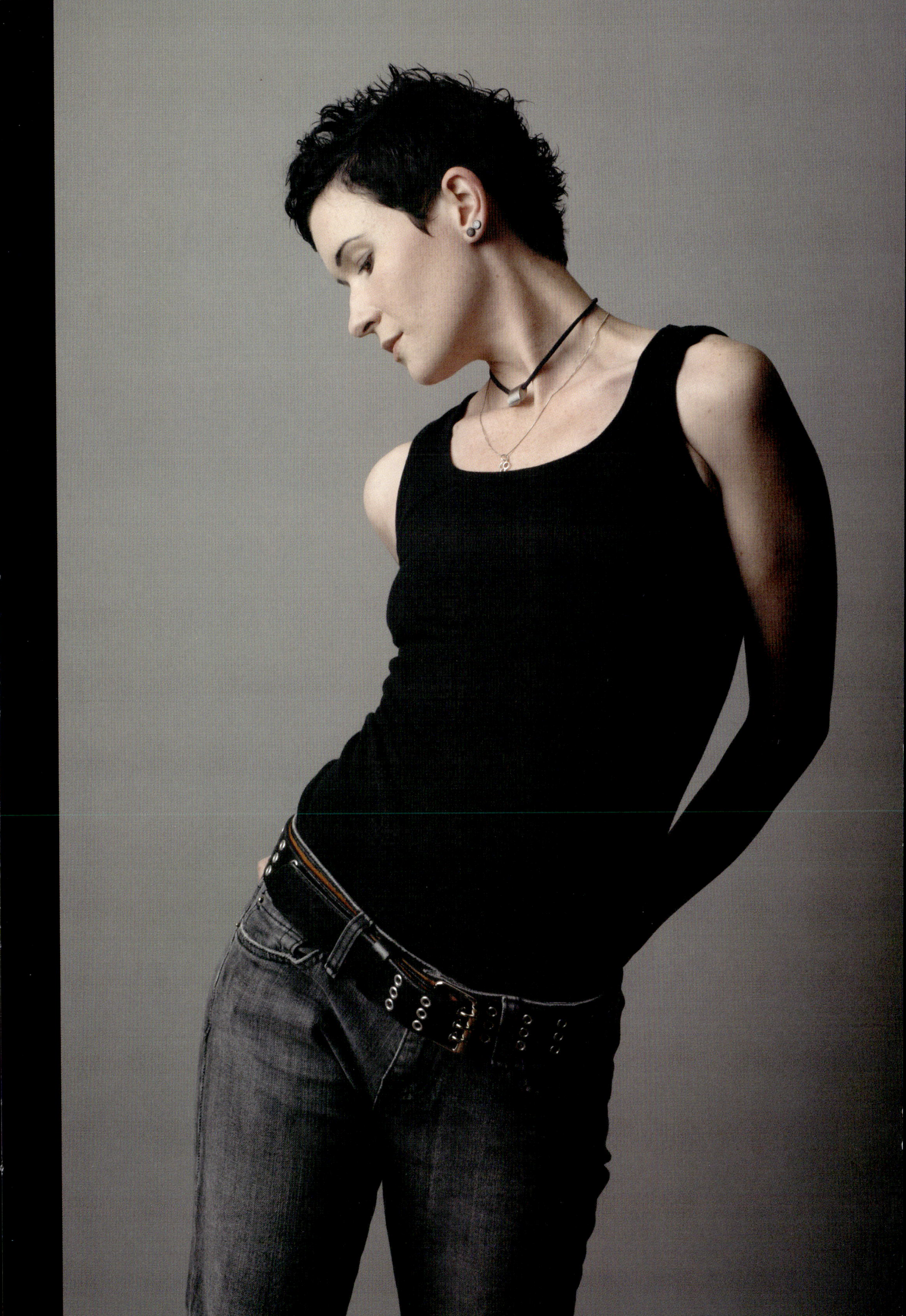

Author photo by Gregory Bojorquez

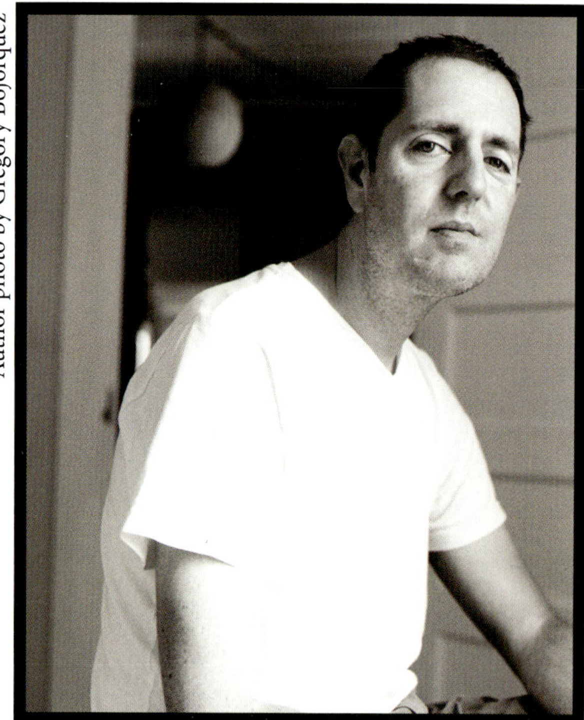

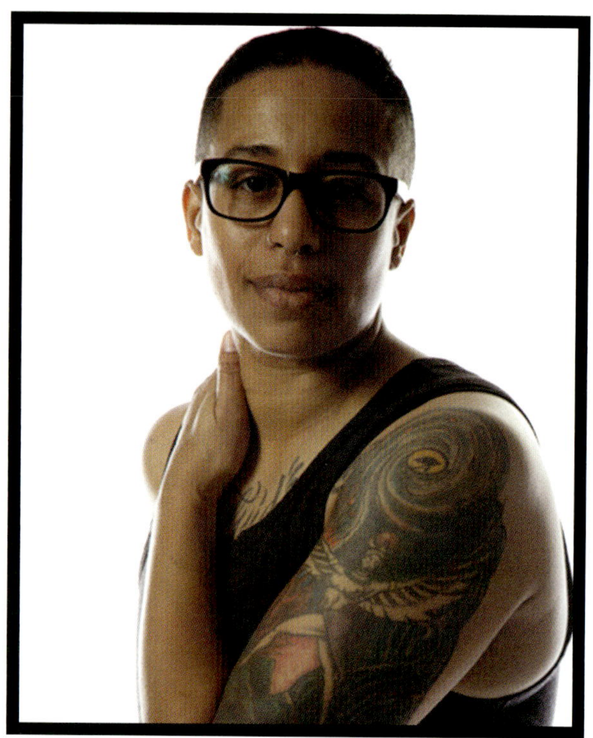

Born in Los Angeles in 1969, Dave Naz is a photographer whose work revolves around the varied identities and personae of our time. He has published seven books, *Genderqueer* is his eighth. Naz's photographs are shown in galleries all over the world. His work has appeard in *GQ*, *Maxim*, *Stern.de*, and *Salon*. He lives in Los Angeles with his wife, Oriana, and their menagerie of artwork and animals.

Ignacio Rivera is a queer, trans, Two-Spirit, Black-Boricua Taíno activist, writer, filmmaker, performance artist, lecturer, and sex educator who prefers the gender-neutral pronoun they. Inspired by lived experiences of homelessness, poverty, and discrimination, Ignacio's work is also driven by identity; their body of work has focused on gender and sexuality including queer, trans, kink, and sexual liberation issues within a race/class dynamic. Ignacio has over twenty years experience in economic justice that includes antiracist and anti-imperialist work as well feminist and LGBTQ movements. Ignacio is one of the founding board members for Queers for Economic Justice and the creator of Poly Patao Productions (P3).

Author photo by Peter Bruno

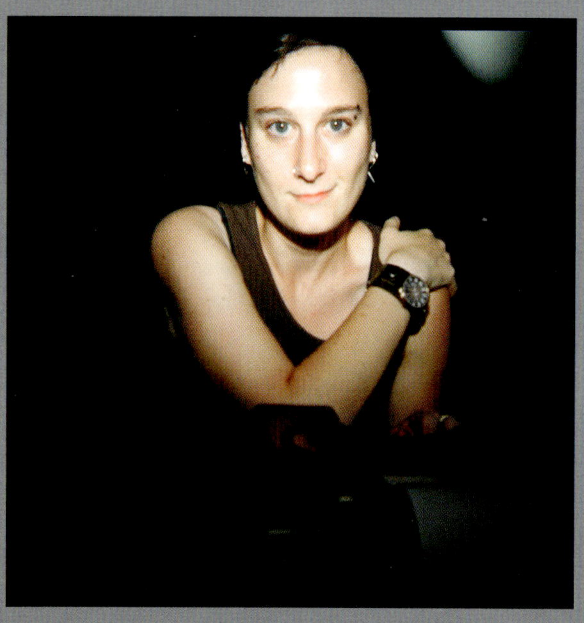

Sarah Burghauser is a Berkeley-based writer and teacher. She holds an MA from Oregon State University and an MFA from California Institute of the Arts, where she has also taught.

She has worked with Semiotext(e) Press in Los Angeles and has been awarded fellowships with the Lambda Literary Foundation Emerging Voices Retreat, The MacDowell Colony, and Vermont Studio Center. Sarah writes for Lambda Literary, Kirkus Media, and *A Café in Space*, the Anaïs Nin literary journal. Her essay "Learning To Be In A Skin" appears in the anthology, *Queer Girls in Class: Lesbian Teachers and Students Tell Their Classroom Stories* (Peter Lang Publishing Group 2011). Currently she is working on a collection of poetry, and finding a home for her first book, *Infringe: A Queer Jewish Memoir*.

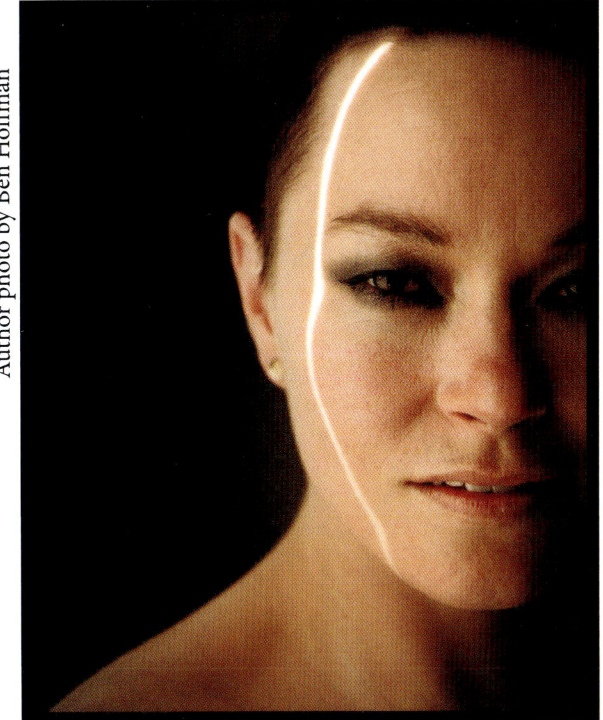

Author photo by Ben Hoffman

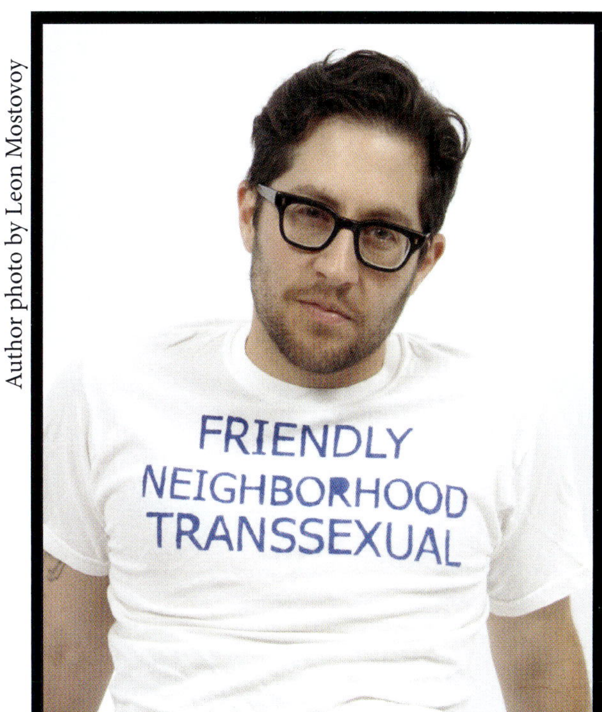

Author photo by Leon Mostovoy

JIZ LEE IS A genderqueer porn performer who has built a name in the adult business by presenting genuine pleasure and unique gender expression on camera. Jiz has worked in over 200 projects spanning six countries within the indie, queer, and mainstream genres. They were awarded Feminist Porn Award's "Boundary Breaker" and have received numerous XBIZ and AVN nominations. Behind the scenes, Jiz moonlights as Marketing Director of Pink & White Productions and runs the erotic philanthropic Karma Pervs. It was through pornography that Jiz began writing, and has since contributed to various publications including Jezebel.com and *The Feminist Porn Book*. Jiz also presents on porn; ever fascinated by the radical potential of sex, love, and art, Jiz blogs at JizLee.com.

MORTY DIAMOND IS AN artist, writer and activist. He has published two anthologies, *From the Inside Out: FTM and Beyond* (Manic D Press) and *Trans/Love* (Manic D Press), focusing on trans and gender variant writers. He is currently finishing his Masters of Social Work at San Francisco State University and is working on an app for suicide prevention in the trans community.

JENNY FACTOR'S FIRST COLLECTION, *Unraveling at the Name* (Copper Canyon Press), was a finalist for the 2002 Lambda Literary Award.

With poems in the *Paris Review*, *Prairie Schooner*, *Ploughshares*, Nerve.com, and more than a dozen anthologies, including *The Best American Erotic Poems* (Scribner, 2008), Jenny's poems have been honored with a Hayden Carruth Award and an Astraea Grant.

Christina Pugh wrote of Jenny in *Poetry Magazine*, "her verseforms sing with idiosyncrasy."

Jenny received her MFA in Literature from Bennington College, and her BA from Harvard College. She serves as Core Faculty in Poetry at Antioch University Los Angeles, the nation's first low-residency MFA program devoted to literature and the pursuit of social justice.

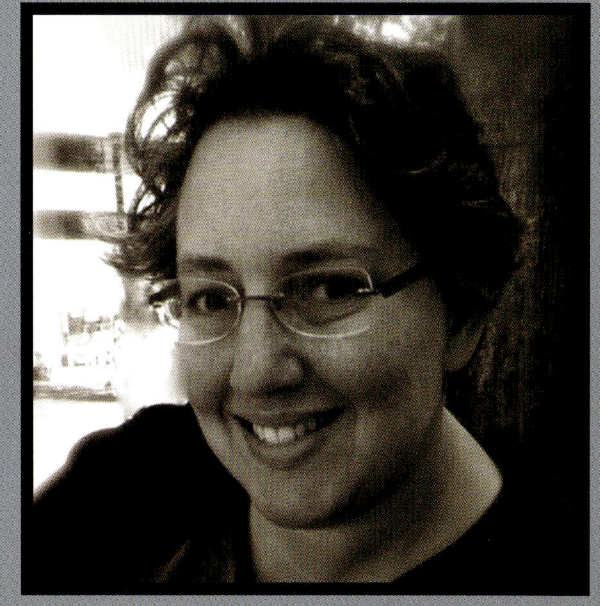

Models: Afro Disiac, Alicia, Alix, Billy Castro, Bing, Britney, Bryn Whipple, Buck Angel, Chandra & Aimee, Colten & Tristan Taormino, Cyd Nova, Drew DeVeaux & Jen Kolmel, Evan & Kelta, Ewan Duarte, Fudgie Frottage, Hans Onher & Clayapeach, James Darling, Jiz Lee, Kez Quin, Kristel, Matty Boi, Nenna, Nica Ross, Nick & Courtney Trouble, Orlan Doe, Pig Pen, Puck Goodfellow, Sarah Burghauser, Shae Flanigan, Shawn, Syd Blakovich, Vid Tuesday, Wolfe Moon.

Thanks to my wonderful wife Oriana & My Family for all of their support, Tyson & Alex Cornell, Julia Callahan, Alice Marsh-Elmer, April Flores, Eric Kroll, Mat & Leigh Gleason, Steve Diet Goedde & Yee, Victor & Susan Lightworship, Cynthia Patterson, Andy Ptashnik, Dave Delucca, Pig Pen & Julie Tolentino, Rick Castro, Coop & Stephanie, Lisa Jenio, Ira & Nina, Ronnie Barnett, Tommi Cahill, Richard Kern, Gregory Bojorquez, Estevan Oriol, Eric Minh Swenson, Violet Blue, Miki Bunge, Ed & Rebekah, Greg & Sheila Cameron, Chris & Lori Shary, Bill & Stacie Stevenson, Dodd Bates, Andi Campognone & Alex, Lisa Derrick, Patrick Hoelck, Maxim Jakubowski, Scott Padgett, Larry & Robyn Hardy, Ed Fox, Lydia Lunch, Sesper & Alexandra, George Pitts, Kris Yenbamroong & Sarah St. Lifer, Tim Armstrong, Dennis McGrath, Octavio & Danielle Arizala, Chris and Andrea, Isac & Emily, David Stowe, Soma & Mike, Rae Threat, Jordan Schwartz, Ramzi Abed.

Thank you to all the models and Jiz Lee, Morty Diamond, Jenny Factor, Sarah Burghauser & Ignacio Rivera for your thoughtful and personal essays.

Jiz Lee and Buck Angel I can't thank you enough for all your help and support with this project.